GRANDPARENTING IN THE UNITED STATES

Edited by
Madonna Harrington Meyer
and Ynesse Abdul-Malak

Society and Aging Series
Series Editors: Madonna Harrington Meyer and
Christine L. Himes

Baywood Publishing Company, Inc.
AMITYVILLE, NEW YORK

Baywood Publishing Company, Inc.
26 Austin Avenue
P.O. Box 337
Amityville, NY 11701
(800) 638-7819
E-mail: baywood@baywood.com
Web site: baywood.com

Library of Congress Catalog Number:
ISBN: 978-0-89503-849-4 (cloth : alk. paper)
ISBN: 978-0-89503-875-3 (paper)
ISBN: 978-0-89503-876-0 (e-pub)
ISBN: 978-0-89503-877-7 (e-pdf)
http://dx.doi.org/10.2190/GIT

Library of Congress Cataloging-in-Publication Data

Names: Harrington Meyer, Madonna, 1959- editor. | Abdul-Malak, Ynesse, editor.
Title: Grandparenting in the United States / edited by Madonna Harrington
    Meyer and Ynesse Abdul-Malak.
Description: Amityville, New York : Baywood Publishing Company, Inc., [2016]
    | Series: Society and aging series | Includes index.
Identifiers: LCCN 2015050522| ISBN 9780895038494 (clothbound : alk. paper) |
    ISBN 9780895038753 (paperbound : alk. paper) | ISBN 9780895038760 (epub) |
    ISBN 9780895038777 (epdf)
Subjects: LCSH: Grandparenting—United States. | Families—United States.
Classification: LCC HQ759.9 .G72345 2016 | DDC 306.874/50973—dc23
LC record available at http://lccn.loc.gov/2015050522

Table of Contents

Dedication

For my sisters, Maura and Rose
Madonna Harrington Meyer

For my mother, Felina
Ynesse Abdul-Malak

http://dx.doi.org/10.2190/GITC1

CHAPTER 1

Grandparenting in the United States*

Madonna Harrington Meyer and Ynesse Abdul-Malak

The role of grandparenting in the United States is diversifying. One-half of those ages 50–64 and 80% of those 65 and older are grandparents (Livingston and Parker, 2010). While some grandparents have little or no contact whatsoever with their grandchildren, others are involved in almost every aspect of the daily care and support of their grandchildren. In between lies the vast majority of grandparents who provide occasional to frequent assistance of a wide variety of types. Spending time caring for grandkids can be very rewarding. A PEW study asked people to rank what they valued most about growing older and 31% of the women and 19% of the men ages 65–74 ranked spending time with their grandchildren as the benefit of aging they valued most (Livingston and Parker, 2010). But it may also be emotionally, physically, and financially exhausting, particularly for those who are employed, providing more intense care, or coping with fewer resources (Harrington Meyer, 2014).

Some grandparents do very little grandparenting. Given the retreat from marriage, the increase in births to single mothers, rising divorce and remarriage rates, and geographical mobility, many grandparents may be unaware they have a grandchild, have no access to that grandchild, or live too far away for meaningful contact. As Cherlin (2010) and Cherlin and Furstenburg (2009) describe, modern American families form and reform, sometimes at dizzying speeds, and the roles that grandparents play may change accordingly. In fact, some grandparents are removed and uninvolved. NACCRRA (2008) found that even among grandparents who live in the same neighborhood as their grandchildren, fully one-half did not provide any grandchild care whatsoever. Some grandparents face too much stress in their relationships with adult children; some face limits on their time, money, or health; and some are busy with other activities and do not wish to be part of an extended family support network. Grandparenting is not for everyone.

*Portions of this chapter are reprinted, with permission, from *Grandmothers at Work: Juggling Families and Jobs,* Madonna Harrington Meyer, 2014, NYU Press.

Conversely, some grandparents do virtually all of the parenting. Indeed, a small but growing group of grandparents provide custodial care to their grandchildren with little or no assistance from the parents. In 2009, nearly 3 million grandchildren were being raised by their grandparents, up from 2.5 million in 2000. Rates of custodial grandparenting are much higher for Blacks and Hispanics and those near the poverty level (Livingston and Parker, 2010). Custodial grandparents face special sets of challenges. Raising another set of children while facing middle-aged health and financial concerns, and struggling with the various reasons that their adult children are not doing the parenting themselves, may be simultaneously emotionally rewarding and physically and financially exhausting (Baker and Silverstein, 2008a, 2008b; Dolbin-MacNab, 2006; Hayslip and Kaminski, 2005).

The majority of U.S. grandparents, however, fall between these two extremes. They are hands-on grandparents and their support comes in all sizes and shapes. Some grandparents send birthday cards with cash, sit and visit the grandkids, or take them on brief outings, such as to the park, zoo, or pizza place. Others pitch in by helping with monthly expenses, childcare, and chores, all in an effort to help the younger generations balance work and family responsibilities. Others pay for soccer camps, scientific calculators, or glorious extended family vacations. Indeed, many U.S. grandparents support their grandchildren in a multitude of ways. In 2009, some 50% of U.S. grandparents reported that they had provided financial assistance to their adult children and grandchildren, 39% had provided grandchild care, and 31% had helped with errands, housework, and home repairs (Livingston and Parker, 2010).

The type of grandparenting depends in part on employment status. Many think of grandparents as retired and readily available, but increasingly, grandparents must balance the role of grandparenting with a job. One-half of Americans are grandparents by age 50 and three-fourths of those in their early 50s are still employed (AARP, 2002; Munnell, 2011; U.S. Bureau of Labor Statistic, 2011). The average age at retirement has increased by two years for men and for women since the mid-1990s, with men now retiring at an average age of 64 and women at an average age of 62 (Munnell, 2011; Population Reference Bureau, 2011; U.S. Department of Health and Human Services, 2008). Studies show that working grandparents are just as likely to provide care as those who are retired, and one-third change their work schedule to accommodate grandchild care (NACCRRA, 2008; Pavalko and Henderson, 2006). Thus, employment may impact grandparenting in competing ways. On one hand, employment may leave less time for grandkids; on the other hand, employment may mean more money available for the younger generations. Many grandparents are readily able to juggle work and care for grandchildren, but some find the multiple roles overly taxing (Harrington Meyer, 2014).

The type of grandparenting also depends in part on the extent of role differentiation. Traditionally, the role of grandparents has been defined differently than the role of parents. Grandparents are supposed to take kids for ice cream, bike rides, or matinees while parents are supposed to worry about proper nutrition, good manners, and algebra (Cherlin and Furstenberg, 2009). Typically, grand-parents were meant to augment childrearing and not be responsible for the basic daily care of children. Traditionally, then, role differentiation was quite high. But over the past few decades, the job descriptions might have become more similar. The role of grandparenting may be intensifying and looking more like the role of parenting, at least for some. Many grandparents may be providing more care than their parents did and more care than they expected to provide. Indeed, for some, the role of grandparenting appears to be intensifying (Harrington Meyer, 2014). In addition to feeding, bathing, and tucking in, grandparents are driving kids to lessons and camps, helping with homework, and watching kids for weeks, months, and even years at a time. Those helping grandchildren with special needs take on even more intensive carework, including therapies, physician visits, and medications. Developmental disabilities are on the rise in the United States, up 14% between 1997 and 2008, with a nearly 300% increase in Autism (Centers for Disease Control and Prevention, 2011; Hogan, 2012). Given the rise in working parents and single parents and the paucity of federal programs that provide job security or paid time off for family responsibilities, grandparenting may be intensifying because some young working families need the help. Many grandparents take the intensification of duties in stride while some are left wishing they were doing a lot less parenting and a lot more traditional, old-fashioned, grandparenting.

Finally, the type of grandparenting also depends on the supply of resources. It may be more difficult to provide support to younger generations for grandparents who have less income, less education, and worse health. Though we do not have statistics for grandparents *per se*, measures of socioeconomic and health status for those ages 65 and older, 80% of whom are grandparents, reveal that some have significantly fewer resources with which to grandparent. First, 10% of people ages 65 and older are poor, and another 6% are near poor (Administration on Aging, 2011). Women are significantly more likely than men to be single and poor in old age; 72% of men but only 42% of women are married. Single people tend to have less income; though the median household income for families headed by a person age 65 or older is $46,000, median income of older single males is $25,704 and single females is $15,072. Second, education has increased dramatically but still varies markedly by race and ethnicity. Between 1970 and 2010, the percentage of older persons who have completed high school rose from 28% to 80%; and 84% of Whites, 74% of Asians, 65% of Blacks, and only 47% of Hispanics have completed high school. Still, only one-fourth of older people have completed a college degree or more. Finally, though 40% of people ages 65 and older report that their health is excellent or good, 60% report that their health is only fair or poor. Certain groups are significantly less likely to report good health: only 28% of Hispanics and 26% of Blacks rate their health as excellent or very good (Administration on Aging, 2011). Grandparents who have less income, less education, and worse health may find it more difficult to buy formula, help with geometry, or chase a toddler. Having enough resources may make it easier to juggle various roles and may lead to role enhancement; having too few resources may make it more difficult and may lead to role conflict (Harrington Meyer, 2014; Cherlin and Furstenberg, 2009).

Increasing Need for Grandparent Care

Why are so many U.S. grandparents providing so much assistance to the younger generations? Several sociodemographic trends contribute to reliance on grandparents. The United States has relatively high levels of single mothers raising children and relatively high levels of employment, particularly full-time employment, among women with children. Moreover, the Great Recession of 2007–2009 has made it more difficult for many younger families to manage on their own and prompted more to turn to grandparents for assistance. Compared to other countries, neither the U.S. welfare state nor U.S. employers offer much support to help working families raise their children. As a result, many young working families juggle the competing responsibilities of kids and jobs by turning to grandmothers for low cost, high-quality childcare.

Many young U.S. families rely on grandparents for childcare or financial assistance because they are single-parent families. The U.S. Bureau of the Census (2008) reports that the share of women who are married has dropped from 66% in 1960 to 53% in 2008. This drop has been more pronounced among Black women. In 2008, some 55% of White, compared to just 34% of Black, women were married. Increasingly, births are to single women. In the 2010 U.S. Census Bureau data, 41% of all births in the United States were to unmarried women, up from 29% in 1980 (Lerner, 2010; Martin et al., 2012). About half of births to unmarried mothers may have been births to cohabitating mothers, but the U.S. Census Bureau does not record those relationships, and nonmarital relationships tend to be more fragile than marriages in the United States (Cherlin, 2010). Asians had the lowest proportion of births to single mothers, 17%, while Blacks had the highest, 72% (Lerner, 2010; Martin et al., 2012). Families headed by a single mother are much more likely to be poor. The U.S. Census Bureau (2012) reports that among families with a child under 18, approximately 19% of all married couples, compared to 41% of female-headed households, are poor. Single parenting is especially difficult for Black and Hispanic mothers—43% of Hispanic and 48% of Black single mothers live in poverty. Many of these single mothers continue to be poor as they reach old age. The Administration on Aging (2011) reports that 41% of single older Hispanic and 32% of single older Black women who live alone are poor. Nonetheless, many of them are providing hours of childcare and dollars of support for the younger generations.

Americans are turning to grandparents for help in part because they are working more hours than workers in any other country, even Japan. U.S. women, particularly those with young children, are increasingly likely to work, and to work full time (Coontz, 2013; Lerner, 2010). Notably, the percentage of women with children under age three working rose from 34% to 61% between 1975 and 2010. Such demographic changes have reshaped U.S. families. Glynn (2012a) reports that only 20% of children currently live in a family with a traditional male breadwinner/female homemaker compared to 45% in 1970. In 2010, the mother was the single or primary breadwinner in 41% of families, up from just 11% in 1970 (Glynn, 2012a). Among families with children, 40% were headed by two working parents, and another 32% were headed by a single parent. Young families have an increasing need for policies and programs that help them balance work and children, but in the United States there are not many options. Understandably, many young families ask grandparents to babysit.

Younger families are also turning to grandparents for help because the Great Recession of 2007–2009 hit many working families hard and there has not been much recovery during the subsequent period. The PEW Research Center (Kochhar, 2012) shows that median household incomes decreased about 4% during the two years of the recession and another 4% in the two years following. Moreover, the poverty rate rose from just over 12% in 2007 to 15% in 2011. Median household wealth fell from $131,016 in 2007 to $79,431 in 2010, a loss of 39%. And the percentage of families that reported at least one unemployed member doubled, from 6% in 2007 to 12% in 2009, and remained above 11% in 2011. Certain groups were especially hard hit. By the end of the recession, the median wealth of White households in 2009 was 20 times that of Black households and 18 times that of Hispanic households, the largest wealth gap on record (Kochhar, Fry, and Taylor, 2011). Bernanke (2012) points out that the Great Recession has made many workers more vulnerable to layoffs as well, making it that much more difficult to balance work and the needs of children. If taking time off for a sick child or a snow day might lead to job loss, many parents may think twice. No wonder they turn to grandma and grandpa for assistance.

Support From the U.S. Welfare State and Employers

Despite growing need, neither the U.S. welfare state nor U.S. employers have been very responsive to the needs of young working families (Chesley and Moen, 2006; Folbre, 2012; Harrington Meyer and Herd, 2007; Heymann, Earle, and McNeill, 2013). Compared to most European nations, the U.S. welfare state provides little support for families as they grow, and this explains part of the reliance on grandparents. Comparisons of different country policies have found that where state supports are more extensive, grandparents provide less care; where state supports are meager, grandparents provide much more support (Igel and Szydlik, 2011; Hughes, Waite, LaPierre, and Luo, 2007). The United States has no federal guarantee for paid vacation, paid sick leave, flexible work schedules, paid family leave, or affordable daycare. Many workers have some benefits through their employers, but these benefits are more readily available to full-time workers with higher salaries and lengthier tenure on the job. Moreover, such coverage has been shrinking in recent years (Glynn, 2012b; Harrington Meyer and Herd, 2007; IWPR, 2007; Lerner, 2010; Mezey, Greenberg, and Schumacher, 2002).

Paid time off is unequally distributed in the United States. Although 127 countries guarantee paid vacations, the United States has no federal vacation policy. The net effect is that one-third of female workers and one quarter of male workers have no paid vacation. In fact, among all working parents, only about 60% have paid vacation days (Glynn, 2012b; Lerner, 2010). Latinos are only one half as likely as Whites, Blacks, and Asians to have those benefits. Lower-income families are hardest hit. Of working parents in the bottom quintile of earnings, only 27% have paid vacation. By contrast, of working parents in the top two earnings quintiles, 76% have paid vacation. Vacations have been linked to higher employee satisfaction and productivity, better physical and emotional health, and stronger family bonds. Additionally, many working parents and grandparents use paid vacation days to schedule time off on days the children would otherwise need childcare (Glynn, 2012b; NACCRRA, 2008). Those without paid vacation time have one less option for providing childcare coverage throughout the year.

Similarly, the United States does not guarantee workers any amount of paid sick leave. Workers receive more or less generous packages through their employers. Ultimately, 44 million U.S. workers do not have paid sick days. Among working parents, only about 60% have paid sick leave, and for Latinos that rate is only about 30% (Glynn, 2012b; Williams, Drago, and Miller, 2010). Of working parents in the lowest earnings quintile, only 24% receive paid sick days compared to 75% in the upper two earnings quintiles. Workers use sick days to cover their own and their children's or grandchildren's illnesses. Those without paid sick days must either go to work when they or their children are ill or take time off with lost wages.

Moreover, the United States does not guarantee flexible work schedules and, as a result, few workers are able to negotiate such arrangements. Even the best educated and highest-paid workers in the United States are often unable to negotiate a flexible schedule when they have children (Stone, 2007). Among workers in the United States, only about 50% have flexible hourly plans that allow them to rearrange their work schedules, 40% have flexible day plans that allow them to alter which days they work, and 25% have flexible location plans that allow them to work from home or another location (Glynn, 2012b). These types of flexible work rules allow parents or grandparents to rearrange their workday to accommodate their children's or grandchildren's snow days, vacation days, early release days, sick days, and all other sorts of irregularities without losing pay or losing their jobs.

The United States does little to regulate the workweek. Many in the United States work much more than a 40-hour workweek. Recent time-use studies suggest Americans work more than employees in any other country, and this makes balancing carework and paid work all the more difficult. By contrast, Great Britain has taken steps to regulate the workweek and make more reduced and part-time work available; children have fared better in terms of health, education, and welfare under these national regulations (Folbre, 2004; Waldfogel, 2010). On the internationally comparative scale of the well-being of young people, Britain moved from 17th place in 2001 to 12th place in 2006. The United States has not taken any such steps.

The lack of paid maternity leave may be what hits U.S. families hardest. Heymann et al. (2013) found that 180 countries offer paid leave to new mothers and 81 offer paid leave to new fathers. The United States does not. The only federal provisions for family leave fall under the umbrella of the U.S. Family and Medical Leave Act, which offers 12 weeks of unpaid leave. However, less than one-half of U.S. workers are able to make use of it either because their employer is exempted for being too small, they have not worked at that firm for a full year, they do not work enough hours, the care recipient does not meet the qualifying criteria (same-sex partners or in-laws are not covered), or they cannot afford time off without pay (Armenia and Gerstel, 2006; Baum, 2006; Folbre, 2012; Han, Ruhm, and Waldfogel, 2009; Heymann, 2013; Lerner, 2010; Rudd, 2004). Those with lower incomes and who are single parents, who are least likely to be able to afford time off without pay, are least likely to take the leaves. Only 39% of workers earning less than $20,000 a year are covered by this law, compared to 74% of those earning over $100,000 (Heymann, 2013; Waldfogel, 2009). Although some women are offered paid maternity leave by their employers, this has dropped from 27% of working women in 1998 to only 16% in 2008 (IWPR, 2007; Lerner, 2010). Coverage by paid maternity leave varies markedly by education. The U.S. Census reports that between 2006 and 2008, some 66% of new mothers with a bachelor's degree or more were able to take paid leave, up from just 15% in the early 1960s (U.S. Census Bureau, 2011). By comparison, just 19% of new mothers with less than a high school diploma were able to take paid leave, the same rate of coverage as in the early 1960s.

Despite the increasing demand, there has been little increase in the supply of flexible, affordable, high-quality childcare. In 2005, about one-fourth of children of employed mothers were in organized childcare facilities, and one-fifth were cared for regularly by a grandparent (Federal Interagency Forum on Child and Family Statistics, 2006). Childcare is often difficult to find, expensive, and of variable quality. Harriet Presser (2003) points out that those with irregular work patterns requiring childcare during late afternoons, evenings, or on only a part-time or rotational basis often find that there are few organized childcare options for them. Moreover, when children are sick, they are not permitted at daycare and working parents have to make other arrangements or stay home from work—or call grandma and grandpa.

The costs for childcare can add up, eroding family earnings. Most families struggle to cope with the "bruising financial burden" (Cohn, 2013). According to Giannarelli and Barsimantov (2000), family daycare expenses are often the second-largest household expense, after the house mortgage. High-quality daycare through the private market is so expensive, Lerner (2010) reports, that families are increasingly being encouraged to pay for it through bank loans. The state provides some supports for families. Middle-income families may be eligible for tax subsidies through the dependent care tax credit. Low-income families may be eligible for tax credits and subsidized childcare, but only about 15% of those entitled to subsidized daycare actually receive assistance. Waiting lists for subsidized daycares and preschools are often so long that some children would be high school-aged by the time they would be admitted (Harrington Meyer and Herd, 2007; Lerner, 2010; Mezey et al., 2002). Finally, concerns about the quality of childcare are persistent. Vandell and Wolfe (2000) show that care is variable and often only fair to poor in quality. The NICHD (2007) established standards for care and reported that most daycare settings do not meet them. Only 10% of daycare settings they evaluated provided what they deemed high-quality care. With few high-quality, affordable options available through the market, many families turn to grandparents for childcare. In fact, grandparents are often defined as the most desirable source of childcare because they tend to have strong bonds with their grandchildren, to be maximally flexible about hours and locations, and to cost little or no money (Folbre, 2012; Harrington Meyer, 2014; NACCRRA, 2008). One survey of adults ages 40 and older found that when grandparents live nearby, more than half provide some amount of childcare every week, and one-half of those provide more than 12 hours a week (NACCRRA, 2008).

The paucity of paid vacation, paid sick leave, flexible work schedules, paid maternity leave, or affordable daycare—either through the U.S. welfare state or through employer benefit programs—leaves many families turning to grandparents for help with grandchildren.

Impact of Grandparenting

As with any type of care work, the impact of grandparenting on emotional, physical, and financial well-being tends to be quite mixed. Some studies show positive outcomes, others show no significant outcomes, and still others show negative outcomes (Baker and Silverstein, 2008a, 2008b; Baker, Silverstein, and Putney, 2008; Blustein, Chan, and Guanais, 2004; Dolbin-MacNab, 2006; Hayslip and Kaminski, 2005; Hughes et al., 2007; Kataoka-Yahiro, Ceria, and Caulfield, 2004; Landrey-Meyer and Newman, 2004; Ludwig and Winston, 2007; Musil, Warner, Zausniewski, Jeanblac, and Kercher, 2006; Nelson, 2000;

Robinson-Dooley and Kropf, 2006; Wang and Marcotte, 2007). With respect to emotional outcomes, grandparenting may bring a great deal of joy. Some grandparents find it to be the most joyful phase of their lives, even more joyful than raising their own children (Folbre, 2012; Harrington Meyer, 2014). But the emotional stresses and strains associated with care work, particularly if care is intense and must be balanced with other roles, can be overwhelming for some (Cherlin and Furstenberg, 2009). With respect to physical impacts, caring for grandchildren can be positive in that it may get grandparents up and moving, focused on a good diet, and committed to setting a good example. But it may also wear out aching joints and leave many grandparents too busy or too tired to attend properly to their own health issues (Baker and Silverstein, 2008b; Harrington Meyer, 2014; Hughes et al., 2007). With respect to financial impacts, grandparenting often results in less money coming in and more money going out. Indeed, many grandparents reduce or rearrange their work schedules to accommodate grandchild care (Harrington Meyer, 2014; Wang and Marcotte, 2007). Moreover many pay for everything from formula and diapers to rent and electric bills. While some grandparents can readily absorb these financial strains, others find they have to postpone travel and other leisure pursuits, delay retirement, or dig out of debt (Cherlin and Furstenberg, 2009; Harrington Meyer, 2014; Wang and Marcotte, 2007). Providing the right amount of the right types of care for grandchildren may leave grandparents rejuvenated and fulfilled; providing too much of the more intensive types of care may leave them depleted and exhausted.

Overview of the Book

Grandparenting in the United States is evolving and becoming more diverse. While some grandparents remain uninvolved, the majority are providing care and assistance even though they may also be employed, providing intensive care, or facing dwindling financial or physical resources. The types and intensities of care and assistance provided are linked to the impacts. Many studies show positive impacts on emotional, physical, and financial well-being, while others show that the transition into grandparenting, particularly when balancing employment, intensive care, and fewer resources, may lead to more negative impacts. The chapters in this book explore the diversity of supports, and the diversity of impacts, of grandparenting in the United States.

The type of support that grandparents provide varies by a variety of socio-demographic and cultural factors. In Chapter 2, Merril Silverstein and Yooumi Lee show just how much immigration and language of origin matter. Using HRS 2008 data, they examine whether the most common types of support—care provided to grandchildren and money transfers to and from younger generations— were differently related among older adults based on their race/ethnicity and language acculturation. They found that grandparents adapt support to various social and cultural conditions. Specifically, Hispanic grandparents preferring

Spanish language tended to provide grandchild care whether or not they provided economic transfers, while less acculturated Hispanic grandparents who received financial support from adult children were more than five times more likely to have provided grandchild care.

Grandparents often provide a lot of financial assistance to the younger generations and at least some do so at their own peril. In Chapter 3, Madonna Harrington Meyer uses qualitative data from the Grandmothers at Work Survey 2008–2012 to explore what sorts of financial assistance grandmothers are providing, why they are providing that assistance, and the impact on such financial contributions on their own retirement plans. Based on 48 in-depth interviews with noncustodial working grandmothers, she reports that nearly all of the grandmothers were providing financial support ranging from gifts to basic necessities to enormous monthly expenses. Most grandmothers helped because their adult children faced job insecurities due to the recession, became single parents, were sick or disabled, or were completing degrees. Others gave even though the help was not needed. Ultimately, she finds that while some grandmothers can readily afford these contributions, others are working more hours, delaying retirement, foregoing travel plans, diverting funds away from their own retirement accounts, or accumulating new debt.

Grandparenting can be particularly challenging for immigrant grandmothers who must traverse multiple sets of customs and expectations. In Chapter 4, Ynesse Abdul-Malak draws on in-depth interviews with 14 immigrant non-custodial grandmothers who immigrated to the United States from Latin America and the Caribbean. She analyzes how grandmothering in the United States varies from the role in their countries of origin. In particular, she focuses on how differences in cultural expectations complicate grandmothering for immigrant women and how providing grandchild care shapes grandmothers' health. She finds that the grandmothers struggling to balance competing expectations about joy vs. duty, tolerance vs. discipline, gendered vs. cultural roles, and economic insufficiency vs. religion abundancy. Most importantly, she finds that the complexities of navigating two sets of cultural expectations while caring for grandchildren may impact ability to exercise, see doctors, eat healthily, and manage chronic diseases.

The rise in childhood disabilities has been noteworthy. To what extent are noncustodial grandparents helping with the growing demands for childcare that accompany various disabilities? In Chapter 5, Peter Brandon explores before- and after-school daycare arrangements for children with disabilities to determine whether they are more likely to be cared for by grandparents. Using Survey of Income and Program Participation (SIPP) data from 1996, 2001, and 2004, he finds that schoolchildren with disabilities are indeed more likely to receive grandparent care and more hours of grandparent care, particularly if the mother is single. Schoolchildren with disabilities spend 50% more time in the care of grandparents when they have a single mother than schoolchildren with or without disabilities who have a married mother. Notably, he finds that the degree of functional limitation, and the type of disability, rather than simply having a disability, better predict whether grandparents will be more likely to provide care.

Though it is still the exception rather than the rule, why has so much scholarly attention been devoted to coresidential and custodial grandparenting families? Because they are becoming increasingly common and face special sets of challenges. Moreover, they have become even more common during and following the Great Recession. The second half of the volume focuses on co-residential and custodial grandparenting. In Chapter 6, Lynne Casper, Sandra Florian, C. Brady Potts, and Peter Brandon use data from the American Community Survey (ACS) to describe coresidential grandparent-grandchildren families. In analyzing class and race differences in these patterns, they find that coresidential grandparent households increased by over 12% following the Great Recession and grandparent-maintained households outnumbered parent-maintained by nearly 3 to 1. They found that while grandparents who maintain their own homes are younger, better educated, more likely to be employed and to act as primary caretakers, custodial grandmothers are significantly more likely to be in poverty.

When multiple generations of families coreside, what roles do grandparents play in building and maintaining family ties? In Chapter 7, Rachel Dunifon, Kimberly Kopko, P. Lindsay Chase-Lansdale, and Lauren Wakschlag explore how multigenerational relationships impact each other in families in which grandparents provide custodial care. They employ a multimethod data-collection system, including interviews and videos with 59 pairs of custodial grandparents and their teenaged grandchildren in New York State. They find that particularly when the relationship between the parent and grandchild was strained, grandparents provided a moderating influence, working hard to build ties and reduce tensions across the generations.

In contrast to numerous studies that explore the impact of custodial grandparenting on grandparent health, in Chapter 8, Megan Dolbin-MacNab explores the health of adolescents raised by grandparents. Using a convenience sample of 81 pairs of adolescents and their custodial grandmothers, and employing an ecological approach, she finds troublesome evidence that grandchildren living in poorer economic and social circumstances may be in worse health and receiving fewer services. Generally, grandchild behavioral and emotional problems were linked to poorer health. More specifically, internalized problems, including depression, have been linked with difficulties with emotional regulation and compromised physical health. Put simply, better grandparent health was linked with better grandchild health and that suggests important policy implications.

Grandparents are often asked how they feel about living with their grandchildren but Chapter 9 turns the tables. Laura Pittman, Micah Ioffe, and Christine Keeports explore young adults' perceptions of what it was like to live with a noncustodial grandparent when they were children. Using a nonrandom sample of 82 college undergraduates, they asked participants to reflect on why they were living with their grandparents and on what the experience was like. Not surprisingly, the results were mixed. Some grandparents moved in with the younger generations while some children moved in with grandparents. The moves were prompted by a wide variety of financial, health, and family tradition considerations. Some students reported feeling closer to their grandparent and enjoying extra assistance with daily life, while others reported that their grandparent was too strict, or yelled or smoked too much, leading to an increase in tension across generations in the household.

To what extent do the perceptions of others contribute to adverse effects of custodial grandparenting? In Chapter 10, Bert Hayslip, Rebecca Glover, and Sara Pollard investigate the perceptions of traditional grandparents about custodial grandparents. Previous research suggests that the job of custodial grandparenting is made even more difficult when others blame the grandparent for poor parenting of the adults who are now no longer parenting. In this study, participants in a nonrandom sample of 610 noncustodial grandparents were randomly assigned to read and react to hypothetical scenarios regarding the reasons a grandparent had to take custody of the grandchildren. The authors found that traditional grandparents predicted less life disruption and need for social support when grandparents took custody of a grandson rather than a granddaughter and when the parent died or had committed child abuse rather than faced hardship. Traditional grandparents perceived the most life disruption and need for services when the grandparent took custody following parental incarceration, drug abuse, or abandonment. To the extent that custodial grandparents feel judged by others, they may find that they face increasing social isolation and poorer physical and mental health.

Collectively, the chapters in this volume underscore how the role of grandparenting is diversifying. Grandparents provide a wide spectrum of emotional, childcare, and financial supports to their grandchildren. While some grandparents provide very little care, others provide routine or comprehensive care. Relying on quantitative sources of data, including the Health and Retirement Survey, SIPP, the American Community Survey, and qualitative sources, including studies of traditional, coresidential, and custodial grandparents, our authors illustrate the complexities of grandparenting and its impact on grandparents and grandchildren's well-being, while paying careful attention to how their situations vary by living arrangements, economic status, education, race, and other key stratifying variables. Taken together, the chapters in this volume highlight the evolving diversification of grandparenting in the United States.

References

AARP. 2002. Grandparenting survey. http://assets.aarp.org/rgcenter/general/gp_2002.pdf

Administration on Aging. 2011. *A profile of older Americans: 2011*. Washington, DC: Administration on Aging. http://www.aoa.gov/AoARoot/Aging_Statistics/Profile/2011/10.aspx.

Armenia, A. and Gerstel, N. 2006. Family leaves, the FMLA and gender neutrality: The intersection of race and gender. *Social Science Research,* 35: 871-891.

Baker, L. A. and Silverstein, M.. 2008a. Depressive symptoms among grandparents raising grandchildren: The impact of participation in multiple roles. *Journal of Intergenerational Relationships,* 6(3): 285-304.

Baker, L. A. and Silverstein, M. 2008b. Preventive health behaviors among grandmothers raising grandchildren. *The Journals of Gerontology Series B: Psychological Sciences and Social Sciences,* 63(5): S304-S311.

Baker, L. A., Silverstein, M., and Putney, N. M. 2008. Grandparents raising grandchildren in the United States: Changing family forms, stagnant social policies. *Journal of Sociology and Social Policy,* 28(7): 53-69.

Baum, C. L. 2006. The effects of government-mandated family leave on employer family leave policies. *Contemporary Economic Policy,* 24(3): 432-445.

Bernanke, B. 2012. *Recent developments in the labor market.* Washington, DC: Board of Governors of the Federal Reserve System.

Blustein, J., Chan, S., and Guanais, F. C. 2004. Elevated depressive symptoms among caregiving grandparents. *Health Services Research,* 39(6): 1671-1689. http://www.c.federalreserve.gov/newsevents/speech/bernanke20120326a.htm

Centers for Disease control and Prevention. 2011. develpomental disabilities increasing in the U.S.. http://www.cdc.gov/features/dsDev_Disabilities

Cherlin, A. J. 2010. *The marriage-go-round: The state of marriage and the family in America today.* New York, NY: Vintage.

Cherlin, A. and Furstenberg, Jr., F. 2009. *The new American grandparent: A place in the family, a life apart.* Cambridge, MA: Harvard University Press.

Chesley, N. and Moen, P. 2006. When workers care: Dual-earner couples' caregiving strategies, benefit use, and psychological well-being. *American Behavioral Scientist,* 49(9): 1248-1269.

Cohn, J. 2013. The hell of American day care: An investigation in to the barely regulated, unsafe business of looking after our children. *The New Republic,* April 15. http://www.newrepublic.com/article/112892/hell-american-day-care

Coontz, S. 2013. Why gender equality stalled. 2/16/13. *The New York Times.* http://www.nytimes.com/2013/02/17/opinion/sunday/why-gender-equality-stalled.html?emc=eta1

Dolbin-MacNab, M. L. 2006. Just like raising your own? Grandparents' perceptions of parenting a second time around. *Family Relations,* 55(5): 564-575.

Federal Interagency Forum on Child and Family Statistics. 2006. *America's children: Key national indicators of well-being.* Washington, DC: U.S. Government Printing Office. http://childstats.gov/americaschildren/tables.asp.

Folbre, N. 2004. A theory of the misallocation of time. In N. Folbre and M. Bittman (Eds.), *Family time: The social organization of care.* New York, NY: Routledge.

Folbre, N. 2012. *For love and money: Care provision in the United States,* N. Folbre (Ed.). New York, NY: Russell Sage Foundation.

Giannarelli, L. and Barsimantov, J. 2000. Child care expenses of America's families. Washington, DC: Urban Institute. http://www.urban.org/UploadedPDF/310028_occa40.pdf

Glynn, S. J. 2012a. *The new breadwinners, 2012 update.* Washington DC: Center for American Progress. http://www.americanprogress.org/issues/labor/report/2012/04/16/11377/the-new-breadwinners-2010-update/

Glynn, S. J. 2012b. *Working parents' lack of access to paid leave and workplace flexibility.* Washington, DC: Center for American Progress. http://www.americanprogress.org/wp-content/uploads/2012/11/GlynnWorkingParents-1.pdf

Han, W. J., Ruhm, C., & Waldfogel, J. 2009. Parental leave policies and parents' employment and leave-taking. *Journal of Policy Analysis and Management,* 28(1): 29-54.

Harrington Meyer, M. 2014. *Grandmothers at Work: Juggling Families and Jobs.* New York, NY: NYU Press

Harrington Meyer, M. and Herd, P. 2007. *Market friendly or family friendly? The state and gender inequality in old age.* New York, NY: Russell Sage Foundation.

Hayslip, B. and Kaminski, P. L. 2005. Grandparents raising their grandchildren: A review of the literature and suggestions for practice. *The Gerontologist,* 45: 263-269.

Heymann, J. 2013. *Children's chances: How countries can move from surviving to thriving.* Cambridge, MA: Harvard University Press.

Heymann, J., Earle, A., and McNeill, K. (2013). The impact of labor policies on the health of young children in the context of economic globalization. *Annual Review of Public Health,* 34: 355-372.

Hogan, D. P. 2012. *Family consequences of children's disabilities.* New York. NY: Russell Sage Foundation.

Hughes, M. E., Waite, L. J., LaPierre, T. A., and Luo, Y. 2007. All in the family: The impact of caring for grandchildren on grandparents' health. *The Journals of Gerontology Series B: Psychological Sciences and Social Sciences,* 62(2): S108-S119.

Igel, C. and Szydlik, M. 2011. Grandchild care and welfare state arrangements in Europe. *Journal of European Social Policy,* 21(3): 210-224. http://esp.sagepub.com/content/21/3/210.full.pdf+html

Institute for Women's Policy and Research (IWPR). 2007. *Maternity leave in the United States.* A131, August, Washington DC: IWPR.

Kataoka-Yahiro, M., Ceria, C., and Caulfield, R. 2004. Grandparent caregiving role in ethnically diverse families. *Journal of Pediatric Nursing,* 19: 315-328.

Kochhar, R., Fry, R., and Taylor, P. 2011. *Wealth gaps rise to record highs between whites, blacks, Hispanics.* Washington DC: PEW Research. http://www.pewsocialtrends.org/2011/07/26/wealth-gaps-rise-to-record-highs-between-whites-blacks-hispanics/

Kochhar, R. 2012. *A recovery no greater than the recession.* Washington, DC: PEW Research. http://www.pewsocialtrends.org/2012/09/12/a-recovery-no-better-than-the-recession/

Landry-Meyer, L. and Newman, B. M. 2004. An exploration of the grandparent caregiver role. *Journal of Family Issues,* 25: 1005-1025.

Lerner, S. 2010. *The war on moms: On life in a family-unfriendly nation.* Hoboken NJ: John Riley & Sons.

Livingston, G. and Parker, K. 2010. *Since the start of the Great Recession, more children raised by grandparents.* PEW Charitable Trusts. http://www.pewtrusts.org/our_work_report_detail.aspx?id=60725&category=304

Ludwig, F. M. and Winston, K. 2007. How caregiving for grandchildren affects grandparents' meaningful occupations. *Journal of Occupational Science,* 14(1): 40-51.

Martin, J. A., Hamilton, B. A., Ventura, S. J., Osterman, M. J. K., Wilson, E. C., and Mathews, T. J. 2012. Births: Final data for 2010. *National Vital Statistics Report,* 61(1). http://www.cdc.gov/nchs/data/nvsr/nvsr61/nvsr61_01.pdf#table15

Mezey, J., Greenberg, M., and Schumacher, R. 2002. *The vast majority of federally-eligible children did not receive child care assistance in FY 2000.* Washington, DC: Center for Law and Social Policy.

Munnell, A. 2011. *What is the average retirement age?* Center for Retirement Research. http://crr.bc.edu/briefs/what-is-the-average-retirement-age/

Musil, C. M., Warner, C. B., Zausniewski, J. A., Jeanblac, A. B., and Kercher, K. 2006. Grandparents, caregiving, and family functioning. *The Journals of Gerontology Series B: Psychological Sciences and Social Sciences,* 61: S89-S98.

NACCRRA. 2008. *Grandparents: A critical child care safety net.* Arlington, VA: National Association of Child Care Resources and Referral Agencies. http://www.naccrra.org/sites/default/files/publications/naccrra_publications/2012/grandparentscriticalchild caresafetynet.pdf

National Institute of Child Health and Human Development. 2007. *The NICHD study of early child care and youth development: Findings for children up to ages 4½ years.* https://www.nichd.nih.gov/publications/pubs/documents/seccyd_06.pdf

Nelson, J. L. 2000. Contemplating grandparenthood. *Ageing International,* 26(102): 3-9.

Pavalko, E. K. and Henderson, K. 2006. Combining care work and paid work: Do workplace policies make a difference? *Research on Aging,* 28, 359-374.

Population Reference Bureau. 2011. The health and well-being of grandparents caring for grandchildren. *Today's Research on Aging,* 23: 1-6.

Presser, H. B. 2003. *Working in a 24/7 economy: Challenges for American Families.* New York, NY: Russell Sage Foundation.

Rudd, E. 2004. Family leave: A policy concept made in America. In M. Pitt-Catsouphes and E. Kossek (Eds.), *Work-family encyclopedia.* http://www.bc.edu/bc_org/avp/wfnetwork/rft/wfpedia/index.html

Robinson-Dooley, V. and Kropf, N. P. 2006. Second generation parenting: Grandparents who receive tanf. *Journal of Intergenerational Relationships,* 4: 49-62.

Stone, P. 2007. *Opting out: Why women really quit careers and head home.* Berkeley and Los Angeles, CA: University of California Press.

U.S. Census Bureau. 2008. *Table MS-1 Marital status of the population 15 years old and over, by sex and race. 1950 to present.* http://www.census.gov/population/www/socdemo/hh-fam.html#ht.

U.S. Census Bureau. 2011. *Maternity leave and employment patterns of first time mothers, 1961-2008.* Washington, DC: Department of Commerce. http://www.census.gov/prod/2011pubs/p70-128.pdf

U.S. Census Bureau. 2012. *Current Population Survey, Annual Social and Economic Supplements.* Social, Economic, and Housing Statistics Division: Poverty. Table 4. Poverty status of families, by type of family, presence of related children, race, and Hispanic origin: 1959 to 2011. http://www.census.gov/hhes/www/poverty/data/historical/families.html

U.S. Bureau of Labor Statistics. 2011. *Women in the Labor Force: A Databook.* Report 985. Table 7. Employment status of women by presence and age of youngest child, 1975-2010. http://www.bls.gov/cps/wlf-databook-2011.pdf

U.S. Department of Health and Human Services. 2008. *Grandparents raising grandchildren: A call to action.* Administration for Children and Families, Region IV. www.acf.hhs.gov/opa/doc/grandparents.pdf

Vandell, D. L. and Wolfe, B. 2000. *Child care quality: Does it matter and does it need to be improved?* Report to the Assistant Secretary for Planning and Evaluation, U.S. Department of Health and Human Services. http://aspe.hhs.gov/hsp/ccquality00/index.htm

Waldfogel, J. 2010. *Britain's war on poverty.* New York, NY: Russell Sage Foundation.

Wang, Y. and Marcotte, D. E. 2007. Golden years? The labor market effects of caring for grandchildren. *Journal of Marriage and Family*, 69(5): 1283-1296.

Williams, C., Drago, R., and Miller, K. 2010. 44 million U.S. workers lacked paid sick days in 2010. IWPR #B293 Washington, DC: Institute for Women's Policy Research. http://www.iwpr.org/pdf/B293PSD.pdf

PART 1

Grandparenting

http://dx.doi.org/10.2190/GITC2

CHAPTER 2

Race and Ethnic Differences in Grandchild Care and Financial Transfers with Grandfamilies: An Intersectional Resource Approach

Merril Silverstein and Yooumi Lee

Grandparents often form the first line of defense in support of their families, allocating valued resources when childcare services and economic assistance are needed. A growing literature has documented the importance of grandparents for the well-being of their adult children and grandchildren (hereafter called grandfamilies), ranging from heroic forms of custodial care for grandchildren whose parents are unable or incapable of engaging in effective parenting, to intermittent childcare that allows parents, mostly mothers, to work in the labor force. Economic support is another strategy by which grandparents elevate the well-being of their grandfamilies by providing financial benefits to adult children that trickle down to also benefit grandchildren. Thus, *time* and *money* are the currencies by which grandparents contribute to, as well as benefit from, their grandfamilies.

This chapter examines time/money tradeoffs in intergenerational grandparent support based on the ethnic and racial identification of grandparents, with particular focus on Black and Hispanic families and their language acculturation. We test the propositions that grandchild care is more interchangeable with providing financial support and more exchangeable with received financial support among ethnic minorities and less acculturated Hispanics than among non-Hispanic Whites.

In this introduction, we first review the extant literature on the contributions of grandparents to their grandfamilies, discuss several theoretical frameworks within which such intergenerational contributions can be understood, and finally discuss the role of race, ethnicity, and immigrant acculturation in structuring intergenerational transfers by grandparents. There are several ways that this chapter differs from much of the literature on grandparent care providers. First, it does not focus on full-time custodial grandparents nor does it focus on grandparents living in skipped-generation households. While we include custodial grandparents in our analytic sample, we note that only 1% of our national sample of grandparents reported that they were raising a grandchild. Thus, we throw a wide net in capturing the broad cross-section of grandparents who provide at least some care for their grandchild. Second, this chapter takes relationships between grandparents and their adult children with their own families as the primary units of analysis. This allows us to focus on individual relationship dynamics and take into account supply and demand factors by which grandparents divide their care among the families of their adult children.

Grandparents as Care Providers

Much research has documented the contributions made by grandparents to their grandchildren and the families of their grandchildren. These contributions range from the prosaic or occasional babysitting to the prolific or custodial caretaking. Although custodial grandparenting is a vitally important social issue and a topic addressed by numerous studies, this phenomenon characterizes only a small fraction of grandparents. On the other hand, caring for grandchildren on a part-time basis is quite common in the United States, with 40% of grandparents providing at least 50 hours of care per year for the children of working parents (Hughes, Waite, LaPierre, and Luo, 2007). Longer-term estimates of prevalence show that over a 10-year period, more than 60% of grandparents provided some care for a grandchild (Luo, LaPierre, Hughes, and Waite, 2012). This result is mirrored in a multinational European study of grandparents 50 years of age and older that found 40% to 60% of grandparents taking care of grandchildren at least occasionally (Attias-Donfut, Ogg, and Wolff, 2005).

One reason why grandparents' care for grandchildren is so prevalent is that women's labor force participation has created demand for the services of grandparents as trustworthy, reliable, and inexpensive sources of childcare in dual-earner and single-mother families. One out of five children below the age of 5 with employed mothers was found to have received care from grandparents as their main source of daycare (Clarke and Cairns, 2001; Ho, 2013). Grandparents appear to allocate their efforts strategically by contributing grandchild care to the families of those parents with greater labor market potential (Dimova and Wolff, 2007). By doing so, grandparents improve the economic status of their grandfamilies by saving them opportunity costs of formal childcare services (Cardia and Ng, 2003; Kritz, Gurak, and Chen, 2000) and reducing their economic hardship by enabling (mostly) maternal labor (Mutchler and Baker, 2009). Supporting these findings from a more macroperspective, several studies found that European countries with higher prevalence of grandparents providing occasional care for their grandchildren also tended to have higher female labor force participation rates (Hagestad and Oppelaar, 2004), as well as more generous social policies that provide incentives for women to work (Hank and Buber, 2009).

Financial Transfers and Care: Substitutable or Reinforcing?

In addition to grandchild care, grandparents are also apt to provide economic assistance to their grandfamilies. Whether grandparent-provided childcare and economic support are substitutable—with each compensating for the absence of the other—or reinforcing—with each complementing the other—has been little considered. Relatively poor grandparents may provide care rather than money to support their grandfamilies, a dynamic observed in other types of family caregiving relationships (Berry, 2006).

There is also evidence that grandparents may use different strategies in allocating time and money resources to their grandfamilies. Downward economic transfers tend to flow to adult children in need, such as the divorced, the unemployed, and single mothers, supporting an altruistic model of giving (Fritzell and Lennartsson, 2005; Künemund, Motel-Klingebiel, and Kohli, 2005; McGarry and Schoeni, 1997). In contrast, supplemental childcare is directed at grandfamilies whose parents have greater education and income (Lee and Aytac, 1998). What this suggests is a dual and contingent strategy on the part of grandparents who help their grandfamilies by targeting childcare services at their more advantaged children and economic support at their more disadvantaged children.

Exchange Dynamics in Families

The contributions of grandparents to their grandfamilies are often couched as altruistically motivated behavior, a form of self-sacrifice for saving the families of their adult children (Hagestad and Oppelaar, 2004). However, particularly in groups and societies characterized by greater scarcity, contributions made by grandparents to their grandfamilies may also be strategically motivated and governed by a norm of reciprocity where grandparents benefit from a return to their time investment. Evidence suggests that grandparents provide care for grandchildren whose parents are most likely to reciprocate by providing upward support (see Friedman, Hechter, and Kreager, 2008).

In developing countries, a time-for-money exchange between generations is a common way for families to adapt to resource constraints and uncertainties, and is institutionalized by filial norms that informally enforce these exchanges. A typical exchange pattern is where grandparents provide care for the children of migrant workers in return for remittances (Cong and Silverstein, 2008; Frankenberg, Lillard, and Willis, 2002). We propose that a similar exchange mechanism exists in groups with a cultural template that prioritizes the centrality of family life and reinforces a general obligation to support family members in need (Fine and Fincham, 2013). In the developed world, the most common type of grandchild care allows women to work, thereby increasing the economic viability of grandfamilies by enabling the accumulation of resources that under particular conditions will allow economic transfers back to the grandparents.

Race/Ethnicity and Acculturation in Grandparenting

Race and ethnic differences have long been observed with respect to styles of grandparenting. African American and Hispanic grandparents tend to be more integrated within their extended families than non-Hispanic White grandparents (Pudrovska, Schieman, and Carr, 2006; Sarkisian, Gerena, and Gerstel, 2006). African American grandparents tend to be more involved with their grandchildren on a daily basis than White grandparents and are more apt than other grandparents to provide discipline, guidance, support, and surrogate care to their grandchildren (Hunter and Taylor, 1998). This difference has been observed with regard to both residential care (Fuller-Thomson and Minkler, 2000) and nonresidential care (Luo et al., 2012). The stronger, more authoritative role taken by Black grandmothers has deep cultural roots, reflecting a tradition of surrogate parenting and extended familism going back to the time of slavery (Hunter and Taylor, 1998; Jimenez, 2002).

Grandparent-grandchild relations in Hispanic families are typically viewed as being more interactive than those in non-Hispanic White families (Strom, Buki, and Strom, 1997), but there is likely to be variation based on acculturation status. Immigrant and less acculturated grandparents often face special challenges such as intergenerational conflict, language incompatibility, and geographic distance from relatives in their nations of origin (Silverstein and Chen, 1999; Treas and Mazumdar, 2002) that may suppress their caregiving for grandchildren. On the other hand, cultural values that privilege in-group family relations provide a basis for intergenerational support and care. Hispanic immigrants to the United States with Spanish-language preference were most likely to provide economic transfers to their parents paralleling similar results among North African immigrants with respect to French-language preference in France (Silverstein and Attias-Donfut, 2010).

As a result of their lower-than-average access to public benefits and concentration in low-wage labor markets, international migrants often engage in mutual cross-generational exchanges of support, both as a survival strategy and as an expression of cultural norms. The question of whether normative structures or lack of alternative sources of care promote resource exchange in immigrant families has yet to be resolved. Divergent views on the role of ethnicity, whether considered a resource or a source of jeopardy, call into question some of the broad assumptions made about support networks in minority and immigrant families and demand more detailed research on intergenerational transfers in these families.

If strong cultural considerations are involved in whether grandparents in minority groups provide care for their grandchildren, then such care may be less conditional on the receipt of money from their adult children. The strong cultural justification for caregiving noted among minority groups (Dilworth-Anderson, Brummett, Goodwin, Williams, Williams, and Siegler, 2005) may imply that grandchild care provided by Hispanic grandparents, particularly less acculturated Hispanic, as well as African American grandparents, is unconditional and may be weakly tied to receiving financial support from children.

On the other hand, we know that upstream intergenerational economic transfers may compensate grandparents for the childcare they provide, particularly among those grandparents in need. In minority families, grandparents' in-kind support to younger generations in the form of childcare may be exchanged for economic support from them in a pattern similar to the time-for-money exchanges observed in less developed societies.

Our central research aims revolve around two questions related to the inter-section of grandchild care and intergenerational financial transfers across several ethnic/racial and language acculturation groups: Are grandparents' contributions of child and economic support to their grandfamilies better characterized as compensatory, rather than complementary, among minority and less acculturated individuals compared to their counterparts? and Are grandparents who receive economic support from their adult children more likely to provide care for grand-children, and is this relationship stronger or weaker among minority and less acculturated individuals when compared to non-Hispanic Whites?

Method

Sample

We used the 2008 Health and Retirement Study (HRS), a biennial nationally representative study of the population 50 years old and older in the United States. Spouses of main respondents under the age of 50 were also included in the survey. We chose the 2008 survey as it is the latest wave for which data about relationships with children were archived in user-friendly format at the time of this writing. We note that the data collection in 2008 took place either just before or just after the financial crisis of that year and the sample is largely untouched by that event. Consequently, the results reported here arguably repre-sent a better depiction of typical family functioning.

For our analyses, we selected 11,981 respondents who had at least one living grandchild, described their race as White or Black, reported their ethnic identity either as Hispanic or non-Hispanic, and who reported about at least one adult child who was a parent. Respondent characteristics were linked to their reports about 23,106 adult children who were the parents of at least one grandchild of the respondent. Because both grandmothers and grandfathers in the same family were included in the study, the procedure generated 34,369 grandparent-adult child/parent records. After omitting 258 records with missing data, the final analytic sample consisted of 34,111 observational units. Because adult children are also parents, we variously refer to them as adult children and/or parents depending on the context.

Dependent Variable

Each grandparent was asked whether he or she provided care for the children or grandchildren of each adult child, and the number of hours they provided such care over the past 2 years. We use the cut-off provided by HRS of 100 hours or more to denote that childcare was provided. This threshold indicates that a nontrivial amount of care was provided. Although number of hours is provided as a continuous variable in the dataset, the percentage of missing values makes use of this information prohibitive. We also note that the amount of time spent providing childcare was asked about both grandchildren and great-grandchildren; however, this information cannot be disaggregated. Assuming that the large majority of care was provided for grandchildren, we refer to this variable as grandchild care.

Independent Variables

We consider a wide variety of personal and family characteristics to predict the provision grandchild care that are organized by whether they describe grandparents or adult children/parents. The main substantive variables are race/ethnicity/acculturation, and economic transfers. Acculturation is proxied by whether or not the respondent completed the interview in Spanish. While a somewhat imperfect measure of acculturation, it serves as a direct indicator of language preference, which much research associates with a traditional cultural orientation.

Race/ethnicity and acculturation are included in combination such that three dichotomous variables are constructed indicating Black, Hispanic with English language preference, and Hispanic with Spanish language preference, with non-Hispanic Whites as the reference group. Economic transfers between generations is measured as whether the respondent provided a financial contribution of $500 or more to each adult child over the past 2 years (1 = yes; 0 = no) and whether the respondent received a financial contribution of $500 or greater from each adult child over the past 2 years (1 = yes; 0 = no).

Among grandparent's characteristics, we control for the following factors known to be associated with providing care for grandchildren: age in years; gender (1 = grandmother; 0 = grandfather); currently married (1 = yes, 0 = no); self-rated health (1 = excellent, 2 = very good, 3 = good, 4 = fair, 5 = poor); years of education (1 = less than high school, 2 = GED, 3 = high school graduate, 4 = some college, 5 = college graduate or more); log of total household income; number of adult children; employed full-time (1 = yes, 0 = no); physical impairment based on self-reported ability to perform seven instrumental activities of daily living

(IADL) (1 = at least one IADL impairment, 0 = no IADL impairment); depressive symptoms based on the abridged CES-D (1 = at least one symptom; 0 = no symptoms); number of children using three dichotomous indicators: two children, three children, and four or more children, with one child as the reference group; number of grandchildren using two dichotomous indicators: six to nine grandchildren, and ten or more grandchildren, with one to five grandchildren as the reference group; and having at least one great-grandchild (1 = yes; 0 = no).

We also take into account characteristics of the adult children as the middle parental generation forms an important relational bridge linking nonadjacent generations (Monserud, 2008). These variables include gender of child (1 = daughter, 0 = son); age in years, college (1 = yes; 0 = no); employed full time (1 = yes; 0 = no); married (1 = yes; 0 = no); lives with parent (1 = yes, 0 = no); and number of children.

Results

We first present descriptive information regarding the grandparents in the sample. Table 1 shows the characteristics of grandparents. We note that 27% of grandparents report providing care for grandchildren at for at least 100 hours, or roughly 2 hours per week, for at least one grandchild over the last 2 years. The distribution across the race/ethnic/acculturation groups reveals slightly higher rates among Blacks (29%) and more acculturated Hispanics (30%) compared to non-Hispanic Whites (27%), but a somewhat lower rate (23%) among less acculturated Hispanics. In terms of financial transfers to and from any child, 36% of the total sample provided a transfer and 5% received a transfer. Differences in other factors fall in predictable ways. Non-Hispanic Whites had the highest rate (39%) of providing a transfer and the lowest rate (4%) of receiving a transfer. Rates of providing transfers to children were particularly low (15%) among less acculturated Hispanics and rates of receiving transfers from children were particularly high (13%) for Blacks. Differences in grandchild care and economic transfers by race/ethnic/acculturation group could be understood by lower education, lower rates of work, and poorer physical and mental health among Black and Hispanic grandparents. However, less acculturated Hispanics had larger families and more grandchildren than the other groups, belying their lower rates of providing care.

Characteristics of adult children who are parents of the respondents' grandchildren are shown in Table 2. These statistics are evaluated on a per-adult child basis. Percentages of adult children who received assistance in childcare were roughly consistent with results at the level of grandparents; children of less acculturated Hispanics were least likely to receive childcare assistance at 8% compared to 12% of children of more acculturated Hispanics, 11% of Blacks, and 12% of non-Hispanic Whites. Again, we see highest rate (15%) of providing economic transfers to children among non-Hispanic Whites and the lowest rate

Table 1. Descriptive Statistics for Grandparents (GP) by
Race/Ethnicity/Acculturation Group (N = 11,981)

	Percentage (%) or Mean				
		Race/Ethnicity			
				Hispanic	
Variable	Total sample	White non-Hispanic	Black	English-preference	Spanish-preference
Total sample (%)	(N = 11,981)	76.71	13.46	4.68	5.14
Grandchild care					
No	72.56	72.66	71.29	69.95	76.91
Yes	27.44	27.34	28.71	30.05	23.09
GP provides financial transfer					
No	63.88	61.48	68.94	65.78	84.74
Yes	36.12	38.52	31.06	34.22	15.26
GP receives financial transfer					
No	94.66	96.19	87.35	92.34	93.02
Yes	5.34	3.81	12.65	7.66	6.98
Gender					
Male	40.31	41.39	34.78	39.75	39.29
Female	59.69	58.61	65.22	60.25	60.71
Marital status					
Married	64.39	67.77	45.44	62.57	65.10
Separated/divorced	12.34	10.25	21.88	18.54	12.99
Widowed	22.19	21.79	27.84	16.22	18.67
Never married	1.09	.18	4.84	2.67	3.25
Educational attainment					
Less than high school	21.75	15.01	34.37	35.83	76.30
GED	4.79	4.75	4.90	8.20	2.11
High school graduate	32.99	35.50	28.60	25.13	14.12
Some college	22.37	23.84	20.53	22.64	5.03
College or above	18.11	20.91	11.60	8.20	2.44
Employment status					
Full-time work	18.50	17.52	21.14	26.20	19.16
Part-time work	13.62	14.09	13.52	12.66	7.79
Not working	67.88	68.39	65.34	61.14	73.05

Table 1. (Cont'd.)

	Percentage (%) or Mean				
	Race/Ethnicity				
				Hispanic	
Variable	Total sample	White non-Hispanic	Black	English-preference	Spanish-preference
Self-rated health					
Excellent	8.65	9.55	5.21	8.73	4.22
Very good	28.83	32.07	21.96	20.86	6.01
Good	32.67	33.02	33.06	35.83	23.70
Fair	20.99	17.67	27.98	21.03	52.44
Poor	8.82	7.70	11.79	13.55	13.64
IADL					
No	85.19	86.51	80.53	83.07	79.71
Yes	14.81	13.49	19.47	16.93	20.29
Mental health: CES-D					
No	45.94	48.86	37.01	34.42	35.23
Yes	54.06	51.14	62.99	65.58	64.77
Number of adult children					
One	5.38	5.45	6.14	5.17	2.44
Two	24.55	26.94	16.99	19.96	12.82
Three	24.59	26.10	19.47	21.21	18.51
Four or more	45.49	41.51	57.41	53.65	66.23
Number of grandchildren					
One to five	50.61	53.69	42.47	43.32	32.47
Six to nine	26.90	27.18	24.92	27.63	27.27
Ten or more	22.49	19.13	32.61	29.06	40.26
Great-grandchildren					
None	60.91	63.10	49.03	59.75	60.16
One or more	39.09	36.90	50.97	40.25	39.84
Age	69.96	70.74	68.03	65.78	67.10
	(9.95)	(9.81)	(9.58)	(10.15)	(10.66)
Total household income	10.47	10.66	9.94	10.27	9.25
(log)	(1.31)	(1.07)	(1.59)	(1.40)	(2.26)

Notes: Standard deviations are shown in parentheses.

Table 2. Descriptive Statistics for Adult Children/Parents by
Race/Ethnicity/Acculturation Group (*N* = 23,106)

	Percentage (%) or Mean				
	Race/Ethnicity				
				Hispanic	
Variable	Total sample	White non-Hispanic	Black	English-preference	Spanish-preference
Total sample (%)	(*N* = 23,106)	71.30	17.41	5.00	6.29
GP provides childcare to adult child					
No	88.34	88.01	88.61	87.68	91.92
Yes	11.66	11.99	11.39	12.32	8.08
GP provides financial transfer to adult child					
No	87.20	85.28	90.80	90.56	96.28
Yes	12.80	14.72	9.20	9.44	3.72
GP receives financial transfer from adult child					
No	97.62	98.18	95.35	96.97	98.14
Yes	2.38	1.82	4.65	3.03	1.86
Coresidence with GP					
No	95.94	97.21	93.13	93.78	90.92
Yes	4.06	2.79	6.87	6.22	9.08
Gender					
Male	48.45	49.23	46.53	46.93	46.11
Female	51.55	50.77	53.47	53.07	53.89
Age					
Less than 25 years old	.98	.53	1.49	3.38	2.82
25–34 years old	11.67	9.51	14.64	20.26	21.13
35–44 years old	31.87	30.78	34.58	34.37	34.76
45+ years old	55.47	59.18	49.29	41.99	41.29
Marital status					
Married	75.82	81.11	54.74	72.21	77.08
Not married	24.18	18.89	45.26	27.79	22.92

Table 2. (Cont'd.)

Variable	Total sample	Percentage (%) or Mean			
		Race/Ethnicity			
		White non-Hispanic	Black	Hispanic	
				English-preference	Spanish-preference
Employment status					
Full-time work	72.11	73.42	69.27	66.73	68.90
Part-time work	8.20	8.35	7.55	9.02	7.36
Not working	19.69	18.23	23.18	24.25	23.74
Educational attainment					
Less than high school	9.85	6.52	13.68	18.10	30.39
High school graduate	38.10	36.19	43.74	42.77	40.52
Some college	24.25	25.06	23.73	22.94	17.57
College or above	27.80	32.22	18.84	16.19	11.51
Number of children	2.47	2.42	2.59	2.60	2.68
	(1.32)	(1.23)	(1.57)	(1.45)	(1.42)

Notes: Standard deviations are shown in parentheses.

(4%) among less acculturated Hispanics. Similarly, the highest rate (5%) of receiving transfers from children was found among Blacks. However, unlike at the grandparent level of analysis, the children of less acculturated Hispanic children had the lowest rate (2%) of receiving transfers, a rate comparable to non-Hispanic Whites (2%), a likely consequence of larger family size among less acculturated Hispanics. Adult children of Black and Hispanic grandparents, and particularly those descended from less acculturated Hispanics, had lower education, less full-time employment, and were more likely to be coresident with a parent compared to adult children of non-Hispanic White grandparents.

We use random effects logistic regression in Stata (StataCorp, 2013) to estimate equations predicting whether or not care is provided for the children of each adult child of the respondent. Because observations are clustered within families, the random effects model provides appropriate estimates and robust standard errors that take into account familywide interdependencies among the observations. We note that the intraclass correlations, indicated by *rho* (ρ in the equations of Table 3, range from 52% to 57%, indicating substantial within-family homogeneity in grandchild care and justifying the use of the random effects model.

Table 3. Logistic Regression Equations Predicting Grandparents
Care for Grandchildren
(Odds Ratio and 95% Confidence Interval)

Variable	Equation 1	Equation 2	Equation 3	Equation 4
Grandparents' (GP) Characteristics				
Black[a]	1.110 (.923~1.334)	1.011 (.823~1.241)	1.030 (.827~1.283)	.953 (.775~1.172)
Hispanic English-preference[a]	.864 (.648~1.153)	.706* (.515~.969)	.855 (.610~1.199)	.732 (.529~1.011)
Hispanic Spanish-preference[a]	.684* (.507~.923)	.449*** (.322~.626)	.498*** (.355~.700)	.390*** (.275~.551)
Grandmother[b]	1.083 (.953~1.231)	1.334*** (1.158~1.536)	1.340*** (1.163~1.543)	1.338*** (1.162~1.539)
Age	.922*** (.915~.929)	.973*** (.963~.982)	.972*** (.963~.982)	.976*** (.967~.985)
Married[c]	1.707*** (1.472~1.978)	1.943*** (1.651~2.287)	1.897*** (1.612~2.232)	1.937*** (1.647~2.278)
Educational attainment	1.084** (1.029~1.143)	1.013 (.956~1.074)	1.012 (.954~1.073)	1.052 (.992~1.114)
Total household income	1.030 (.977~1.086)	.998 (.943~1.056)	.998 (.943~1.056)	1.031 (.974~1.091)
Self-rated health	.951 (.891~1.015)	.950 (.885~1.021)	.951 (.885~1.022)	.940 (.875~1.009)
At least one IADL[d]	.697*** (.563~.863)	.629*** (.498~.796)	.637*** (.504~.805)	.642*** (.509~.811)
At least one depressive symptom[e]	.969 (.935~1.004)	.955* (.918~.993)	.955* (.918~.993)	.962* (.925~1.000)
Two children[f]	.626*** (.521~.751)	.690*** (.565~.842)	.687*** (.563~.839)	.679*** (.557~.828)
Three children[f]	.441*** (.353~.550)	.552*** (.433~.705)	.551*** (.431~.703)	.521*** (.409~.664)
Four or more children[f]	.317*** (.245~.410)	.437*** (.328~.581)	.436*** (.328~.580)	.385*** (.290~.511)
Six to nine grandchildren[h]	.911 (.763~1.087)	.812* (.666~.990)	.807* (.662~.984)	.799* (.656~.973)

Table 3. (Cont'd.)

Variable	Equation 1	Equation 2	Equation 3	Equation 4
Ten or more grandchildren[h]	1.109 (.877~1.403)	.844 (.646~1.103)	.834 (.638~1.090)	.837 (.642~1.093)
One or more great-grandchildren	.407*** (.347~.477)	.526*** (.441~.627)	.529*** (.444~.632)	.513*** (.430~.611)
Adult Children/ Parents' Characteristics				
Coresidence with GP[i]		2.629*** (2.041~3.385)	2.696*** (2.095~3.469)	2.640*** (2.053~3.394)
Female[j]		1.726*** (1.553~1.918)	1.731*** (1.557~1.924)	1.750*** (1.576~1.943)
Age		.316*** (.287~.348)	.316*** (.287~.348)	.300*** (.272~.330)
College education or more[k]		1.312*** (1.162~1.481)	1.330*** (1.178~1.501)	1.241*** (1.101~1.400)
Number of children		1.180*** (1.131~1.231)	1.180*** (1.130~1.230)	1.187*** (1.138~1.238)
Employed full-time[l]		1.514*** (1.317~1.741)	1.528*** (1.329~1.756)	1.511*** (1.316~1.735)
Employed part-time[l]		1.443*** (1.171~1.779)	1.437*** (1.166~1.772)	1.502*** (1.221~1.848)
Married[m]		.949*** (.830~1.084)	.941 (.823~1.076)	1.044 (.915~1.191)
GP provides financial transfer[n]		2.981*** (2.596~3.424)	3.129*** (2.685~3.646)	
GP receives financial transfer[o]		2.552** (1.829~3.560)		2.189*** (1.433~3.342)
Interaction Terms				
Black by GP provides financial transfer			1.096 (.737~1.629)	

Table 3. (Cont'd.)

Variable	Equation 1	Equation 2	Equation 3	Equation 4
Hispanic English-preference by GP provides financial transfer			.377** (.190~.747)	
Hispanic Spanish-preference by GP provides financial transfer			.305* (.112~.829)	
Black by GP receives financial transfer				1.415 (.708~2.829)
Hispanic English-preference by GP receives financial transfer				.366 (.101~1.323)
Hispanic Spanish-preference by GP receives financial transfer				2.460$^+$ (.883~6.853)
Constant	19.591*** (8.265~46.439)	4.447** (1.708~11.579)	4.574** (1.757~11.903)	3.556** (1.367~9.249)
rho (ρ)	.523 (.495~.550)	.573 (.545~.601)	.574 (.545~.601)	.572 (.544~.599)

Note: 95% confidence intervals are shown in parentheses.
[a]Reference group = White non-Hispanic
[b]Reference groups = grandfather
[c]Reference group = not married
[d]Reference group = no IADL problem
[e]Reference group = no depressive symptoms
[f]Reference group = only one child
[g]Reference group = no great-grandchild
[h]Reference group = one to five grandchildren
[i]Reference group = not living with grandparent
[j]Reference group = male
[k]Reference group = below college education
[l]Reference group = not working
[m]Reference group = not married
[n]Reference group = no financial transfer provided by grandparent
[o]Reference group = no financial transfer received by grandparent
$^+p < .10$; $^*p < .05$; $^{**}p < .01$; $^{***}p < .001$.

The equations were built hierarchically, first including only grandparent characteristics, next introducing adult child characteristics, and finally adding interaction terms for providing and receiving economic transfers by race/ethnicity/acculturation groups in the final two models. A model that simultaneously included all interaction terms was considered too complex to illustrate predicted values, and these results did not alter substantive findings.

Table 3 shows the estimates for the random effects models. In equation #1, we note that less acculturated Hispanic grandparents were less likely than non-Hispanic Whites to provide grandchild care. In addition, younger, married, higher educated, and less impaired grandparents were more likely to provide childcare than their counterparts, providing support for the argument that social, health, and status resources enhance the ability to care for grandchildren. Competition for the services of grandparents reduced the likelihood that any one adult child received childcare assistance as having more children and being a great-grandparent lowered the odds that such help was provided.

In equation #2, characteristics of adult children and their families were entered. Here we see changes emerge in the effects of several grandparents' characteristics. In this model, Hispanic grandparents, regardless of language acculturation, were less likely to provide care for grandchildren compared to non-Hispanic White grandparents. In addition, grandmothers were more likely than grandfathers to provide care, as were grandparents with no depressive symptoms compared to those with at least one symptom. Education of grandparents was no longer significant. The receipt of childcare assistance was enhanced for those adult children who, compared to their counterparts, lived with their parents and had more children, and who were daughters, younger in age, and college educated. Providing economic transfers to children and receiving economic transfers from children were both positively related to the provision of grandchild care.

Interactions between race/ethnicity/acculturation groups and economic transfer variables were added in the next two equations. In equation #3, interaction terms for providing economic support to adult children were significant and negative in direction both for more and less acculturated Hispanic groups. This pattern indicates that the connection between providing childcare and providing money to grandfamilies was weaker among Hispanic grandparents than among non-Hispanic White grandparents. In order to better interpret the interaction terms, we plotted predicted probabilities for the eight groups involved in the interactions with other covariates in the equations held constant at their mean values. The predicted probabilities in Figure 1 show that among Hispanic grandparents, the distribution of childcare services was almost equal between those who provided an economic transfer and those who did not provide an economic transfer. Among Black and non-Hispanic White grandparents, childcare and economic provisions tended to occur together.

In equation #4 of Table 3, none of the interactions with receiving economic support from adult children was significant at the .05 level; however, a trend

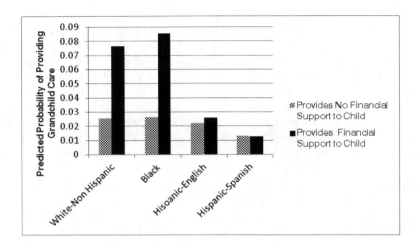

Figure 1. Predicted probability of providing grandchild care by whether financial support is provided to children and race/ethnicity and language acculturation of grandparent.

($p = .09$) for less acculturated Hispanics revealed a positive interaction. Predicted probabilities shown in Figure 2 reveal that the association between providing grandchild care and receiving economic support from adult children was proportionately greatest among less acculturated Hispanics, with the probability of providing care increasing by a factor of five between 1% of those who were not receiving economic support and 7% of those who were receiving economic support.

Discussion

The contributions of grandparents to their grandfamilies during extraordinary times and in response to family crises are well known, but less attention has been paid to routine types of childcare that provide for family stability on a more casual basis. In this chapter, we approached grandchild care from a resource-based perspective, considering such care as time contributions that intersect with monetary contributions, both scarce resources that were hypothesized to be interchangeable with each other and exchangeable across generations. Consideration of race/ethnicity and acculturation as moderators of the interplay of time and money resource transfers was based on theories of immigrant adaptation and cultural templates of filial interdependence.

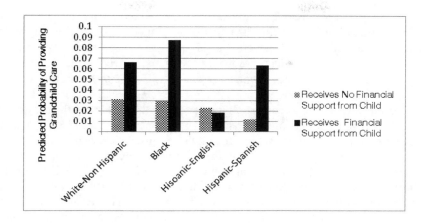

Figure 2. Predicted probability of providing grandchild care by
whether financial support is received from children and
race/ethnicity and language acculturation of grandparent.

Using random effects logistic regression, we found that in contrast to non-Hispanic Whites, Hispanic grandparents, particularly those preferring Spanish language, were similarly likely to provide grandchild care whether or not they provided economic transfers to adult children, and less acculturated Hispanic grandparents who received financial support from adult children were more than five times more likely to have provided grandchild care compared to those who did not receive financial support from children. While we found no evidence that minority grandparents used a compensatory strategy that selectively substitutes money and time contributions to grandfamilies, we did find that childcare and economic provisions were independent among Hispanic grandparents, particularly among the less language acculturated. By contrast, time and money contributions from non-Hispanic White and Black grandparents were more commonly found together. That the decision to provide childcare was not contingent on the provision of economic support suggests that unique needs among adult children may drive these two types of contributions to Hispanic grandfamilies. It is conceivable that grandparent-provided childcare lowers the need for economic contributions among Hispanic parents because the increase in marginal wages enabled by greater labor force participation of adult children obviated their need for economic assistance.

Our most surprising finding was that Hispanic grandparents, particularly the less acculturated, were less likely to provide care for grandchildren compared to other groups. That this result held when health and socioeconomic factors were controlled points to possible family factors such as geographic dispersion and alternative childcare arrangements available to grandparents of different backgrounds. Older and younger generations in immigrant Hispanic families may be separated by national borders, producing a barrier to meeting the demand for care. In addition, childcare in Hispanic families tends to be provided by a greater variety of family actors, rendering grandparents singly less important than in other ethnic groups (Goodman and Silverstein, 2006). Considering the possibility that intensity of care rather than prevalence of care may reveal ethnic differences, we examined number of care hours among those providing care but found lower values for Hispanic grandparents than for other grandparents.

Less acculturated Hispanic grandparents, many of whom were immigrants, represent the group most likely to be engaged in a time-for-money exchange with their adult children. Whether economic benefits received from children are payment for childcare services provided by grandparents cannot be concluded from this research, but the evidence is consistent with a pattern of exchange characteristic of marginalized groups and traditional cultures. In this way, families maintain their well-being and equilibrium in the face of the economic and social challenges associated with acculturation to the host society.

That Black grandparents were not more likely than White grandparents to provide care for grandchildren is likely a finding related to our consideration of prevalence rather than intensity of care, as Black grandparents tend to provide more hours of care. What this implies is that Black grandparents are less likely than other grandparents to provide low levels of care. As older Blacks tend to experience greater fluidity in their family networks compared to older Whites (Peek, Koropeckyj-Cox, Zsembik, and Coward, 2004), casual caregiving for grandchildren may be more unstable in this racial group.

There are several limitations of the analysis that deserve mention. First, we cast a wide net by considering all types of care and ignore heterogeneity related to the intensity of care. While it was an intentional strategy to use a low threshold in determining whether grandchild care was delivered, more intensive providers are treated equally with those contributing much fewer hours of care. Second, the data used are cross-sectional and preclude causal interpretations of the findings. Longitudinal analysis will be necessary to establish temporal ordering of the main constructs. Third, the measure of acculturation is likely an imperfect representation of cultural integration, as some respondents who preferred a Spanish language interview may have been bilingual. Still, this variable as a parsimonious, if crude, measure has face-validity and has been used effectively in a variety of studies.

In spite of the above shortcomings, the current analysis was able to demonstrate intriguing patterns and interrelationships that are suggestive and consistent with the mechanisms proposed. We conclude that grandparents provide resources to their grandfamilies and receive resources from them in ways that suggest an adaptation to particularistic cultural conditions and resonate with larger social issues such as immigrant incorporation. In this chapter we have framed the issue in such a way that future research will consider grandchild care not in isolation but as one of several strategies by which grandparents help their grandfamilies during challenging times and under more typical conditions, as well as within the context of a two-way flow of transfers that potentially benefits all generations.

References

Attias-Donfut, C., Ogg, J., and Wolff, F.-C. 2005. European patterns of intergenerational financial and time transfers. *European Journal of Ageing,* 2(3): 161-173.

Berry, B. 2006. What accounts for race and ethnic differences in parental financial transfers to adult children in the United States? *Journal of Family Issues,* 27(11): 1583-1604.

Cardia, E. and Ng, S. 2003. Intergenerational time transfers and childcare. *Review of Economic Dynamics,* 6(2): 431-454.

Clarke, L. and Cairns, H. 2001. Grandparents and the care of children: The research evidence. In *Kinship care: The placement choice for children and young people* (pp. 11-20). London: Russell House Publishing.

Cong, Z. and Silverstein, M. 2008. Intergenerational time-for-money exchanges in rural China: Does reciprocity reduce depressive symptoms of older grandparents? *Research in Human Development,* 5(1): 6-25.

Dilworth-Anderson, P., Brummett, B. H., Goodwin, P., Williams, S. W., Williams, R. B., and Siegler, I. C. 2005. Effect of race on cultural justifications for caregiving. *The Journals of Gerontology Series B: Psychological Sciences and Social Sciences,* 60(5): S257-S262.

Dimova, R. and Wolff, F.-C. 2008. Grandchild care transfers by ageing immigrants in France: Intra-household allocation and labour market implications. *European Journal of Population/Revue européenne de Démographie,* 24(3): 315-340.

Fine, M. A. and Fincham, F. D. 2013. *Handbook of family theories: A content-based approach.* New York, NY: Routledge.

Frankenberg, E., Lillard, L., and Willis, R. J. 2002. Patterns of intergenerational transfers in Southeast Asia. *Journal of Marriage and Family,* 64(3): 627-641.

Friedman, D., Hechter, M., and Kreager, D. 2008. A theory of the value of grandchildren. *Rationality and Society,* 20(1): 31-63.

Fritzell, J. and Lennartsson, C. 2005. Financial transfers between generations in Sweden. *Ageing and Society,* 25(3): 397-414.

Fuller-Thomson, E. and Minkler, M. 2000. African American grandparents raising grandchildren: A national profile of demographic and health characteristics. *Health & Social Work,* 25(2): 109-118.

Goodman, C. C. and Silverstein. M. 2006. Grandmothers raising grandchildren ethnic and racial differences in well-being among custodial and coparenting families. *Journal of Family Issues,* 27(11): 1605-1626.

Hagestad, G. O. and Oppelaar, J. A. 2004. *Grandparenthood and intergenerational context* (pp. 19-23).Washington, DC: Annual Meeting of the Gerontological Society of America.

Hank, K. and Buber, I. 2009. Grandparents caring for their grandchildren findings from the 2004 Survey of Health, Ageing, and Retirement in Europe. *Journal of Family Issues,* 30(1): 53-73.

Ho, C. 2013. Grandchild care, intergenerational transfers, and grandparents' labor supply. *Review of Economics of the Household* , 13(2): 359-384.

Hughes, M. E., Waite, L. J., LaPierre, T. A., and Luo, Y. 2007. All in the family: The impact of caring for grandchildren on grandparents' health. *The Journals of Gerontology Series B: Psychological Sciences and Social Sciences,* 62(2): S108-S119.

Hunter, A. G. and Taylor, R. J. 1998. Grandparenthood in African American families. *Handbook on grandparenthood* (pp. 70-86). Connecticut: Greenwood Publishing Group.

Jimenez, J. 2002. The history of grandmothers in the African-American community. *Social Service Review,* 76(4): 523-551.

Kritz, M. M., Gurak, D. T., and Chen, L. 2000. Elderly immigrants: Their composition and living arrangements. *Journal of Society and Social Welfare,* 27: 85.

Künemund, H., Motel-Klingebiel, A., and Kohli, M. 2005. Do intergenerational transfers from elderly parents increase social inequality among their middle-aged children? Evidence from the German Aging Survey. *The Journals of Gerontology Series B: Psychological Sciences and Social Sciences,* 60(1): S30-S36.

Lee, Y.-J. and Aytac, I. A. 1998. Intergenerational financial support among whites, African Americans, and Latinos. *Journal of Marriage and the Family,* 60(2) : 426-441.

Luo, Y., LaPierre, T. A., Hughes, M. E., and Waite, L. J. 2012. Grandparents providing care to grandchildren: A population-based study of continuity and change. *Journal of Family Issues,* 33(9): 1143-1167.

McGarry, K. and Schoeni, R. F. 1997. Transfer behavior within the family: Results from the Asset and Health Dynamics Study. *The Journals of Gerontology Series B: Psychological Sciences and Social Sciences,* 52(Special Issue): 82-92.

Monserud, M. A. 2008. Intergenerational relationships and affectual solidarity between grandparents and young adults. *Journal of Marriage and Family,* 70(1): 182-195.

Mutchler, J. E. and Baker, L. A. 2009. The implications of grandparent coresidence for economic hardship among children in mother-only families. *Journal of Family Issues,* 30(11): 1576-1597.

Peek, C. W, Koropeckyj-Cox, T., Zsembik, B. A., and Coward, R. T. 2004. Race comparisons of the household dynamics of older adults. *Research on Aging,* 26(2): 179-201.

Pudrovska, T., Schieman, S., and Carr, D. 2006. Strains of singlehood in later life: Do race and gender matter? *The Journals of Gerontology Series B: Psychological Sciences and Social Sciences,* 61(6): S315-S322.

Sarkisian, N., Gerena, M., and Gerstel, N. 2006. Extended family ties among Mexicans, Puerto Ricans, and Whites: Superintegration or disintegration? *Family Relations,* 55(3): 331-344.

Silverstein, M. and Chen, X. 1999. The impact of acculturation in Mexican American families on the quality of adult grandchild-grandparent relationships. *Journal of Marriage and the Family,* 61(1): 188-198.

Silverstein, M. and Attias-Donfut, C. 2010. Intergenerational relationships of international migrants in developed nations: The United States and France. *The Sage Handbook of Social Gerontology* (pp. 177-189). London: Sage Publications.

StataCorp. 2013. Stata Statistical Software: Release 13. College Station, TX: *StataCorp LP*.

Strom, R. D., Buki, L. P., and Strom, S. K. 1997. Intergenerational perceptions of English speaking and Spanish speaking Mexican-American grandparents. *The International Journal of Aging and Human Development,* 45(1): 1-21.

Treas, J. and Mazumdar, S. 2002. Older people in America's immigrant families: Dilemmas of dependence, integration, and isolation. *Journal of Aging Studies,* 16(3): 243-258.

http://dx.doi.org/10.2190/GITC3

CHAPTER 3

Grandmothers' Financial Contributions and the Impact on Grandmothers*

Madonna Harrington Meyer

Deanne and her husband had nearly paid off their own home in preparation for their retirement. But when their daughter divorced and nearly lost her house, Deanne and her husband bought it. Though she is working, Deanne's daughter is unable to make the monthly payments because she is trying to complete her college degree and raise three sons on her own. Deanne's husband is self-employed and disabled. The economy has been bad for construction workers lately, so he is rarely working and earns very little income. Additionally, Deanne and her husband took a second mortgage on their own home to further assist their daughter during the divorce. At age 57, Deanne is now paying three mortgages: the first and second mortgage on her own home, as well as her daughter's mortgage. Because so much of Deanne's paycheck goes toward mortgages, she is not saving for her own retirement. At a time when she is supposed to be accumulating a nest egg, Deanne is diverting funds to the younger generations and accumulating debt.

Deanne is not alone. Studies show that in the United States, the flow of cash from parents to adult children and grandchildren can be enormous and may become even more so during hard economic downturns (Ashton, 1996; Folbre, 2012; Gladstone, Brown, and Fitzgerald, 2009; Glenn, 2012; Harrington Meyer, 2014; Waldrop and Weber, 2005; Wilson, 1987). This chapter uses qualitative data from the Grandmothers at Work Survey, 2008–2012, to highlight financial contributions made by working grandmothers during hard times and the financial implications of those contributions for their own old-age financial security. The interviews overlapped with the Great Recession of 2007–2009 and the subsequent lackluster recovery. When I interviewed 48 grandmothers in the United States

*Portions of this chapter are reprinted, with permission, from *Grandmothers at Work: Juggling Families and Jobs,* Madonna Harrington Meyer, 2014, NYU Press.

41

about a wide variety of topics, nearly all noted the amount of financial assistance they were providing but only a few linked that assistance to the recession.

Nearly all of the grandmothers said that their own parents provided little financial assistance when they were young parents. A few of the grandmothers were keeping with that tradition and told me they expected their children to raise their grandchildren independently. In these families, grandmas buy gifts, but little else. But the majority of the working grandmothers I interviewed were breaking with tradition. Some help with one-time expenses like college, a first car, or a first home. Others help with daily and monthly expenses such as rent, electricity, food, clothes, formula, and diapers. Others buy homes or businesses, pay for summer camps or private tuitions, and cover housekeeping or daycare expenses. Particularly if their adult children face employment challenges such as layoffs, unemployment, or new jobs, or if their adult children are single parents, ill or disabled, or completing degrees, grandmothers tend to provide a great deal of financial help. But in several cases, the financial assistance did not appear to be needed at all, yet the grandmothers kept giving. These latter cases were particularly troubling when the grandmother's giving was undermining her own financial security. Thus, the types of, and the impetus for, financial assistance working grandmothers provide to the younger generations are diverse.

The impacts of such financial contributions are equally diverse. Providing financial assistance to adult children and grandchildren often brings joy and eases worries. But for many it also adversely affects nest eggs. Some working grandmothers can readily afford even substantial financial contributions. But others, even some of the wealthiest grandmothers I interviewed, are working more hours, delaying retirement, foregoing travel plans, diverting funds away from their own retirement accounts, and accumulating new debt, all in an effort to provide financial assistance to the younger generations.

Lifecourse Approach

To assess the positive and negative impacts of the financial assistance working grandmothers provide, I employ a lifecourse perspective that highlights the cumulative effects of various choices, opportunities, policies, and programs at different stages of life (Elder, 2006; Moen and Spencer, 2006). A lifecourse approach allows us to analyze the sort of financial juggling that women undertake across the lifecourse (Baca Zinn and Dill, 2005; England, 2005; Harrington Meyer, 2000). Trying to raise a young family and launch a new career may work very differently in periods of economic growth than it does in periods of recession, when it can be much riskier to take time from work for a sick child or a snow day (Bernanke, 2012). Similarly, organizing retirement travel plans may be much more difficult during a recession in which many lost their pension investments, left work prematurely, or unexpectedly spent a great deal of money on their adult children and grandchildren.

Each stage of the lifecourse may present different challenges and conse-quences. Young mothers, who may have low earnings and little savings face different sets of issues than grandmothers, who may have relatively higher earnings and established investments but may be willing to forfeit some of the economic security to improve the economic security of their adult children and grandchildren. The costs incurred at any one stage may not seem like much, but the cumulative impact of providing so much financial assistance may lead to reduced savings, investments, and pensions in old age (Folbre, 2012; Harrington Meyer and Herd, 2007).

The impact of expenditures may have been particularly problematic during and following the Great Recession. The percentage of families with retirement accounts declined, and the value of those accounts declined as well. Between 2007 and 2010, families headed by a person ages 35–44 lost 20% and families headed by persons ages 45–54 lost 10% of the median value of their retirement accounts (U.S. Congress Joint Economic Committee, 2012). Many middle-aged people lost substantial portions of their old-age investments and have little time left in the labor force to attempt to recover those losses. Wealth gaps between Whites, Blacks, and Hispanics have risen to record sizes (Kochar, 2012; Kochar, Fry, and Taylor, 2011) As a result, many are delaying planned switches from full-to part-time work, while others are delaying retirement altogether. My inter-views suggest that while some working grandmothers are readily able to absorb the impact of their financial contributions, others struggle to find enough dollars to cover their own needs and the needs of the younger generations.

Increasing Need for Grandmother Contributions

Grandparents have long provided various types of financial assistance but that giving may well be growing, particularly during tough economic times. Whether or not they are providing childcare, many grandparents provide financial support for their adult children and grandchildren (Ashton, 1996; Chesley and Moen, 2006; Folbre, 2012; Gladstone et al., 2009; Glenn, 2012; Loe, 2011; Waldrop and Weber, 2005; Wilson, 1987). As pointed out in Chapter 1, reliance on grandparents may be increasing because of the unprecedented rise in births to single mothers, the ongoing increases in women of all ages being employed, increasing hardships related to the Great Depression, and the lack of federal guarantees for paid vacations, flexible work schedules, paid sick leave, paid family leave, affordable daycare, or universal access to preschool programs (Harrington Meyer, 2014; U.S. Bureau of Labor Statistics, 2011; U.S. Census Bureau, 2012). Thus, the need for help among many younger working families may be growing, and given that the U.S. welfare state has not stepped up, in many families, grandparents, and specifically grandmothers, have. Studies suggest that the amount of financial support, and the impact of that support, varies by gender, race, class, and marital status (Harrington Meyer, 2012; Loe, 2011). Those with greater resources and supports may be better able to absorb such expenditures, while those with fewer resources may become impoverished or go into debt.

Data and Methodology

For the Grandmothers at Work Survey 2008–2012, I interviewed 48 women across the United States who were employed for any number of hours and who cared for grandchildren for any number of hours. I did not interview custodial grandmothers because they have a special set of concerns. Though custodial grandparenting is growing in the United States, the vast majority of grandparents do not have custody of their grandchildren, and I was interested in learning more about this more routine situation. Of the 48 women I interviewed, 77% were White, 67% were married, 81% had at least some college education, 79% lived in the northeast, and 81% worked at least 40 hours a week.

I conducted the interviews over 5 years, from 2008 to 2012. Though I did not ask any questions about the Great Recession, which was coincidental with my project, I did ask questions about income, expenditures, and retirement savings. Many of the grandmothers mentioned that they, their partners, and their adult children had been touched by the recession through loss of work, reduction of hours, lower wages, and greater job insecurity. Many of the grandmothers also mentioned that the consequences of the recession had caused them to rethink their retirement plans, postponing retirement as they tried to recover lost investments, embellish savings, and pay off mortgages.

Because there was no way to draw a random sample, I employed a convenience snowball sample, asking colleagues, friends, and relatives to help me find grandmothers who were employed and caring for their grandchildren. Then I asked the women I interviewed for the names of two other grandmothers who did not know each other and who met my criteria. I emphasized variation in race, age, marital status, class, and geographic location.

Most of the interviews were done face-to-face in the grandmothers' homes, workplaces, or coffee shops of their choosing. Some were done by phone when I could not arrange to fly to them or if they preferred a phone interview. My response rate was 100% in the sense that everyone I actually managed to ask to do an interview agreed to do one. Some phones and email messages were never answered, so those grandmothers were never asked to participate. Each interview lasted about 1 hour, and I transcribed as we talked, typing the words on my flamingo-pink Dell laptop. The questions were all open-ended except a set of multiple-choice questions that I asked everyone at the end. Though I asked a wide array of questions about work, family, finances, and health, here I focus on the portions of the interviews that explored what types of financial assistance grandmothers were providing and how such contributions were affecting their own economic security. Grandmothers' identities are confidential. Each woman is referred to by an alias, and her family members are referred to by their relationships rather than their names. I transcribed the interviews verbatim and the only change I made was to change the names.

In Good Times and Bad

Though a few grandmothers report that they do not provide financial assistance, most in fact provide quite a bit. Their aim is often to ease financial strain during difficult times. But a few provide more financial help than is needed or more than is advisable, given their own financial situation.

I never help them with money

It is important to note that a few grandmothers provide very little financial support. For example, Betty says that she never gives her daughter any money. She is also one of only a few who in fact receive money from their adult children. Betty is a 59-year-old high school graduate who lives in a city in the northeast. She completed high school and as a licensed practical nurse receives a private pension as well as income from her current job, generating an annual income of just under $40,000. She lives in a well-maintained home in a very rundown part of a northeastern city. Betty spends money on the grandchildren because she often picks up the kids and drives them around, using mostly her own car and gas. She also feeds the grandchildren dinner most weeknights. But Betty's daughter, who lives with her four children in a house she owns less than a block away, holds a nursing job that pays relatively well. She never pays her mom to provide care, but she sometimes gives Betty cash for the car or groceries. "I never help her with money. She makes more than I do anyway. Sometimes she pays me, like if I go pick them up and she gives me gas money."

In lower-income families, money often flows in all directions. Paula is never paid for providing care but describes a constant stream of cash between all the adults in her family. Sometimes she gives, sometimes she receives. Paula is a 48-year-old divorced mother of four and grandmother of seven. Her annual income is below $20,000 and she is providing temporary custody to one grandson and caring for the others almost daily.

> We have ups and downs but we are very family oriented. People can be across town and we will all take care of them. We are tight. We give each other rides, everything. Everyone keeps coming to my house. If someone doesn't have money, we pitch in, give money to the one who needs it. I take my son packages in prison every month. And I am paying for everything for his son.

When cash is tight, families concentrate their financial help on whoever needs it most at that time.

> I will help my married daughter with money but she helps me with money sometimes, too, for gas with the car, or for food, or whatever I need. My

daughter who has the 7-year-old doesn't need my money. She works, but I babysit a lot for her daughter. She helps me with money sometimes.

Ironically some grandmothers say that they do not provide financial support but in fact they do. Lucinda says that she and her husband provide quite a bit of grandchild care for their only granddaughter but do not provide financial assistance. Lucinda, a 52-year-old who works full time as a physical therapist, said her daughter and son-in-law, a cashier and construction worker, respectively, have enough money. When her daughter's family was house hunting, they moved in for 6 months. But it was not rent-free.

> I never buy them things, in fact, when they lived with us for that 6 months, while they looked for a house to buy, I charged them rent. Is that terrible? I made them pay rent. I did not want them to think they could just live with us. Of course we put that rent in an account and later used that money to help with things they needed, like the washer and dryer we bought for their new house.

Lucinda was the only grandmother I interviewed who charged her adult child and grandchild rent, though it hardly counts as rent if it was returned in the form of a washer and dryer. Even though Lucinda says they never buy things for the kids or grandkids, in fact they do. During the interview, she gave several examples of gifts they had purchased, in addition to the washer and dryer.

We wanted to be able to help the kids with financial strain

When grandmothers see the bills piling up, they often intervene to assist with finances. Indeed many of the working grandmothers I interviewed reported helping with expenses during difficult times such as a divorce, foreclosure, job loss, disability, or when goals were being pursued, mainly college degrees or first mortgages. Marsha and her husband covered the costs of expensive therapies for their grandsons when their adult children could not foot the bill. Marsha is 64 and would have liked to retire already but cannot afford to do so. She has a personal income of about $30,000 and together she and her husband have a household income just over $100,000. But they have paid quite a bit for therapies for their twin grandsons, one who is diagnosed with autism and the other with Down syndrome.

> I would have retired if I could have but financially we could not. We needed more money and we wanted to be able to help the kids with financial strain. It was a big financial strain on the kids to have two sons with special needs. While my son stayed home for 2 years with the boys, we paid about $500 a month for therapy for the boys. Now that he is back at work we really do not help financially anymore. They can afford the therapy the boys need. The speech therapy for my grandson with autism worked really well, worth every penny. I would gladly pay it again twice over.

Their financial situation is not what they planned because when the twins were diagnosed they moved to a new city to be close to the boys. Marsha and her husband both changed careers, and invested in additional education, in their early 50s. Additionally, they have already helped with some of the boys' expenses and plan to continue to do so as they reach adulthood. Even though both parents are working now, their financial situation remains somewhat strained. As a result of providing so much assistance to the younger generations, Marsha and her husband find that their own incomes, and their nest eggs, are all much smaller than they expected. They both expect to work for another 10 years, until Marsha is 74.

> I plan to work for a long time, and so will my husband because he is a lot younger. We both went back to school and started second careers. We lived off our savings for years, and so we do not have much put aside for retirement. I think I will probably work another 10—as will he. I would plan to still be helping the boys; I will probably always be pretty involved in their everyday lives.

When their adult children are unable to do so, some grandmothers pay for daycare, house payments, and other monthly expenses. Janet and her husband provide a lot of financial support to both of their adult daughters but provide quite a bit more to the daughter who has children. At 61, Janet works full-time for a little over $30,000 a year. She and her husband provide substantial financial assistance to that daughter and grandchildren, including monthly house payments, food, and childcare. Janet says they provided more financial help when the young couple could not support themselves, but provide less now that they are more economically stable.

> We pay for our granddaughter's after-school daycare, about $250 a month. Until she was in first grade, we paid for her daycare. That was quite a lot more. My granddaughter could go home with her dad after school, but her little brother is there, so she would rather go to daycare. We have helped a lot financially. We have covered several mortgage payments, groceries, clothes. But now my daughter has a different job, so they are handling it more themselves.

I like to be able to help my kids financially

Some working grandmothers reported helping with expenses even when it was not clear that their help was needed. Natalie pays for daily necessities in addition to gifts and splurges for the kids and grandkids. Though it is not clear they need this much help, Natalie and her husband provide a great deal of financial assistance to all three of their children. Natalie works full time, earning about $70,000 a year. She would like to retire in about 8 years but may not be able to if they keep up this level of support for the adult children. For their adult children, she and her husband help pay for education, cell phones, clothes, travel, sports, workouts, and much more. In addition, Natalie pays for many of her grandchildren's expenses, including diapers and clothes. "I buy the grandkids a lot of things. I buy diapers, formula, clothes. I do not help with rent."

Like most of the grandmothers I interviewed, Natalie has rearranged her work schedule to provide grandchild care on evenings and weekends, and she spends a sizable portion of her paycheck on expenses for her adult children and her grandchildren. This was one of a few cases that appeared to be more about the grandmother's need to give than the adult children's or grandchildren's need to receive.

Some grandmothers keep their jobs primarily so that they can continue to provide financial support. Diane had always hoped to be a hands-on grandma and is very grateful that her daughter moved nearby when her only grandchild turned one. Diane loves caring for her granddaughter; something she does at least three or four times a week. She also loves her job. When her granddaughter was born she shifted from full-time to part-time work. She gave up paid vacations and paid sick days but gained a flexible schedule. And now that the job fits well with her grandchild care demands, Diane intends to keep her 30-hour-a-week job as an interior designer as long as possible. She loves the creative challenges it poses, and the income allows her to buy more for her children and grandchild.

> I do not ever want to stop working. I love my job. It is a creative outlet for me. I sell furniture; the company loves having me because I make them money. I may go 3 days a week. Another lady worked there till she was 75. That is what I would like to do. I need stimulation. Besides, I like to be able to help my kids financially. My son is a gifted artist and he will never have a lot of money. And I like to work to help them financially. I want to be able to help my children. I have started a college fund for my granddaughter. I contribute $50 a month to that. And I buy her lots of pretty clothes and love her to death. My children are so not selfish; they never ask me for anything. Ever. . . . That makes you want to give even more.

Our parents did not help us with anything, but we will be helping our kids forever

Even though they say that their own parents did not help them, some grandmothers are providing much more financial assistance than they want to be providing. Sarah, 67, and her husband have paid for nearly everything for their grandson, who is now 17. Because their son and his girlfriend became pregnant while in high school, and because her son has been in and out of work in the years since, Sarah and her husband paid for the down payment on their son's first house, nearly every article of clothing their grandson has ever owned, and activities like tennis lessons and trips. Their son has little money, but Sarah and her husband have a household salary over $200,000 a year and they use a sizable portion of it to provide a middle-class lifestyle for their grandson. They can readily afford to provide the support but struggle to decide whether doing so is a good idea. Starting next year, they will pay for college. Increasingly they are paying for more things for their daughter and her family as well. Their daughter's marriage is on the rocks and in the past few years, Sarah and her husband have cleared out all of their daughter's credit card debt twice, added their granddaughter to their cell phone plan, and much more. Sarah never expected to provide so much financial assistance; her own parents certainly never did. She keeps trying, and failing, to set limits.

> With our son, he is always in financial trouble. We always say this is the end. Then there is a crisis and we give him more money. We give him money constantly. Then my daughter and her husband separated for 5 months this summer and so I helped her then. Two different times we have helped her by clearing out a huge credit card debt. I feel that it is endless. . . . Our parents did not help us with anything, but we will be helping our kids forever.

Sarah and her husband try to limit the financial help, and the childcare, they provide. But both seem to keep escalating. As she looks ahead, she has decided she would rather pay more money than let them move back home.

> I imagine us keeping up this level of caring for the grandkids but I am not willing to do more. . . . It is a scary thought: what if my daughter gets divorced? The worse thing would be if she moved into my house. I would rather give them money than have her move in. Both of my kids would love to move into my house and have me take care of things. I would not do that . . . I know I could not. That would wreck my life. I like peaceful time. I like privacy. I like them over for 2 hours then, okay, go home. I would rather buy her house than have her live in my house. I would give them money to stay where they are. That is the limit, what I could not do, have them live with me.

Her husband is already retired and Sarah may join him within a few years. After years of taking care of her own disabled mother, her ill father, her son and daughter, and now all three grandchildren, she feels the time has come to refocus her energies on her marriage and her husband. To do that, she must effectively limit how much financial and grandchild care she will provide—and keep the kids from moving back into the house.

Yes, I do spend too much on them sometimes

Some grandmothers are clearly giving more financial assistance than is needed—and more financial assistance than they can readily afford. Janelle is a 67-year-old mother of two and grandmother of two. She plans to continue working full time until she is 70, in part because 3 years ago her husband of 35 years left her for another woman. Money has been tight but she buys a lot of gifts for the grandchildren even though her adult children ask her to stop.

> They do not want me spending so much money. They say I should not buy all that stuff. I buy the grandkids clothes, toys, magazines, everything. It is

> terrible. I spend a lot, and they will say I did not have to. I am cognizant that
> I should not spoil them. It is me. I want to buy the clothes, the toys. It is
> about me. Yes, I do spend too much on them sometimes, and every now
> and then I worry about my own future, my own finances.

Because the divorce settlement is not yet complete, she really is not sure of her financial situation. She earns less than $40,000 a year and has spent quite a bit of her nest egg on the grandchildren. She tries to put these worries out of her mind.

> I am going to get some money from the divorce that will go into my retire-
> ment account. But I am still waiting to get it to see what my account will
> look like. I am not good with this stuff. I am not really sure. I guess I am
> all right. It is the fear of the unknown. I don't know what it will cost, what
> I will have. I have not put a lot into my retirement account. So I guess I am
> just not focusing on it. A little out of sight, out of mind.

Janelle is providing much more financial assistance than the younger generations need or even want, and by doing so she is making her already perilous financial situation even more perilous. She is one of a few grandmothers I interviewed who is giving too much and doing so to her own financial detriment.

Amelia is another working grandmother who is giving more financial assistance than she or her husband feels she should. When Amelia and her husband's 17-year-old daughter had a baby while still in high school, they did what many new grandparents would do. They moved their new grandson into their home and provided a tremendous amount of grandchild care and financial support. As the years have passed and her daughter and grandson have moved out, they are still providing substantial financial assistance. She and her husband sometimes disagree about how much help they should be providing, particularly when it comes to money.

> We will occasionally disagree: I will want to give more help than he does.
> He feels sometimes I do too much, not worried about the time but the
> money. We help her financially. We gave her the car. She lived with us. We
> helped with her tuition. She is on my insurance. We give her credit card to
> pay for her groceries. I don't want to know how much we help her. I buy
> a lot of our grandson's clothes. My husband worries that we need to make
> sure she is standing on her own two feet. He is more worried that my grandson
> will not get what he needs—will she be able to help pay for his sports, etc.
> We will help if she can't afford those things.

Given that most of the respondents mentioned that their own parents provided little if any financial assistance, why are so many of these grandmas giving their adult children and grandchildren so much money? My interviews suggest that the answers to this question are numerous. The economic recession has affected some of the families with respect to both employment and pension investment security. Some of the adult children face lay-offs, unemployment, and the insecurity of new jobs. Moreover, several of the adult children appear to be in particularly difficult financial situations due to divorces, illnesses, disabilities, or attempts to complete college degrees. But some grandmothers are giving to give. Their assistance does not appear to be needed, and in some cases, is not even wanted. Broadly, then, grandmothers may be providing more financial assistance than they did in previous generations, even when it is not needed and when money is in short supply. In the end, some grandmas appear to be providing a much-needed, temporary helping hand while others appear to be overly, even adversely, involved in their children's household economies.

Depleted Nest Eggs and Debt

Some grandmothers are readily able to provide financial assistance, whether large or small, to their children and grandchildren. But others have given so much that their own nest eggs are diminished or depleted. As middle-aged women, they are at the stage of life at which they should be saving for their own old age. They should be diverting as much money as possible into pension plans and investments so that they have enough resources for retirement and any rainy days that await. But most of the grandmothers I interviewed are not putting much aside. Most are spending money on the kids and grandkids, some are taking money out of pension investment accounts, and some are taking out new loans to provide financial assistance to the younger generations. The concerns of the grandmothers I interviewed reflect the concerns of middle and older aged persons nationwide. In 2014, some 36% of all respondents in the Retirement Confidence Survey, and 68% of those in families earning less than $35,000 a year, reported they have less than $1,000 saved for retirement. In addition, 58% of workers and 44% of retirees reported problems with their level of debt (Helman, Adams, Copeland, and Van Derhei, 2014).

We do not have enough

Candi is one of several working grandmothers who is providing a lot more financial assistance than she would like to be, and she can ill afford to maintain this level of support. But she provides the support because her older son and daughter are both single parents with little income. They cannot afford even the basic necessities for their own children and Candi pitches in when needed. Candi, a 43-year-old high school graduate who works 50 hours a week as an LPN, is the mother of three and the grandmother of three. Her youngest daughter is living at home with her in Section 8 housing. She spends so much of her money on necessities for her grandkids that she often does without such basics as gas, oil changes, or movies.

> I can't go to movies because I have to buy Pampers. . . . I have to buy diapers to see my grandson because his mom drops him off with nothing. So out of my $20 I'm taking $11 to buy Pampers, praying I don't run out of gas on the

way to work. And I have to buy him a decent outfit, because his mom drops him off with nothing, no clothes . . . I took money I had planned for an oil change for my car, and bought Pampers, and it's not my job to take care of either of you.

Given the daily struggle to cover basic necessities, it is understandable that saving for retirement is not even on the radar. Candi expects to work until she no longer is able—to cover daily needs for three generations. She does not expect to put anything aside for a rainy day.

Bennie and her husband have struggled with disabilities and an insatiable urge to spoil their grandchildren. As a result, their finances are in trouble. Bennie works full time, despite her recent knee replacement. Her husband is out of work due to a disability and now receives Social Security benefits. They have no savings, no nest egg built up, but Bennie says she spends a lot of money on the grandchildren. It is not that they need her financial help. In fact, they have told her to stop. It is that she wants to give it.

Our total income is just $40,000 a year but I spend a lot of money on the grandkids, for backpacks, school supplies, clothes, electronics, four-wheelers, Kindles. . . . I buy all sorts of things for the grandkids. Remote-control cars. I do not help my kids with rent or mortgage, but I will pay for gas, groceries, school things, clothes. And my youngest daughter lives here with me now and she pays nothing for food or rent. I would be happy to have all my kids and grandkids living with me here.

The combination of having low-paying jobs, health problems at fairly young ages, and her husband out of work due to disability has left Bennie and her husband with fewer resources than they ever imagined. But the paucity of income has not prevented her from showering her grandchildren with gifts. She is worried about having enough money for their old age, and her husband is even more worried.

But I never imagined we would be this disabled this young, me with the second knee replacement and him with the bad back and now the heart attack. He is 47, and disabled, and out of work. So the money is much less than we thought it would be, and much less than we need to buy things we want. I thought we would be working, traveling, spending on the grandkids, not struggling with health and money. But I love to spoil the kids now, and I love to spoil the grandkids. My kids are always telling me I buy too much for the grandkids. That I spend too much money. I do. I am very worried we will not have enough. My husband is worried too.

Money is in short supply. Bennie keeps spending on the kids and grandkids. In exchange, she is watching her retirement plan slip away. She and her husband had hoped to move to a quieter neighborhood and to travel. That plan is becoming increasingly unlikely.

> We do not have enough. We are young and we have so much disability already. We want to move but we need more money to do that. We need to move to a quieter neighborhood. This one is loud, busy, crazy, not as safe as I would like. He worries about the money, especially now that he is disabled. He worries we might run out. He feels we should do more for ourselves. He would like us to travel more. And move to a better neighborhood.

Similarly, Janet has neither the money nor the time to travel. She is too busy helping her grandkids. Janet and her husband had hoped to retire around age 60 and travel, as her parents had done. But now they are providing a great deal of care to their grandchildren and financial assistance to their daughter and her husband. She told me that the economy has not been good and when the stock market tumbled they watched much of their retirement investments slip away. They will now have to work at least until age 65, maybe longer, forfeiting their dreams of retirement excursions.

> In my ideal, my parents retired when they were 60 and traveled a lot. That would have been our plan, to retire and travel. But we can't afford to retire with the economy like this. And we don't travel much because we are helping with the grandchildren. But I am glad that I am working. . . . When we retire at 65, I hope we will travel. It depends on the stock market. It has been stressful watching our retirement accounts dwindle.

I have no money saved up at all for when I am old

Jamica has diverted so much of her meager income to the younger generations that she has gone without proper medical and dental treatment for years. A 49-year-old divorced mother of four and grandmother of three, Jamica works full time as a housecleaner so that she can control her schedule. Her annual income is less than $30,000 a year and she has no health or dental insurance. Her adult children have little income and at times, she has paid for nearly everything for her grandchildren.

> I help my kids a lot financially. When my oldest daughter had her baby, and they lived with us, I paid for nearly everything. And I was a single mom, raising four children on my own. When my second daughter had her baby, she did not want much help, and even now when I help her and the two boys financially, she tries to pay it back. But my oldest girl, she still wants help. She is 30, married, and her husband is about 90% disabled, can't work. So she got way behind on the rent, and I paid some of it. Some other bills too. My two sons are in college. The oldest is at community college and the tuition is covered but I have to help with his apartment and food. My youngest son got a full scholarship. Very lucky. I have no money saved up at all for when I am old. I have no health insurance and have not been to the doctor in 8 years. No dental insurance.

Thanks to an intervention by one of her clients, she is now contributing to Social Security, but that is all she will have. As a result, there is no hope of retiring.

> The kids are worried that I do not have money saved, but then they ask for money. For a long time, I was not paying into Social Security and Medicare. Then one of my customers, a professor, sat me down and told me I had to. So he sent the papers to all of my customers and they all filled in the forms. Now I have been paying into both for 12 years, so I will be eligible when I am older.

Some grandmothers provide so much financial assistance that they can no longer cover their own living expenses and are worried about falling below the poverty line in old age. When there is not enough money for a new heater, there is not enough money for travel or other leisure pursuits that were supposed to accompany retirement. Corey, a 57-year-old woman, has helped her daughter and three grandchildren by paying for virtually everything for more than 4 years. Corey and her lesbian partner bought a house for them to live in rent free. Though Corey's daughter, who is recovering from substance abuse, has no job or money, her boyfriend sometimes now pays some expenses. Nonetheless, Corey and her partner have paid for the house, food, clothes, medical expenses, gifts, summer camps for the grandson with autism, and much more. Despite working 40–60 hours a week, Corey has no nest egg, no savings of any kind, and growing debt. Increasingly she is struggling to make ends meet. She needs a new heater but has no resources with which to make the purchase.

> My daughter has recently slowed down what she asks for. But before last summer, she would ask me for things till I was dry. Ask for every single thing she can. But since last summer she has taken pride in raising her own family. And so she tries to ask for less. I sometimes really struggle to pay my bills. I have only recently told her that I am struggling financially. I had to get a new furnace, and I did not have the money for it. I do not make enough to cover. I probably should have told her years ago that I am struggling.

Corey's partner disapproves of the constant flow of time and cash and is struggling to set limits on the supports that go to the daughter and grandchildren. They fight about it all the time. Corey said the relationship is over and she would end the relationship today if she could afford to do so. But she plans to stay with her until the grandchildren are in college and then leave her partner.

> My partner is opposed to all the time and money that I spend with my daughter. I would leave my partner today if I had the money. I recently nearly left her. I am so tired of living with her complaining that I am spending time and money on my grandkids and daughter. I can't stand my partner anymore. She will not see the kids at all. When they come over she stays in the bedroom. She will not go to their house at all. I have to get so that I can live

independently, then I will leave my partner. I will hang in for 8 years, and then the grandkids will be in college and I will sell the house in 8 years.

Though she would like to retire now, Corey will work until she is 67 and eligible for full Social Security benefits. She is very worried that even so she will not have enough money for the basics like housing, much less retirement dreams of travel.

> Very concerned. Very concerned about poverty when I retire. I do not allow myself to think about it. To change that, I have to stop supporting my daughter and I will not change that. So I am just going to keep supporting her even though it isn't wise. I am scared to death of being really poor.

I have shame over this debt

Grandmothers who have spent all of their retirement savings and taken on new debt in their efforts to assist their children and grandchildren have to give up all dreams of traveling or retiring. Estelle has given financially until it hurts. Estelle had been enjoying her empty nest but then her adult daughter asked if she could live at home for 3 months. During that time she became pregnant. Over the years, Estelle has provided a great deal of financial support for her three children and six grandchildren, but now much of the money goes toward the youngest daughter and her 7-month-old son, who live in Estelle's home. Estelle's daughter does not have a job right now and is not paying for her own or her son's expenses.

> She is putting me in the poorhouse. I have always put a lot of money into my daughters and their kids. I will pay a phone bill or bring gifts or buy school supplies. I have always been in debt because I have chosen to support my kids and grandkids financially. But this last year with my daughter living with me has sunk me. I am now in serious financial problems. . . . Her daycare is $200 a week. She has no health insurance, but at least my grandson does. She is looking for jobs but can't find one she can keep. She has applied for unemployment and other things, but she has not gotten anything yet. She doesn't have a dollar—I just paid her car insurance. She gets food stamps.

Providing so much support for her daughter and all of her grandchildren has taken a tremendous toll on Estelle's financial situation.

> I have taken most of my retirement account over the years, so it is nearly empty. I have a total of eight existing loans against my retirement account. My entire end-of-the-month paycheck pays that loan back. I have closed my credit card accounts because they were maxed out. I know where the money went. I know I was not gambling. I have been caring for my kids and grandkids. But I still have shame. I make a decent salary, but I have used it all. I have shame over this debt.

Estelle will never be able to retire or travel. She told me she will likely have to die at her desk.

> My daughter especially doesn't see that my money is gone. She thinks I am a never-ending fountain of money. She wants independence, and I want it for her. But she doesn't have it and I do not see it any time soon. But I am 63, and I should be traveling and getting ready for retirement, but I am not even close. But I love going home to my grandson. He is the most precious child in the world. I am paying for nearly everything for him.

Even the wealthiest grandmothers sometimes give more to the kids than they have and then delay retirement and travel plans as they try to rebuild their nest eggs. Renee and her husband have provided tremendous amounts of money to their children and grandchildren. She covered all of the expenses when her niece, and then later her daughter, were in serious car accidents. "We help our kids financially all the time. We helped them each with a down payment of $25,000 and $50,000 for a down payment for the first house. I put them all through college."

But by far the largest financial payout involved helping her son who lives nearby. He asked her to pay $500,000 for a business venture that she knew would not be successful. After endless badgering she gutted her retirement account. He then lost all of the money and she is now repaying that $500,000 loan to her retirement account. This debt is the only thing that prevents her from retiring.

> I have helped one with a business, gave them $500,000 for his business. That is why I am still working. The business failed and closed. He has massive debt. He owned a printing business but then it went bankrupt, and I am paying off the $500,000 loan I gave him. Otherwise I would be retired. I took that $500,000 out of my retirement account. Financially, I have helped my kids with over $1 million.

Once the business venture failed, Renee's son began to ask for help with many more daily expenses for her granddaughter, including summer camps, clothes, and school supplies. She clearly articulates why she provides so much assistance. She does not want her granddaughter to suffer.

> My granddaughter called one day and said we do not have power and my son had not been able to pay the power bill, and so I have jumped back in to be in my granddaughter's life. I am trying to let them figure it out without opening my checkbook. I have no problem letting my son suffer to figure this out. But I do not want my granddaughter to suffer. So I get her clothes, her Ugg boots, her volleyball camp, her trip to Florida to see Grandma. She doesn't even know I am paying for all of this. She thinks her parents are. I bought the calculator for her school, $125, her parents could not afford.

Though her household income is well over $200,000 a year, she cannot afford to retire because the nest egg is gone. She is feeling her age and finds work more tiring. Because she works full time and has very little time to spend with her granddaughter. She would like to reverse the arrangement and work less and spend more time with her granddaughter. She would also like to spend 3 months in

Florida every winter with her husband, who retired years ago. But none of this is possible because she gave the nest egg to her son.

> I never imagined we would be helping our kids this much. Never. Not financially. But when these things happen you just jump in and you do it. So then now I have to work longer. But then I have less time with the grandkids. I am older now. I can't work as hard and fast as I used to, so now since 65 I have not been able to run as fast. So it takes longer to get things done. Some days you just do. I have hoped to retire for years now, but I think I have to work at least another 2 years. The stock market crash made me lose a lot, and then giving the kids so much money, my portfolio took a double whammy. The things you thought you had, you just did not have. You can't be mad. I do not have time to be mad. I have to feel blessed that I had it to give to them.

I have debt now, too, because I have helped them so much

Some grandmothers give enormous amounts of money to reduce the amount of time they are expected to spend with the grandchildren. But then they delay retirement to pay off the debts. Christine's salary, even in semiretirement, is over $150,000 a year and she dedicates a significant proportion of it to her daughter, son-in-law, and two granddaughters. At first they lived with her and she paid for everything. She took out loans to help them buy their first businesses. Then they moved out after Christine took out additional loans to cover much of the costs of their new home. Even though Christine's parents never helped her financially, she pays for her daughter's housekeeper, and her granddaughters' sports teams, private school tuition, tutors, camps, clothes, and much more.

> I have bought a good part of their house, which they now live in. I have since given them all but 5% of that house, so that we can keep the loan. I still help them. I give them $400 a month of their monthly $1,400 mortgage; I have done that for 10 years. This was not expected. I had not expected to do it, and they do not expect me to do it. My parents did not support me. They did not ask me, but I wanted to help them. I took out loans; I took out a $75,000 loan for the first business, and then $150,000 on the second business. I have been giving them more and more of the ownership. I pay $300 a month for their housekeeper. I pay a $100 a month for their sports club for them.

It seems a bit like guilt money. When I gently asked her if it was, she nodded and shed more tears. She said her daughter complains that she is not a hands-on grandmother and so Christine pays for more of her expenses. Unwilling to part with her professional career, she parts with her money instead.

> I have insisted on helping them with these things. I felt that if they were going to come live near me, that is how my daughter presents it, that they are here for me, then I wanted them to be in a good place where they would want to stay. It was important to see them thrive and enjoy where they are. I

have also helped pay for my granddaughter's tutors, $400 a month for reading. And I pay for camps, lessons, and $2,000 for each child into a 529 each year for their college. And I spend a lot on toys, costumes, clothes, for the kids. I have bought most of their clothes.

Despite her high income, Christine has debts to repay. She says she has to stop spending on her daughter and granddaughter, but she gives them money because she is not giving them as much of her time as they would like.

I have debt now, too, because I have helped them so much. They do not ask, I insist. It is one way I can help them. I help them financially because I am not giving them the time they want—I give them the money but not the time. But that isn't enough for my daughter. The first 2 years of my granddaughter, I paid $2,000 a month for her daycare. I can't continue to pay all of this though . . . some of this spending has to stop.

Discussion

Nearly all of the grandmothers I interviewed are helping financially. Some are helping in modest ways with occasional expenditures for gas, food, clothes, and gifts. But many are also helping with major monthly expenses such as electric, rent, or daycare bills. In some cases the financial assistance is much needed because the adult children are single parents, unemployed, in foreclosure, completing degrees, disabled, or newly hired. In other cases, the assistance is much more than is needed and has more to do with the grandmother's need to give than the younger generations' need to receive.

Providing financial assistance to the younger children creates a real conflict for middle-aged women who are at a stage in the lifecourse where they should be saving resources for their own old age. Retirement planning is particularly important given the repercussions of the Great Recession of 2007–2009. During hard times, grandmothers may well pitch in, but many do so at their own financial peril. Some have high enough earnings and savings to take these expenditures in stride, but for many it creates financial hardship. Indeed, many are deflecting contributions from retirement accounts to their children and grandchildren. And they do so even though their own retirement investments were hit hard during the recession. Some are spending their own retirement savings and a few are incurring new debt. The net effect is that many are reducing their own expenditures for travel, downsizing their dreams, and delaying their retirement so that they can continue to earn money. Most worrisome is that many will enter old age with little to no accumulated savings to cover the years of retirement that lie ahead.

The financial contributions of many grandmothers were enormous though only some appeared to be linked to the Great Recession. Some families had faced job insecurity and investment losses due to the recession. But hard times come from many sources. Many are responding to periods of great need caused by layoffs, divorces, illnesses, prison, or other challenging events. Though they are quick to say their own parents did not help them much, or at all, they are also quick to open their wallets for the younger generations. Some appear to be providing more assistance than their adult children want or more than their partners and friends think advisable. Those with more meager resources make these contributions at their own financial peril.

Whatever prompts the financial contributions, it is clear that many of the grandmothers are paying for more than just electricity or diapers. They are paying for peace of mind. Though they say that they are generally fine with their adult children doing without, or learning at the school of hard knocks, they do not want their grandchildren to do so. They love their grandkids and do not want them to suffer. Some would rather that they, and not their grandkids, do without.

References

Ashton, V. 1996. A study of mutual support between black and white grandmothers and their adult grandchildren. *Journal of Gerontological Social Work,* 26(1-2): 87-100.

Baca Zinn, M. and Dill, B. T. 2005. What is multiracial feminism? In J. Lorber (Ed.), *Gender inequality: Feminist theories and politics* (3rd ed., pp. 202-207). Los Angeles, CA: Roxbury Publishing.

Bernanke, B. 2012. Recent developments in the labor market. Washington, DC: Board of Governors of the Federal Reserve System. http://www.c.federalreserve.gov/newsevents/speech/bernanke20120326a.htm

Chesley, N. and Moen, P. 2006. When workers care: Dual-earner couples' caregiving strategies, benefit use, and psychological well-being. *American Behavioral Scientist,* 49(9): 1248-1269.

Elder, G. 2006. Life course. In G. Ritzer (Ed.), *The Blackwell encyclopedia of sociology* (pp. 109-131). Volume 1479. Maldon, MA: Blackwell.

England, P. 2005. Emerging theories of care work. *Annual Review of Sociology,* 31: 381-399.

Folbre, N. (Ed.). 2012. *For love and money: Care provision in the United States.* New York, NY: Russell Sage Foundation.

Gladstone, J., Brown, R., and Fitzgerald, K.-A. 2009. Grandparents raising their grandchildren: Tensions, service needs and involvement with child welfare agencies. *International Journal of Aging and Human Development,* 69(1): 55-78.

Glenn, E. N. 2012. *Forced to care: Coercion and caregiving in America.* Cambridge, MA: Harvard University Press.

Harrington Meyer, M. (Ed.). 2000. *Care work: Gender, labor, and the welfare state.* New York, NY: Routledge.

Harrington Meyer, M. and Herd, P. 2007. *Market friendly or family friendly? The state and gender inequality in old age.* New York, NY: Russell Sage Foundation.

Harrington Meyer, M. 2012. US grandmothers juggling work and grandchildren. In V. Timonen and S. Arber (Eds.), *Contemporary grandparenting: Changing family relationships in a global context* (pp. 71-90). Bristol, UK: Policy Press.

Harrington Meyer, M. 2014. *Grandmothers at work: Juggling families and jobs.* New York, NY: NYU Press.

Helman, R., Adams, N., Copeland, C., and Van Derhei, J. 2014. The 2014 retirement confidence survey: Perceived savings needs outpace reality for many. *EBRI Issue Brief*, (397). http://www.ebri.org/pdf/surveys/rcs/2014/EBRI_IB_397_Mar14.RCS.pdf

Loe, M. 2011. *Aging our way: Lessons for living from 85 and beyond.* New York, NY: Oxford University Press.

Kochhar, R., Fry, R., and Taylor, P. 2011. Wealth gaps rise to record highs between whites, blacks, Hispanics. Washington, DC: PEW Research. http://www.pewsocialtrends.org/2011/07/26/wealth-gaps-rise-to-record-highs-between-whites-blacks-hispanics/

Kochhar, R. 2012. A recovery no greater than the recession. Washington, DC: PEW Research http://www.pewsocialtrends.org/2012/09/12/a-recovery-no-better-than--the-recession/

Moen, P. and Spencer, D. 2006. Converging divergences in age, gender, health, and well-being: Strategic selection in the third age. In R. H. Binstock and L. K. George (Eds.), *Handbook of aging and the social sciences* (6th ed., pp. 127-144). New York, NY: Academic Press.

U.S. Bureau of Labor Statistics. 2011. *Women in the labor force: A databook.* Report 985. Table 7. Employment status of women by presence and age of youngest child, 1975-2010. http://www.bls.gov/cps/wlf-databook-2011.pdf

U.S. Census Bureau. 2012. Table 4. Poverty status of families, by type of family, presence of related children, race, and Hispanic origin: 1959 to 2011. In *Current population survey, annual social and economic supplements.* Social, Economic, and Housing Statistics Division: Poverty. http://www.census.gov/hhes/www/poverty/data/historical/families.html

U.S. Congress Joint Economic Committee. 2012. *Retirement security after the Great Recession: Middle-income and middle-aged Americans feeling the squeeze.* Washington, DC: U.S. Congress. http://www.jec.senate.gov/public/index.cfm?a=Files.Serve&File_id=4bc4e022-4bc8-476c-a91a-268852d8ff0e

Waldrop, D. P. and Weber, J. A. 2005. Grandparent to caregiver: The stress and satisfaction of raising grandchildren. In F. J. Turner (Ed.), *Social work diagnosis in contemporary practice* (pp. 184-195). New York, NY: Oxford University Press.

Wilson, G. 1987. Women's work: The role of grandparents in inter-generational transfers. *Sociological Review*, 35(4): 703-720.

http://dx.doi.org/10.2190/GITC4

CHAPTER 4

Health and Grandparenting Among 13 Caribbean (and one Latin American) Immigrant Women in the United States

Ynesse Abdul-Malak

How does the involvement in childcare shape immigrant grandmothers' health? How does health shape the ability to care for grandchildren? The answers to these questions vary with the cultural contexts of grandmothering.

There is a dearth of scholarly works regarding new immigrant grandparents and health, mostly those who emigrated from the Caribbean. In 2010, more than 50% of all U.S. immigrants were from Latin America and the Caribbean (Grieco, Acosta, de la Cruz, Gambino, Gryn, Larsen, Trevelyan, and Walters, 2012). This is a change in U.S. immigration patterns of the past 50 years whereby new immigrants are originating from non-European countries. This study explores the special challenges immigrant grandmothers from Latin America and the Caribbean face as they provide care for their grandchildren. Using a lifecourse approach and emphasizing the impacts of cumulative inequality, I conducted in-depth interviews with 14 immigrant noncustodial grandmothers from the Caribbean and Latin America who provide care for their grandchildren. I examine the lived experiences of these grandmothers and how they perceive their grandmothering role in the United States contrasted with the cultural expectations of their native countries. First, I explore the links between health and grandmothering to see how cultural expectations complicate grandmothering for immigrant women: I find that the grandmothers struggle to balance competing expectations about joy vs. duty, tolerance vs. discipline, gendered roles vs. cultural roles, and economic insufficiency vs. religion abundancy. Then I explore how providing grandchild care shapes grandmothers' health, including their ability to exercise, see doctors, eat healthily, and manage chronic diseases. I find that taking care of their grandchildren may have an impact on these healthy behaviors.

Grandmother Care and the Impact on Health

In general, in response to the lack of public alternatives for childcare and increased women's participation in the labor force, grandparents play a pivotal role in caring for their grandchildren (Harrington Meyer, 2012; Lerner, 2010). Some families depend on grandma as a safer and better childcare provider. Additionally, as with any other groups in the United States, immigrant grandparents provide care for grandchildren when their adult children are in need of assistance either because of single parenthood or because of mental and physical illnesses, drug abuse, and/or incarceration (Goodman and Silverstein, 2002; Kelley, Yorker, and Whitley, 1997). Many grandparents provide childcare because their adult children are in need of financial assistance and are unable to pay for childcare (Harrington Meyer, 2014). According to the 2009 American Community Survey, more than 470,000 of the 1.9 million immigrant grandparents are responsible for their own grandchildren under the age of 18 (U.S Census Bureau, 2009). Providing care for grandchildren could be a rewarding yet physically demanding job for grandparents and thus it may have mixed consequences for their health. Some studies show that grandparenting might have negative effects on the mental and physical health of the grandparents (Bachman and Chase-Lansdale, 2005; Hughes, Waite, LaPierre, and Luo, 2007; Musil and Ahmad, 2002; Musil, Gordon, Warner, Zauszniewski, Standing, and Wykle, 2011), especially when it is combined with other roles such as labor-force participation. However, some grandparents might benefit emotionally from providing care for their grandchildren (Dolbin-MacNab, 2006; Goodman and Silverstein, 2001; Pruchno and McKenney, 2002).

Caring for grandchildren can include physically and emotionally demanding tasks. There is a growing body of evidence suggesting that grandparental caregiving may worsen grandparents' health, particularly for those who provide high numbers of hours of care. Minkler and Fuller-Thomson (2001) examined the links between physical health and various degrees of childcare on a national survey of 3,260 grandparents and found that extensive caregiving was linked to higher levels of depression and some limitations in activities of daily living. In a similar study, Butler and Zakari (2005) found that grandparents assuming parenting roles experienced adverse mental health effects.

Conversely, some studies show few negative health impacts. Hughes, Waite, LaPierre, and Luo (2007) examined a sample of 12,872 grandparents aged 50 through 80 from the Health and Retirement Study and found no adverse health effects of grandparents taking care of grandchildren. They suggested that the negative health effects associated with grandparent caregivers are mostly seen among coresidential and custodial grandparents. They found that grandchild care does not lead to health declines unless it is compounded by previous health problems and scarce resources. They asserted that, "For most grandparents, the demands of grandchild care appear to be balanced by the benefits of caregiving and available resources. Only when demands are heavy and resources scarce will grandchild care itself lead to health declines" (Hughes et al., 2007, p. S115). A survey of 149 grandmothers and great-grandmothers found that grandparent caregivers reported high levels of emotional health such as feeling of greater life satisfaction (Goodman and Silverstein, 2001).

The health impact of grandparent caregivers is inconclusive, with some studies reporting deteriorating physical and emotional health while others reported good health. Research on the impact of grandmothering on women's emotional and physical health is mixed and mostly focused on native-born Americans. In the coming years, the United States will become more ethnically diverse. It is projected that in 2050, the aggregate minority will become the majority among the general population and 42% of the adult population of 65 years and older (Administration on Aging, 2010). With the rapid growth of non-Western-origin immigrants, the health status of this new wave of immigrants has not received considerable attention in scholarly works. We know little about the daily experiences of immigrant grandmothers. Thus, qualitative research is warranted to fully discover the cultural frames that immigrant grandmothers use to navigate between cultural expectations and the impact of grandmothering on their health. Grandmothers from different cultures experience disparate cultural expectations in caring for their grandchildren. This cultural complexity inadvertently shapes grandmothering and the health of grandmothers.

Conceptual Framework

This research draws on a lifecourse perspective and cumulative inequality theory. These two paradigms highlight how inequality accumulates over the life course and produces diverging health trajectories among different groups. Lifecourse perspective and cumulative inequality could be usefully linked to understand health, as suggested by Ferraro and Shippee (2009).

Lifecourse Perspective

I employ a lifecourse perspective to better understand the positive and negative health impacts of providing care to grandchildren. Lifecourse perspective provides a framework to understand intergenerational family members across different life stages (Elder, 1974). Different individuals in the families' "linked lives" interact depending on the developmental stages. Providing childcare is one aspect of grandparents' interaction with younger grandchildren. The lifecourse perspective elucidates how the cumulative effects of various choices that these women made from the decision to migrate and the available opportunities, programs, and policies at different stages of their lives and how these facilitate or hinder good health. Additionally, it allows me to see the complex interplay of biography and history at different stages of these women's lives (Moen,

Spencer, Binstock, and George, 2006). In sum, lifecourse perspective highlights the cumulative effects of various choices, opportunities, and policies originating from the immigrant's country of origin and on the receiving country. It informs my research question by elucidating how the age and lifecourse position of immigrants from diverse countries influence grandmothers' cultural and health experiences in the United States. For example, those who immigrate later in life and in good health may be able to absorb the stresses of grandmothering with few adverse health effects, while those who already have chronic conditions when they immigrate may have even more adverse health effects from caring for grandchildren.

Cumulative Inequality Theory

The cumulative inequality theory provides insight into the differences that exist in immigrants' health status. This theory stems from Dannefer's (2003) cumulative advantage-disadvantage theory, whereby with initial access to economic resources during the life course influences one's life trajectories, including health status. Ferraro and Shippee (2009) generated the cumulative inequality theory to study aging and the accumulation of inequality, positing that lifecourse trajectories are shaped by disparities in resources, accumulation of risk, and human agency. Cumulative inequality points out the systematic linking of age-related trajectories to individual health outcomes. It informs this study by revealing how immigrant grandmothers' health status is linked to early life trajectories, such as lack of resources in their native countries and current economic inequalities in the United States. It provides insight into how country of origin and time of migration are important factors in determining health status. Cumulative lifecourse exposure to low socioeconomic conditions can lead to chronic diseases (Pollitt, Rose, and Kaufman, 2005; Wakabayashi, 2010). For example, those with fewer resources early in life in their home countries often continue to have fewer resources in the United States and as a result they struggle with more adverse health effects when they care for their grandchildren.

Taken together, these two theories help us to see how caring for grandchildren may impact immigrant women's health and vice versa. New waves of immigration, specifically those from the Caribbean, may have diverging health outcomes, and different cohorts from different countries have different health statuses. Country of origin may be a determining factor of immigrant health. Indeed, immigrants from some Caribbean countries may not be experiencing the Healthy Immigrant Effect or the Hispanic Health Paradox, which has been pervasive in immigrant's health research (Abraido-Lanza, Chao, and Florez, 2005; Abraido-Lanza, Dohrenwend, Ng-Mak, and Turner, 1999; Franzini, Ribble, and Keddie, 2001; Hummer, Rogers, Amir, Forbes, and Frisbie, 2000). Though these theories have been widely supported in the literature for explaining Hispanics' better than expected health trajectories, Caribbean grandmothers might not be extra-healthy. Haitian immigrant poverty levels are higher than Black Americans and therefore are expected to follow similar or worse health trajectories than most immigrants (Williams, 2005). Therefore, I conjecture that the time of migration and country of origin are important predictors of later-life health outcomes.

Methods and Data

This qualitative study is based on a snowball convenience sample of in-depth interviews with 13 Caribbean and one Latina grandmothers in the New York City area. I recruited the research participants by contacting colleagues in New York City. I began by contacting participants who attend a predominantly Black church that is well frequented by immigrants from the Caribbean. Each grandmother signed a standard consent form before the interview. After interviewing a grandmother, I would ask her to refer me to another grandmother. These grandmothers for the most part were daycare grandmothers who provided regular care to their grandchildren on a daily or weekly basis. My sample included a couple of coresidence grandmothers because their daughters were relatively young and were still living at home when they got pregnant and gave birth. The interviews lasted 45 minutes to 2 hours. Most of the interviews were conducted in their own houses. Four were conducted at the church and one at a local café. All interviews were audio recorded and subsequently transcribed. The interviews were fully analyzed for recurrent themes and then were coded. Each grandmother was given an alias to protect her identity.

Most of the women I interviewed were from the Caribbean except for one who was from Mexico (see Table 1). More than 50% were from Haiti and Jamaica. One-third of the sample had less than a high school education, three grandmothers had master's degrees, and the remainder had high school, some college, or college education. My objective was to see how cultural expectations complicate grandmothering for immigrant women and how providing grandchild care shaped grandmothers' health, including their ability to exercise, see doctors, eat healthily, and manage chronic diseases.

Everyday Challenges of Immigrant Grandmothers

How does culture shape grandmothering? Some of the common themes that emerged from the interviews derived from many tensions that grandmothers experienced while taking care of their grandchildren. Some of the tensions stemmed from the complexity of grandmothering while others were the result of cultural differences. Immigrant grandmothers are navigating an arena wherein cultural norms from their native countries are not always in sync with those of the United States. Throughout the interviews, immigrant grandmothers invariably raised the issue of cultural differences and how that complicated their

Table 1. Demographic Characteristics

Alias	Age	Country of origin	Education	Number of children	Number of grandchildren	Number of chronic illnesses	Physical limitations	Exercise at least once a week
Barbara	50	Barbados	Graduate degree	3	2	0	No	No
Harriet	52	Haiti	Less than HS	3	2	4	Yes	Yes
Jermaine	60	Jamaica	Less than HS	6	8	2	No	No
Glenda	50	Grenada	Less than HS	3	4	1	No	No
Paula	72	Puerto Rico	College	2	5	2	Yes	No
Maria	54	Mexico	Graduate degree	3	1	0	No	No
Susan	50	Saint Lucia	High school	3	9	2	No	No
Janet	60	Jamaica	College	2	7	1	Yes	No
Hoda	66	Haiti	Less than HS	2	2	2	Yes	No
Hanna	72	Haiti	Less than HS	2	3	3	Yes	No
Jane	41	Jamaica	College	4	3	1	No	No
Jenna	60	Jamaica	Less than HS	4	8	1	Yes	No
Harmonie	55	Haiti	Graduate degree	2	3	1	Yes	Yes
Hanrietta	65	Haiti	Some college	2	1	0	No	Yes

grandmothering experiences. They talked about the joy of grandmothering combined with a sense of duty. This sense of duty could be because their children are in financial need and are unable to afford paid childcare. They also talked about cultural differences in disciplining grandchildren and how that could generate some stress and even tension with their children. Gendered and cultural expectations to care for their grandchildren leave them very little time for themselves. Finally they talked about the importance of religion in their lives and how that helped them overcome economic insufficiency and even deal with their health and manage their chronic diseases.

Joy vs. Duty

Most grandmothers love spending time with their grandchildren and feel a sense of joy. Nonetheless, many confer a sense of duty that encompasses this form of carework. The theme of joy is consistent across all the interviewers (Harrington Meyer, 2014). Pruchno and McKenney (2002) found that caring for grandchildren could be a rewarding task. The sense of duty or obligation that grandparents feel is commensurate with parental obligations that grandparents feel toward their adult children (Draper, 2013; Gibson, 2002). The sense of duty is more prevalent in the case of working-class grandmothers and with those who experience poorer health or who are needed to watch their grandchildren because their children are unable to afford paid childcare services.

The feeling of joy is derived from being able to help their children, to spend time with their grandchildren, and at the same time the feeling of being productive. Paula is a Puerto Rican middle-class retired grandmother. Paula is 72 years old, overweight, and is battling a debilitating neurological condition that affects her mobility and breathing. She is a grandmother of five. She talks about the joy that she experiences while watching her 7-, 5-, and 3-year-old grandchildren, in order to give her daughter some free time. Even though Paula struggles with health issues and is unable to physically run after the grandkids, she gleefully talks about the joy that spending time with her grandchildren brings her. "Well it stresses me physically, but emotionally I feel better because again I'm still productive. Yes it does make me happy because I'm productive. I'm not a lump sitting on the couch." When Paula talks about her grandchildren, she exudes a sense of joy. While recounting many funny stories about her grandchildren, she would erupt in contagious laughter, which oftentimes ended with a coughing spell from her medical condition.

Grandmothers from the working class also experience this sense of joy while caring for their grandchildren. Glenda is 50 years old from Grenada; she coresides with her unmarried daughter and her 4-year-old granddaughter. Glenda works full time as a housecleaner. She goes to great lengths to talk about her experiences when her daughter, then a college student, came home pregnant. She was very disappointed with her daughter because she wanted her "to make something of herself and to stop the cycle of poverty." She goes on to explain how her granddaughter changed her life.

> Well, you know at first I did not approve that my daughter was pregnant because she was going to college and she didn't finish college. That kind of had me, you know. So it took me a long time to recognize this pregnancy. But once the child is born, it changes everything. I will take back all that I said, back then, you know, to the mother and everything, because my grandchild changed my life. Yeah, she did . . . I can't get enough of her. I can't. You know even on my worst day she just makes me happy . . . I don't know how to say, but from the minute that I see her she makes me happy.

Even though she knows that her daughter needs her help with childcare, that sense of duty is compounded by a sense of joy.

A sense of duty is also pervasive across the interviews but more so among the working-class women. Harriet is a 52-year-old from Haiti. She lives in a one-bedroom apartment with her three sons and 1-year-old grandson. She has another 4-year-old grandson in Haiti. Harriet works a full-time night shift as a home health aide while she cares for her grandson during the day. Harriet suffers with high blood pressure, high cholesterol, and diabetes, and she had a stroke 2 years earlier. She takes care of a grandson in Haiti financially because the father is 27 years old, with no college education, and has not been able to hold a steady job. She talks about her obligations to take care of her two grandsons. She does not think that she has a choice in that matter. In fact she goes into detail on how she viewed her grandchildren as if they were her own children.

> I take care of them. The one in Haiti, I send money for his mother to take care of him, my son is not working. . . . You know, his parents are young, and I take care of the one here too. . . . You know it is always hard because you have to help. It is an extra "baggage" that is added to your load. They don't have money. The kid needs stuff and I have to buy. You understand? When I go to the supermarket and I see something he might need, I have to buy it for him. You understand?

Harriet's sense of duty is also paired with the sense of joy caring for her grandchildren brings her. She talks about how she loves to talk on the phone to the grandson in Haiti and she is delighted when he said to her on the phone he loves her. The grandson who currently lives with her also makes her happy.

> I love him. He is so much fun. Had he been here, you would have seen him. He would have been laughing. Whenever he sees people he starts laughing. I love him a lot. Now he is not here, I miss him.

Grandmothers performing this type of grandmothering do it because of the joy that caring for their grandchildren brings them and also because they feel that it is their parental duty and obligation to help their children in need (see Draper, 2013). In this instance, the joy might be conducive to better emotional and physical health, but as the remainder of the chapter illustrates, the duty may cause them to do more than they should, ignore their own health needs, and leave them emotionally weary and in poorer health. However, representative data is warranted to unravel how the sense of joy couples with the sense of duty might be impacting grandmothers' health.

Tolerance vs. Discipline

Immigrant grandmothers attempt to reconcile the forms of discipline from their home countries and what they perceive as the tolerance that is pervasive in Americans' childrearing practices. Discipline is one of the most salient issues that many grandmothers raise during the interviews. Many grandmothers bring up the topic of discipline and how it engenders some emotional stress. Jermaine, a 60-year-old Jamaican grandmother of eight, suffers from high blood pressure. She finds that taking care of her grandchildren could be a source of added stress. At one point, her granddaughter, at the time 7 years old, was living with her because her parents were going through a difficult divorce. She finds that the granddaughter could be disrespectful at times and she was not sure on how to deal with her behavior issues.

> Back home, you can spank them, you can't do it here in the system they grow here. Back home you can talk to your kids, here you can't. Most kids here don't show respect, they don't have it. I believe back home is better.

In their research in New York City on West Indian immigrant families, Waters and Sykes (2009) found that the issue of discipline was ubiquitous among West Indian parents. My research corroborates that discipline could be a source of stress for the grandmothers. Many immigrant grandparents deplore the American's childrearing practices and perceive it to be the source of behavioral problems that are pervasive among immigrant youth. Many grandparents believe that corporal punishment is necessary and is a proper form of discipline. Jenna, a 60-year-old grandmother of eight and great-grandmother of three, contrasts the childrearing practices of her native country of Jamaica with the United States. She has been living in New York City for 30 years and she still finds it difficult to care for her grandchildren and great-grandchildren and to refrain from corporal punishment as a form of discipline.

> I used to slap them back home. That's what we know growing up. But we didn't know it was abuse, but God, nothing went wrong with them. They're turning out to be good. We didn't murder our kids or abuse them. We believe in disciplining them because my mother grow me up with sharp pain, with the belt. Even when we used to go to school my teacher would use the cane when we're talking in class. Whoops! [She mimics spanking motion.] These kids can't straighten up themselves.

Conversely, some grandmothers leave the disciplining to the parents and find that their role is to be as tolerant toward their grandchildren. Paula underscores this point.

> Oh, I'm much more lenient with my grandchildren because they have parents to take care of their discipline. It's my turn to enjoy, OK? That's what it's all about. Now they jump on the couch to a limit and my daughter says, "How come you never let me do this or that?" My son especially, "How come they can do all that, I could never do that?" And I go, "It's a different story." And if they ask me for something or if they don't want to finish their dinner I go, "Oh that's OK, don't worry about it." With my kids they had to finish they're meal, they couldn't get any dessert if they didn't finish. But I said that's their job now. I don't have to worry about that.

Many grandmothers underscore the cultural differences in the form of discipline that complicate grandmothering. Grandmothers attempt to adapt to U.S. disciplinary practices that often clash with their native country's childrearing practices. They reluctantly conform to the U.S. form of discipline, which many perceive as being counterproductive to children's acceptable behaviors. This cultural clash engenders a type of emotional stress that could adversely impact their health. It seems clear that the stress that accompanies the decision that some grandmothers have to make regarding the form of discipline may inadvertently affect or worsen their physical health. In particular, many grandmothers deal with health issues such as high blood pressure. The added stress may be deleterious to their already fragile health. Future research could explore how the cultural chasm adversely affects immigrant grandmothers' health.

Gendered vs. Cultural Expectations

Gendered and cultural expectations for childcare arrangements were emerging themes across many of the interviews. Goodman and Silverstein (2002) highlighted that a normative view of grandchild care is contingent on race, ethnicity, and social class. Many immigrant grandmothers perceive their role as grandmother to be unequivocally nonnegotiable. Many come from cultures in which grandmothers are fully involved in their grandchildren's lives. Intergenerational residence or living in close proximity to family members facilitates childcare. Most of the grandmothers received help from their mothers when they were raising their own children. Grandfathers are not expected to provide hands-on childcare. In fact many grandfathers encourage their wives to help their children with their grandchildren. As in the case with physical limitations and chronic illnesses, grandmothers struggle to fulfill these gendered and cultural expectations.

Gendered expectation is more salient in cases in which the grandmothers are in worse health than the grandfathers. Hoda is a soft-spoken working-class immigrant from Haiti. She is a 67-year-old mother of two and grandmother of two. She immigrated from Haiti 30 years ago and has been living off her disability insurance for the last 10 years because of a back injury she sustained from lifting a patient from her previous job as a home health aide. The back injury is exacerbated by a recent fall. Hoda also has high blood pressure and high cholesterol. Hoda's son is incarcerated and her daughter-in-law works full time. With limited resources, Hoda is expected to provide unpaid childcare to the two grandchildren from her incarcerated son. With a bad back, Hoda struggles to take care of her 15-month-old granddaughter. Even when she is physically unable to babysit, her husband insists that she does.

> Everyone knows that I fell last week and I'm in a lot of pain in my arms. I just did an MRI so I'm not really supposed to be taking care of the kids. But my husband has a lot to do with that. Even if I can't at times, he tells them to bring the kids.

Paula, with a neurological condition, from Puerto Rico, talks about the role that her husband plays in encouraging her to watch their grandchildren.

> My husband is really tolerant; he likes for the kids to be here all the time. Even when I say I can't, he insisted on the daughter-in-law to bring the kids here even if he knows he won't be home. I told him that this cannot go on like this. It is very difficult for me to take care of the kids.

Cultural expectation is one of the main reasons why many grandmothers believe that they have to provide care for their grandchildren. They frequently bring up comparisons between grandmothers in the United States and in their native country. Most of the grandmothers value this type of expectation. They find it to be an important aspect of their culture, the fact that everybody helps each other. They say that they believe that the collectivism that is pervasive in their native country is conducive to family unity and it helps every member of the family. They deplore the individualistic American's way of life.

Maria, a 54-year-old Mexican, is a full-time teacher and a new grandmother of a 1-year-old baby boy. She is on her second marriage and both husbands are American. She talks about her role as a new grandmother and contrasts her Mexican family with her American in-laws. She reminisces about an inter-generational household in Mexico and the importance of different members of the family helping each other.

> I think the grandmothers here tend to be a little more removed. I've heard some grandmothers say, "I don't want to babysit all the time, I don't want to be a babysitter." Where, when I was growing up, usually, the family, you know, that's what the family was. Grandma always lived with you and you were so much a part of each other's lives.

While Maria was raising her three children, her husband's family was not par-ticularly helpful at assisting her. She finds great difficulty understanding why American grandmothers choose not to interfere as compared to what she was accustomed to with her Mexican grandmothers.

> But they're different in that way; they're very kind to my kids, very generous, but they stay away unless I ask something to them. They don't really interfere too much. . . . Whereas, Mexican grandmas are very much part of the family, and you would turn to a grandma and ask for advice. You would turn to a grandma and whatever grandma would say that would be kind of the rule. It's not that way here. The culture is different. Even though I lived here a long, long time it's still really different.

Now that it is her turn to be a grandma to her grandson, she is negotiating between her Mexican and American cultural expectations.

> I think I try to be an American grandmother, an American mother-in-law you know, type of thing where you stay away. You just kind of mind your own business and if they come and ask you, then fine. But that's the way I see it; whereas, Mexicans, they're all in there, everybody knows your business. They care very much about you that you will never be alone ever. You would never consider yourself alone. If you had a big decision, family would be right there with you. Here, I still am alone, I feel. Even though with my new husband's family, and my ex, I still see his family but it's still removed. For some reason, I feel like I'm doing the same thing, I'm a little removed. I guess I don't want to be too much the other way cause if so, maybe they would think it's too much.

Paula reiterates the same concept of collectivism and cultural expectations. She refuses to conform to what she perceives as the American culture of grand-mothering, whereby American grandmothers are preoccupied with youth and do not want to play the grandmother role. Paula has the greatest physical limitations of the grandmothers I interviewed, yet her cultural expectations of childcare are nonnegotiable.

> Growing up we had a lot of grandparents, because they lived with their kids, who did step in and watch the kids. In the culture here, the Anglo culture, there's so much focus on youth. I see a lot of these. . . . For instance I see my daughter's mother-in-law had facial work done and she wants to look young and she wants to do this and that. It's more a self-absorbed culture I think. I don't think they are as willing to put out.

Most of the grandmothers I interviewed cherish their role as care providers for their grandchildren. Some grandmothers hope to find other alternatives for childcare, but in many situations the lack of resources constrains their ability to find other possibilities for childcare such as daycare or paid babysitters. Hoda, because of her poor health, wishes to find another alternative for childcare for her 15-month-old granddaughter, but the family does not have the money for paid childcare. "The parents are always at work and I don't work. If they have to pay for babysitting it would be too much money for them and they don't have it. If I was working it would have been different." Hoda sees that it is equally her responsibility to provide or to pay for childcare for her granddaughter, as dictated by cultural expectations.

Globally, women mostly perform this type of carework, caring for their children and grandchildren. The immigrant grandmothers I interviewed conform to the gendered and cultural expectations of providing childcare to their grandchildren while juggling other responsibilities such as paid employment. While many of the grandmothers in their native countries did not have paid employment, in the United States, many find that they are at a disadvantage because they have to work and still provide unpaid childcare. Women in different stages of their lives have different expectations. Immigrant grandmothers have to constantly negotiate their new position in the United States and the cultural expectations. Immigrant grandmothers I interviewed report that they are still expected to provide grandchild care even when their health is less than ideal. This cultural or gendered expectation may inadvertently impact grandmothers' ability to exercise, see their doctors, or manage their chronic conditions because of lack of time. Future investigations could provide more insight into the impact of carework on immigrant grandmothers' health.

Economic Insufficiency vs. Religious Abundancy

Many of the grandmothers find refuge in their church while struggling with meager finances and poor physical health. The lack of economic resources was ever-present in most of the interviews. Many grandmothers spend hours in church and believe that their current situation would improve with God's help. In fact, many believe that their emotional health is not affected by their poor physical health because their spirituality helps them to overcome hardships. Additionally, many grandmothers believe that they have a Christian duty to take care of their grandchildren. This is in line with the research carried out by Gibson (2002), wherein she found that African American custodial grandparents believed that the Lord had an active role in their decision-making process to take care of their grandchildren.

About half of my sample is working grandmothers who constantly have to navigate within limited resources. Harriet finds that she is always running out of money, and she knows that her two grandchildren add an extra burden to her finances. Susan, a 50-year-old housecleaner from St. Lucia, talks about her economic struggle since her daughter was deported and she has to provide for her granddaughter. She had just lost two of the five houses that she cleaned weekly. She believes that God will provide. "I lost two but the two I lost was paying very, very well. These 2 days work was paying $320. Yeah, but they moved to a different state so I lost these two. Now, God is on my side."

The economic difficulty of working-class immigrant women is another added stress. Hoda talks about how she is using her disability money from Supplemental Security Income to feed her grandchildren and also to pay lawyer's fee for her son who is incarcerated. At the same time, she clashes with her daughter-in-law when she takes the grandchildren to church.

On Saturday we go to the Seventh-day Adventist church. She gets mad when we take them to church; she said that the kids are not Adventist. Sometimes she lets a friend watch them so that we don't take them to church.

Many grandmothers I interviewed believe that religious institutions help them to overcome economic insufficiency and poor health. Most of the participants consider themselves to be very religious. Janet, a 60-year-old from Jamaica, is recovering from two knee replacement surgeries and also suffers from high blood pressure. She finds it very hard to provide continuous care to her seven grandchildren. She blames her bad knees from arthritis that she developed from years of working as a nurse. She does not provide too much childcare but she helps her daughters financially. When I ask her about her emotional health, she talks about the importance of her faith.

I learn to use my faith and don't let anything bothers me. I don't get depressed, nothing bothers me. If I don't have a penny today, it's not gonna matter. I know how to control myself; I use my faith. That's a big part for me, this church, we pray about everything.

Hanna makes similar remarks about her faith: "My church is my life; that's where I get my strength, that's where I laugh, that's my life. I say if somebody take away my church, you may kill me."

Many of these grandmothers have accumulated a lifetime of economic disadvantages. Their early life trajectories impact their current social position in the United States. In line with a lifecourse perspective and cumulative inequality theory, immigrant grandmothers' lack of resources in their native countries and current economic inequalities in the United States shape their grandmothering experiences. However, these grandmothers use religion to deal with their economic disadvantage and find that they are well equipped to handle their emotional and physical health. Their religiosity may help them to deal with the emotional stress that comes with living with limited material resources. Many grandmothers express the importance of religion for helping them deal with emotional stress and poor physical health. For example, the social support that stems from religious abundancy may be conducive to or even protective of good health (see George, Larson, Koenig, and McCullough, 2000).

Health Impacts of Grandmothering

Given the multitude of competing cultural expectations that immigrant grandmothers must navigate, how does caring for grandchildren, along with other responsibilities, shape grandmothers' health? In return, how does health shape the ability to care for grandchildren? Most of the immigrant grandmothers in this study were not providing intensive care to their grandchildren. Therefore, deteriorating health effects from caregiving is not expected. Studies reporting deteriorating health conditions are usually in the case of custodial grandparents or those who provide extensive care (Bachman and Chase-Lansdale, 2005; Minkler and Fuller-Thomson, 1999, 2001; Musil and Ahmad, 2002; Musil et al., 2011). However, in the case of most of my participants, grandmothering may create some stressful situations and interfere with grandmothers' time to attend to their own needs, such as exercising and management of chronic diseases (Baker and Silverstein, 2008; Hughes et al., 2007). Additionally, physical limitations may hinder grandmothers' abilities to take care of their grandchildren. Indeed, many interviewed grandmothers reported physical limitation as one aspect that makes taking care of their grandchildren problematic. Given the unrepresentative nature of this sample, this study raises questions that should be further explored by future studies.

Diet, Exercise, and Management of Chronic Conditions

Most of the grandmothers I interviewed report good to excellent health (see Table 2). This is a sample of relatively young grandmothers who work full time. Some of them have school-age children. However, I was astonished at the prevalence of chronic illnesses among these relatively young women. Most of the grandmothers have multiple chronic conditions such as high cholesterol, diabetes, and high blood pressure. Most are not actively engaged in preventative measures such as exercising (see Table 1). However, many mention that they are watching their diet. Many blame lack of time as one of the main reasons they are not able to exercise. Brenda, a 50-year-old from Barbados, works full time as a kindergarten teacher with disabled children. She finds her job to be very demanding and stressful. She looks forward to summer vacation to join a gym with a friend. She had just received a call from her son asking her to watch her 3-year-old grandson during the day while he and his wife are at work. She understands that her son and daughter-in-law have financial constraints and they desperately need her help. But she finds that it is unfair that they want her to use her summer vacation to care for her grandson while she was planning to go to the gym with her friend during the summer days.

Table 2. Distribution of Self-Reported Health among Immigrant Grandmothers

	Count	Percentage
Excellent	3	21
Good	6	43
Poor	4	29
Very poor	1	7
Total	14	100

> I plan to join with a friend this new gym over here during the summer. I can, you know, go there and do something. . . . I don't like babysitting, but I do it sometimes if I have to do it. He wants my grandson to be here 2 months, July and August. They're not saying, "Please mom take care of him"; they ask me if I would. In other words, I don't have to; they are just asking if I would. So I said, "Well I don't think it's fair to ask to take care of him for 2 months knowing that I work with kids from September to June, little kids, and now you want me to have another little kid for 2 months straight." I need a break, I do not do Sunday school for a reason, and I need the time for myself.

Many grandmothers face difficulties finding time to take care of themselves when they are expected to care for their grandchildren. Harriet, with multiple chronic conditions, finds that managing her chronic illnesses is difficult because she works the night shift so that she can take care of her grandson during the day. At times, she forgets to take her antihypertensive medications.

> This is what happened with my high blood pressure. I was only taking the med when I feel something is wrong and I wasn't taking it regularly because I'm so busy. That's why I had the stroke. They said that you have to take the pills every day. Now I don't spend a day without taking my blood pressure pills.

Immigrant grandmothers who are working and providing extensive grandchild care have more difficulty finding time and energy to exercise and manage their chronic conditions. Navigating within limited resources, immigrant grandmothers are providing this type of carework compounded by paid employment, which leaves them very little time to take care of themselves, either by exercising and managing their chronic conditions. Again, those with life course trajectories that are marred with economic deprivation are more likely to experience poorer health and have greater difficulty at grandmothering.

Physical Limitations

Physical limitations are not pervasive among the interviewed grandmothers. However, some of the grandmothers report some types of arthritis or back/joint pain. Harmonie is 55 years old but suffers from advanced rheumatoid arthritis. She has recently retired. However, she splits her time between her two daughters' houses to help them with their young children. She finds it especially difficult to watch her two young grandsons because taking care of them requires more physical labor.

> I used to lift them up. Now, I can't run after them. If I have to change them, I can't lift them. My doctor told me not to lift them. I spoke to the parents and told them, "If you come here and find them dirty, don't blame me because I can't change the diapers."

Janet, who just had knee-replacement surgeries, finds that she can no longer provide childcare for her grandchildren, as much as she would love to; instead, she mostly helps her children with financial expenses. However, she still takes her grandchildren to the park as much as she can.

For the most part, the physical limitations that many grandmothers are dealing with do not seem to be related to grandmothering *per se*. Almost all the grandmothers report physical limitations that are the results of early life processes and previous occupations. In line with a lifecourse perspective and cumulative inequality theory, immigrant grandmothers have special challenges to provide childcare because of earlier disadvantages, notably holding physically demanding jobs during their early years. Consequently, immigrant grandmothers who came to the United States from countries with limited resources might experience greater physical limitations, which inadvertently shape their grandmothering experiences. Future research with representative samples, especially longitudinal data, can unravel the level to which health is shaped by early life events or later lifecourse circumstances.

Discussion

Immigrant grandparents caring for grandchildren go through very diverse grandmothering experiences. With such diversity in country of origin, socio-economic status, health status, and intensity of care, how does caring for grandchildren impact grandmothers' health? Using in-depth qualitative research has provided nuanced analyses that have been lacking in large datasets. Although not conclusive, there is evidence of a cumulative disadvantage over the life course. Most of the participants describe their immigration as a direct result of limited economic resources in their native countries. Those from countries with limited economic resources, such as Haiti, experience poorer health and are financially worse off. This finding is consistent with a life course perspective and cumulative inequality theory. Overall, my findings are consistent with previous scholarly works that suggest that grandparents' caregiving could be beneficial for emotional health (Goodman and Silverstein, 2001; Pruchno and McKenney, 2002). This research shows that most of the grandmothers provide childcare in response to their adult children's financial needs. This study has uncovered the cultural frames that immigrants use to negotiate gendered and cultural expectations.

In general, immigrant grandmothers find joy in taking care of their grandchildren. This sense of joy is pervasive, even among those who provide care because there are no other alternatives. Many grandmothers rely on their religion as a source of support to help them deal with lack of economic resources or their emotional health. Nevertheless, the cultural frames that some grandmothers have to navigate do engender some emotional stress, especially when it involves the issue of disciplining their grandchildren. Furthermore, taking care of their grandchildren leaves them very little time to take care of their health by seeing doctors, exercising, and managing their chronic conditions. Given the nonrandom nature of this sample, more research is warranted to unravel the health impact of grandmothering among immigrant grandmothers.

References

Abraido-Lanza, A. F., Chao, M. T., and Florez, K. R. 2005. Do healthy behaviors decline with greater acculturation?: Implications for the Latino Mortality Paradox. *Social Science & Medicine (1982)*, 61(6): 1243.

Abraido-Lanza, A. F., Dohrenwend, B. P., Ng-Mak, D. S., and Turner, J. B. 1999. The Latino Mortality Paradox: A test of the "Salmon Bias" and healthy migrant hypotheses. *American Journal of Public Health*, 89(10): 1543-1548.

Administration on Aging. 2010. The next four decades—The older population in the United States: 2010 to 2050. Retrieved December 4, 2013 from http://www.aoa.gov/AoARoot/Aging_Statistics/future_growth/DOCS/p25-1138.pdf)

Bachman, H. J. and Chase-Lansdale, P. L. 2005. Custodial grandmothers' physical, mental, and economic well-being: Comparisons of primary caregivers from low-income neighborhoods. *Family Relations*, 54(4): 475-487.

Baker, L. A. and Silverstein, M. 2008. Preventive health behaviors among grandmothers raising grandchildren. *The Journals of Gerontology Series B: Psychological Sciences and Social Sciences*, 63(5): S304-S311.

Butler, F. R. and Zakari, N. 2005. Grandparents parenting grandchildren: Assessing health status, parental stress, and social supports. *Journal of Gerontological Nursing*, 31(3): 43-54.

Dannefer, D. 2003. Cumulative advantage/disadvantage and the life course: Cross-fertilizing age and social science theory. *The Journals of Gerontology Series B: Psychological Sciences and Social Sciences*, 58(6): S327-S337.

Dolbin-MacNab, M. L. 2006. Just like raising your own? Grandmothers' perceptions of parenting a second time around. *Family Relations*, 55(5): 564-575.

Draper, H. 2013. Grandparents' entitlements and obligations. *Bioethics*, 27(6): 309-316.

Elder, G. H. 1974. *Children of the great depression: Social change in life experience.* Chicago, IL: University of Chicago Press.

Ferraro, K. F. and Shippee, T. P. 2009. Aging and cumulative inequality: How does inequality get under the skin? *The Gerontologist*, 49(3): 333-343.

Franzini, L., Ribble, J. C., and Keddie, A. M. 2001. Understanding the Hispanic paradox. *Ethnicity & Disease*, 11(3): 496.

George, L. K., Larson, D. B., Koenig, H. G., and McCullough, M. E. 2000. Spirituality and health: What we know, what we need to know. *Journal of Social and Clinical Psychology*, 19(1): 102-116.

Gibson, P. A. 2002. African American grandmothers as caregivers: Answering the call to help their grandchildren. *Families in Society: The Journal of Contemporary Social Services*, 83(1): 35-43.

Goodman, C. and Silverstein, M. 2002. Grandmothers raising grandchildren family structure and well-being in culturally diverse families. *The Gerontologist*, 42(5): 676-689.

Goodman, C. C. and Silverstein, M. 2001. Grandmothers who parent their grandchildren: An exploratory study of close relations across three generations. *Journal of Family Issues,* 22(5): 557-578.

Grieco, E. M., Acosta, Y. D., de la Cruz, G. P., Gambino, C., Gryn, T., Larsen, L. J., Trevelyan, E. N., and Walters, N. P. 2012. The foreign-born population in the United States: 2010. *American Community Survey Reports.*

Harrington Meyer, M. 2012. Grandmothers juggling work and grandchildren in the United States. In S. Arber and V. Timonen (Eds.), *Contemporary grandparenting: Changing family relationships in global contexts* (pp. 71–90). Bristol, UK: Policy Press.

Harrington Meyer, M. 2014. *Grandmothers at work: Juggling families and jobs.* New York, NY: NYU Press.

Hughes, M. E., Waite, L. J., LaPierre, T. A., and Luo, Y. 2007. All in the family: The impact of caring for grandchildren on grandparents' health. *The Journals of Gerontology Series B: Psychological Sciences and Social Sciences,* 62(2): S108-S119.

Hummer, R. A., Rogers, R. G., Amir, S. H., Forbes, D., and Frisbie, W. P. 2000. Adult mortality differentials among Hispanic subgroups and non-Hispanic whites. *Social Science Quarterly,* 81(1): 459-476.

Kelley, S. J., Yorker, B. C., and Whitley, D. 1997. To grandmother's house we go . . . and stay. Children raised in intergenerational families. *Journal of Gerontological Nursing,* 23(9): 12-20.

Lerner, S. 2010. *The war on moms: On life in a family-unfriendly nation.* New York, NY: John Wiley and Sons.

Minkler, M. and Fuller-Thomson, E. 2001. Physical and mental health status of American grandparents providing extensive child care to their grandchildren. *Journal of the American Medical Women's Association,* 56(4): 199-205.

Minkler, M. and Fuller-Thomson, E. 1999. The health of grandparents raising grandchildren: Results of a national study. *American Journal of Public Health,* 89(9): 1384-1389.

Moen, P., Spencer, D., Binstock, R. H., and George, L. K. 2006. Converging divergences in age, gender, health, and well-being: Strategic selection in the third age. In R. H. Binstock and L. K. George (Eds.), *Handbook of Aging and the Social Sciences,* (6th ed., pp. 127-144). San Diego, CA: Academic Press.

Musil, C. M. and Ahmad, M. 2002. Health of grandmothers A comparison by caregiver status. *Journal of Aging and Health,* 14(1): 96-121.

Musil, C. M., Gordon, N. L., Warner, C. B., Zauszniewski, J. A., Standing, T., and Wykle, M. 2011. Grandmothers and caregiving to grandchildren: Continuity, change, and outcomes over 24 months. *The Gerontologist,* 51(1): 86-100.

Pollitt, R., Rose, K., and Kaufman, J. 2005. Evaluating the evidence for models of life course socioeconomic factors and cardiovascular outcomes: A systematic review. *BMC Public Health,* 5(1): 7.

Pruchno, R. A. and McKenney, D. 2002. Psychological well-being of black and white grandmothers raising grandchildren examination of a two-factor model. *The Journals of Gerontology Series B: Psychological Sciences and Social Sciences,* 57(5): P444-P452.

U.S Census Bureau. 2009. American Community Survey, 2009. Retrieved May 14, 2013 from http://factfinder2.census.gov/faces/tableservices/jsf/pages/productview.xhtml?pid=A CS_09_1YR_B10053&prodType=table)

Wakabayashi, C. 2010. Effects of immigration and age on health of older people in the United States. *Journal of Applied Gerontology,* 29(6): 697-719.

Waters, M. C. and Sykes, J. E. 2009. Spare the rod, ruin the child. First- and Second-Generation West Indian Childrearing Practices. In Foner, N. (Ed.), *Across generations: Immigrant families in America* (pp. 72-97). New York, NY: NYU Press.

Williams, D. R. 2005. The health of U.S. racial and ethnic populations. *The Journals of Gerontology,* 60B: 53-62.

http://dx.doi.org/10.2190/GITC5

CHAPTER 5

Grandparent-Provided Childcare for Families Raising Elementary School-Aged Children with Disabilities

Peter D. Brandon

For several reasons, there has been growing interest in disability among school-children. First, the Americans with Disabilities Act (ADA) focused national attention on children with disabilities, the impact of social organizations and physical structures on such basic activities as children with disabilities getting to school, and the potential for rehabilitation and enablement. Second, the increased number of infants with very low birth-weight and the dramatically improved survivorship of these children and other children with chronic medical conditions has increased the number of children with high risk of disability. Third, attention to such emergent childhood afflictions as attention deficit hyperactivity disorder and better diagnosis of acute asthma has expanded the risk pool for children with disabilities. Fourth, the costs of continuing newly developed programs to support the healthy and productive development of children with disabilities have increased due to the expansion in the number of children eligible, availability of innovative new services, and increasing costs associated with each enrolled child.

Despite growing interest in childhood disability and governmental recognition that it is time to better understand the well-being of the nation's approximately 2.8 million schoolchildren with disabilities, there are still few national studies of childhood disability among schoolchildren (Brault, 2011). Though there are only a handful of studies, they show that (a) nearly all of these schoolchildren live with their parents and attend regular school; (b) a sizable proportion of all schoolchildren experience a disability, which could include some form of limitation in mobility, self-care, communication, or learning; and (c) research at the national level on the impact of childhood disabilities on family well-being and family organization is inadequate.

One area that requires further research is the childcare arrangements before the schoolday starts or after it ends for schoolchildren with disabilities. Possibly, out-of-school childcare for children with disabilities is unnecessary because their parents successfully schedule work hours around the hours of the schoolday. Or out-of-school childcare might not be utilized by these particular children because there are not enough programs to meet their special needs or because their parents would incur added out-of-pocket expenses for care. Or perhaps, as investigated here, disabilities among schoolchildren increased odds that grandparents are relied upon rather than school programs or market childcare providers. In any case, until now the care and supervision of schoolchildren with disabilities before or after school is still largely unknown.

Thus, it is timely to use the Survey of Income and Program Participation (SIPP) to explore the out-of-school childcare arrangements of schoolchildren with disabilities by family structure. My aim is to better grasp whether disabilities among schoolchildren lead families to rely more on grandparents than before- or after-school programs or market providers of childcare. SIPP data permitted examining the bond grandparents have with schoolchildren with disabilities and addressing questions such as (a) What were the patterns in childcare use among schoolchildren with disabilities, and do those patterns differ from schoolchildren without disabilities? (b) If grandparents are more likely to care for schoolchildren with disabilities outside of school hours, are the out-of-pocket costs lower while the hours of care longer? (c) Do characteristics of mothers of schoolchildren with disabilities using grandparent care differ from characteristics of other mothers? (d) Once the maternal labor force decision and factors related to out-of-school childcare choices are considered, do schoolchildren with disabilities still have a higher likelihood of receiving grandparent care rather than care from their parents? And finally, (e) Does grandparent care for schoolchildren differ by type of disability and family structure?

Background

Estimates vary by data source and definition of disability, but the central fact is inescapable: many schoolchildren living at home have a disability. Even if lower-bound estimates of disability from the census are used, which does not include functional limitations, the proportion of all children aged between 5 and 17 years with a disability in 2010 was about 5%, or about 2.8 million children (Brault, 2011). If the National Health Interview Survey (NHIS) is used, which includes activity limitations and has a broader age range of 3 to 17 years, the estimated proportion for 2011 rises to about 8%, or 4.7 million preschool and school-age children (Bloom, Cohen, and Freeman, 2012). Previous estimates from the 1990s reinforce the fact that large numbers of families raise schoolchildren with disabilities. Adler (1995), for example, estimated that about 7% of all children younger than 18 years of age had a disability in 1990; McNeil (1997) estimated that about 13% of school-age children had a disability in 1995; and lastly, Hogan, Msall, Rogers, and Avery (1997) estimated that in the early 1990s about 12% of children had some form of disability.

Until the studies from the 1990s and the 2000 census, there were no national population estimates of disabilities among school-aged children. As a consequence, national policies concerning childhood disability were made in a vacuum. Plainly, the government statistics indicated that childhood disability among children is a feature of everyday life for millions of families. Despite this fact, studies of how this sizable number of families balance work responsibilities and the demands of raising schoolchildren with disabilities are unknown. Hence, investigating use of out-of-school childcare by children with and without disabilities is critically important because it provides insights into this ongoing juggling act while raising broader questions about the institutional structures that enable families to manage the exceptional tasks of raising school-age children with disabilities.

Though ostensibly logical that childhood disabilities might push parents to use grandparent-provided out-of-school childcare as substitutes for themselves or other childcare modes, scant evidence exists to substantiate the presumption. Yet research on grandparenting suggests that many American grandparents are tied into their adult children and grandchildren's lives (Fuller-Thomson and Minkler, 2001).

Grandparent-provided childcare is a transfer of time to adult children. Using the Health and Retirement Study (HRS), Luo, LaPierre, Hughes, and Waite (2012) found that 61% of grandparents provided at least 50 hours of care annually for grandchildren between 1998 and 2008. Other researchers using an earlier wave of the HRS also reported sizable intergenerational time transfers; Soldo and Hill (1995) and Cardia and Ng (2003) reported that nearly 46% and 43%, respectively, of grandmothers spent more than 100 hours caring for grandchildren annually.

Also, for millions of families, grandparent-provided childcare is preferred over market-provided alternatives. Today, about 24% of all preschool-aged children receive their primary childcare from grandparents, making this activity a substantial intergenerational transfer of time within families (Laughlin, 2013). Between 1985 and 2005, grandparent care was the primary childcare mode for 16% to 19% of preschoolers with employed mothers (U.S. Census Bureau, 2008). Over these 20 years, proportions of preschool-aged children receiving childcare from grandparents equaled proportions of preschool-aged children using daycare centers (U.S. Census Bureau, 2008). Among the 10.9 million preschool-aged children receiving childcare in 2008, some 21% had grandparents as their primary caregivers while mothers worked (U.S. Census Bureau, 2011).

Clearly, grandparent-provided childcare is integral to the lives of millions of families. It would seem ill-considered to assume away the potential impact that childhood disability among schoolchildren could have on use of grandparents to provide out-of-school childcare. Our knowledge about the extent of grandparent-provided childcare, motives for intergenerational transfers of care time, and barriers facing families raising schoolchildren with disabilities makes it prudent to analyze the effects of childhood disabilities on the odds of families using grandparent-provided out-of-school childcare. Lastly, pursuing this inquiry is vital since schoolchildren today confront a different reality than the reality of their parents. The new reality is working mothers rather than stay-at-home mothers; families with only one parent instead of two; and neighborhoods that are unsafe and disconnected, not secure and cohesive.

Theoretical Perspectives and Hypotheses

Grandparent-provided childcare is conceptually an intergenerational transfer of time (Fuller-Thomson and Minkler, 2001). Disciplines like sociology, economics, and human development draw upon theories about altruism and caring, evolutionary genetics, and exchange and reciprocity to explain intergenerational time transfers (Bianchi, Hotz, McGarry, and Seltzer 2008). Each theory offers insights, but I argue that grandparent-provided childcare is more closely tied to a theory of altruism than to theories of exchange and reciprocity or evolutionary genetics. I theorize that altruism for adult children and grandchildren drives grandparents, and that this caring for the welfare of subsequent generations is amplified when grandparents know adult children face added strains and challenges when raising children with disabilities. *Quid pro quo* motives or propagating genetic traits are less persuasive, I argue, once the demands of raising children with disabilities are appreciated. Thus, my hypotheses rest on the notion that grandparent-provided childcare is a transfer of time "flowing down" to subsequent generations (Caldwell, 2005).

In the context of altruistic intergenerational support, parents' decisions regarding out-of-school childcare for schoolchildren are likely based on need, resources, perceived risks to children, characteristics of children, and preferences. The model I develop assumes that the care chosen has the highest value and is the optimum alternative to parental care for school-aged children during the workday. So if grandparent care is chosen, it is the best alternative, reflecting parental preferences, availability of resources, including a second parent to share care, child characteristics, and assessment of perceived risk in the immediate environment. Since I lack measures of neighborhood risks perceived by parents, I have to indirectly measure those risks using children's ages and spatial location. Plainly, a parent must first decide to work in the labor market, but this decision is modeled as a joint decision with the childcare decision.

My main hypothesis is that the decision by employed parents to use grandparents for out-of-school childcare depends upon schoolchildren's degree of autonomy, which is not necessarily just a function of age, and chances of enrollment at market-provided childcare sites. A school-aged child's ability to act autonomously or independently before or after school in the absence of parental supervision may not only depend upon his or her maturity but also upon the presence of disabilities or functional limitations. Likewise, resource inadequacies could prevent a school-aged child with a disability from attending a childcare center. So, besides a child's ethnicity and age, my model tests whether mobility; cognitive or developmental limitations; or physical, communicative, or behavioral disabilities among schoolchildren lead employed parents to choose grandparent childcare over alternatives, thereby minimizing perceived risks related to self-care or uncertainties linked to market childcare.

I further conjecture that a measure of a child having a disability or not might fail to detect an effect of childhood disabilities on employed parents' choice to use out-of-school grandparent-provided childcare. Employed parents' decisions about childcare for school children with disabilities, if tied to concerns about balancing perceived risks against independence, might mean that grandparent-provided childcare is more closely tied to specific types of limitations or disabilities that restrict children's capabilities to care for themselves or cope at market-provided childcare. Though I have no hypotheses as to which particular limitations or disabilities lead schoolchildren to have less autonomy, I separately evaluate the effects of types of disabilities and functional limitations to discover which particular disabilities or limitations are more closely linked to employed parents' decisions to use grandparent childcare. If children's ages are reasonable proxies for maturity in both types of families, I expect older children are less likely to receive care from grandparents after accounting for disabilities.

Another hypothesis tested is that parental employment status is related to the grandparent childcare decision. It makes sense that parents working full time will need reliable and longer hours of childcare. I hypothesize that employed single and married parents working full time are more likely to choose grandparent care since grandparents are dependable, invested in their grandchildren, and have more flexible schedules to accommodate early morning drop-offs and late afternoon pick-ups compared with market childcare providers.

A key reason exists to anticipate differences in the way employment status is related to the grandparent childcare choice among single mothers and married parents. Married parents working full time often share care with spouses by working different schedules (Presser, 1989), which is an option unavailable to single mothers. A big difference, therefore, is the differential availability of all the options, with single mothers having less access to the other "parent" option. Thus, it is essential to examine childcare separately for schoolchildren of single and married parents since the childcare choice sets differ even when other characteristics are similar.

The choice of grandparent out-of-school care also depends on family resources, such as availability of appropriate caregivers. I expect that children of single mothers who do not have a spouse to provide regular care are more likely to substitute grandparent-provided childcare or self-care (Cain and Hofferth, 1989). The number and ages of other children in the family are also important. While more children in a family increases the cost of nonfamilial care and may increase the likelihood of using grandparent care, older siblings may also serve as childcare providers. I conjecture that for single and married mothers, more children will increase the cost of nonfamilial care and decrease the odds of using school-based and nonrelative childcare because older siblings can provide childcare.

Poverty status is another aspect of family resources identified in the model. Most market childcare requires payment. Hence, greater economic disadvantage for both types of families should decrease the use of formal care and increase the use of nonpaid care such as grandparent care. Past research hypothesized that because low-income parents may be unable to pay for childcare arrangements, children would be more likely to care for themselves (Seligson, 1983), but other studies find no association (Laird, Pettit, Dodge, and Bates, 1998; Smith and Casper, 1999) or a positive association between income and self-care (Cain and Hofferth, 1989). Single mothers experience both lack of the parental care option and low income. Distinguishing by family structure first, then testing for the effects of economic disadvantage should point to the effects of economic disadvantage on the decision to use grandparent care for schoolchildren.

Parental preferences should also be associated with the childcare chosen. Parents' preferences may reflect their attitudes and beliefs regarding the monitoring and supervision schoolchildren need. Because parents' levels of education, their ethnicity, and ages play a part in forming preferences, I include measures of all three. Research on the childcare decisions of mothers of preschool-age children suggests that mothers with higher levels of education choose formal daycare programs more often than mothers with lower levels of education (Hofferth, Brayfield, Deich, and Holcomb, 1991). But that research may not carry over for choice of grandparent care for school-aged children. I hypothesize that limited educational attainment among mothers with schoolchildren, for example, lacking a high school diploma, may reflect past family stress or curtailed opportunities when mothers were themselves adolescents. If so, I argue that single mothers and married parents with high school diplomas or better will choose grandparent care for schoolchildren more frequently than parents who did not complete high school because their own family histories were less likely to lack educational opportunities or achievements.

To repeat, the chief difference between the choices of single and married mothers is the unavailability of spouses for single mothers. Hence, other forms of childcare should be used more frequently. And income is a vital consideration for single mothers when they choose market childcare. Though lower-income mothers may have access to childcare subsidies and are thus more likely than higher-income mothers to use market childcare and school-based programs, I conjecture that maternal traits could be more important to low-income mothers' choice of out-of-school childcare than their income.

Data, Measures, and Statistical Model

Data Description

Data for this study are from the 1996, 2001, and 2004 panels of the Survey of Income and Program Participation (SIPP). The SIPP is a longitudinal survey of a random sample of the U.S. population (U.S. Census Bureau, 2001). Each wave of the SIPP panels was conducted quarterly, so every participant was interviewed three times a year about his or her monthly experiences over the past 4 months. Thus, these data provide monthly information on household composition, labor market behavior, and income sources. Overall, the SIPP is well suited for this study since it collected economic and demographic data on households and because it gathered detailed information on the childcare arrangements of school-aged children and on types of disabilities and functional limitations among school-aged children.

Childcare Arrangement Measures

Childcare questionnaires in wave four directed parents to report childcare expenditures for their three youngest children and hours each of the children spent in alternative types of childcare. Types included childcare provided by (a) the other parent or step-parent, (b) a brother or sister over 15 years of age, (c) a grandparent, (d) another relative, (e) a nonrelative, (f) a day or group care center, (g) a nursery or preschool, (h) a school, (i) the child, that is, self-care, (j) a parent working at home, and (k) a parent at the workplace. I collapsed the 11 childcare types into six childcare categories[1] so that I could estimate the statistical model: (1) parent, (2) grandparent (3) other relative, (4) self-care, (5) market care, and (6) before- or after-school care.

Disability and Functional Limitation Measures

A measure of disability status and alternative measures of disability types and functional limitations among children are my chief independent variables of interest. My disability status measure and other measures of disability types and functional limitations are derived from the rich array of comprehensive disability questions that form the specialized modules contained in wave five of each of the three SIPP panels; that module aimed to collect a large amount of disability and functional limitation data for every member of a household. The data gathered by the module included both restrictions on activities of daily living and limitations in performing age-appropriate social roles. Types of information collected for

---

[1] Parent care consisted of types (a), (j), and (k); other relative care consisted of types (c) and (d); nonrelative consisted of types (e), (f), and (g); school-based consisted of type (h); and self-care consistent of type (i).

children include whether children use wheelchairs, canes, crutches, or walkers; whether they have difficulty or an inability to communicate, lift everyday household items, ambulate, or use telephones; whether they find difficulty with or need the help of others with self-care or socializing; and whether they have a learning disability, mental retardation, or any other developmental disability, or mental or emotional condition. If a SIPP respondent answered "yes" for a child in the household to *any* items, I coded the child as having a disability; then I capitalized on the detailed items on types of disabilities and functional limitations to create more specific measures guided by the literature (Hogan et al., 1997; Wells and Hogan, 2003; McNeil, 1997; Stein, Silver, and Bauman, 2001; World Health Organization, 2001). Two typologies resulted: the first identified three types of functional limitations, namely, cognitive, mobility, and communication; the second identified three types of disability conditions, namely, learning, developmental, and behavioral.

The SIPP data permit combining the childcare and disability information and then matching that data to other SIPP data collected on mothers' demographic characteristics, work schedules, health status, income sources, living arrangements, and state of residence. The extensive childcare and disability data once merged with data on the mothers and families of these children offered an excellent opportunity to learn about the childcare arrangements of children in elementary school, especially out-of-school grandparent care, and compare those arrangements by family structure. The combined panels yielded a sample of 14,585 children between the ages of 5 and 10 with a married or single mother using one of the six types of out-of-school childcare.

Statistical Model

A chief aim of my empirical strategy was incorporating a parental decision to enter the labor force into the model of her childcare choice. To achieve my aim, I exploited a bivariate probit model. The bivariate probit model is a model that can estimate whether two situations, that may appear "seemingly unrelated" (Agresti, 2010) are in fact related. The underlying statistical association is estimated by the coefficient for the variable "Rho" in the multivariate regressions. Hence, in my model, the decision to work and the decision to use a particular type of childcare are simultaneously estimated and the hypothesized unobserved correlation between the two decisions is taken into account.[2] By controlling for variation in mothers' propensities to enter the labor force, the model permits testing my

---

[2] If decisions about work and childcare were uncorrelated with each other, the estimated effects of variables should match those generated by a probit model predicting choice of a type of childcare. When I compared estimates from the probit regressions with estimates from bivariate probit regressions, I found that the coefficients from the former overestimated effects of the independent variables.

theory that the employment decision influences a mother's childcare decision for her school-aged children and it also generates consistent estimates of the effects of children with disabilities, economic disadvantage, employment status, and demographic and household characteristics on that childcare decision.[3] (See Brandon and Hofferth [2003] for a description of applying this model to childcare choices.)

Because I contend that differences exist in the choice process for single and married mothers, I estimate separate bivariate probit models for children living with single and married mothers. For both groups of children, models estimate the probability that mothers work or do not work (first dependent variable) and the likelihoods of mothers choosing either grandparents, school-based programs, other relatives, market- or self-care (second dependent variables), compared to using parental care. My control variables include mother's age, race/ethnicity, education level, work status, nativity status, poverty status, and welfare use. To capture salient characteristics of the family and state, I include number of children in the family, children's age structure, region of the country, and state unemployment rates.

Findings

Descriptive statistics in Table 1 suggest that nearly three-quarters of the schoolchildren lived with married parents. The 25% of schoolchildren living with single mothers were more likely to have mothers with disabilities themselves compared to schoolchildren living with married parents. And schoolchildren living in single-mother households faced greater economic disadvantage, even though their mothers were more likely to work in the labor force. The households of schoolchildren with single mothers compared to those of schoolchildren with married parents had lower household income, greater reliance on welfare, and higher poverty levels. Married parents were less likely to have dropped out of high school and more likely to at least have a college degree than the single mothers. Though family structure had no association with children living in urban areas, with mothers' ages, or with their own gender (more likely male than female), schoolchildren with single mothers were more likely to have a disability (18%) compared to their peers with married parents (12%). Also, schoolchildren with single mothers were more likely in minority families than schoolchildren with married parents.

Lastly, Table 1 shows that, except for self-care and out-of-school childcare programs, the childcare arrangements for schoolchildren differed by family

---

[3] I also examined interactions between variables and family structure. These regressions yielded results similar to those reported. Because fit statistics (Long, 1997; Raftery, 1995) suggested that models by family structure yielded better predictions, I kept separate models.

Table 1. Selected Descriptive Statistics for Children
Aged 6 to 10 Years by Family Structure

	Single mothers	Married mothers
Northeast	0.19	0.17
South	0.38	0.34
Midwest	0.22	0.26
West	0.21	0.23
Live in metro area	0.79	0.78
Working	0.73	0.68
Household monthly income (\$2001)[a]	\$2,149.9	\$5,621.7
At or below poverty line	0.43	0.12
Receive welfare	0.31	0.05
Mother's age	33.9	36.3
Mother disabled	0.29	0.16
High school dropout	0.2	0.12
High school only	0.33	0.28
Some college	0.38	0.33
College plus	0.09	0.27
Child's age	7.74	7.74
Child has disability	0.18	0.12
Number of children	2.34	2.39
White	0.45	0.71
Black	0.34	0.08
Hispanic	0.17	0.15
Other race/ethnicity	0.05	0.06
Male child	0.52	0.51
Primary out-of-school childcare arrangement		
Parent	0.423	0.621
Self-care	0.027	0.023
Grandparent	0.186	0.096
Other relative	0.148	0.082
Market provider[b]	0.087	0.056
Before/after-school program	0.128	0.122
$N =$	3.705	10,880

Source: SIPP 1996, 2001, 2004 panels.
[a]In \$2001.
    [b]Market providers are nonrelatives, family daycare providers, and childcare centers offering before- or after-school programs for school-aged children; Disability measures based on wave five topical modules.

structure. Schoolchildren in single-mother households are more likely to receive childcare from grandparents and other kin than schoolchildren in two-parent households (about 8% for nongrandparent kin and 10% for grandparents). And schoolchildren with single mothers are more likely to receive childcare from a market provider, for example, a childcare center offering programs, than care from their mothers, while the reverse holds for schoolchildren with married parents.

Focusing now on patterns in grandparent out-of-school care, Table 2 indicates that single mothers and married parents using grandparent care as their primary out-of-school childcare arrangement differ from single mothers and married parents using other types of childcare. Among married parents with school-children, those using grandparent care are more likely to work compared with married parents using other types of out-of-school childcare. Patterns suggesting greater economic disadvantage or higher prevalence of maternal or child disability among married parents using grandparent care, however, were undetectable. By contrast, married parents using grandparent care for schoolchildren were younger, less likely White, and more likely Black compared to other White and Black married parents using other types of out-of-school childcare.

While no clear patterns emerged for married parents, Table 2 indicates that single mothers using grandparent care were one of the two least likely groups of single mothers to have disabilities themselves, but the most likely group of single mothers to raise children with disabilities. Alongside single mothers who used before- or after-school care or used market care, single mothers using grandparent out-of-school care were more likely to work compared with single mothers using themselves or other relatives to care for schoolchildren out of school, or with single mothers letting children care for themselves, that is, self-care. Interestingly, children living with single mothers using grandparent care had the highest average monthly household income among all children in single-mother households. Also, these children and those using school childcare programs were less likely to live below the poverty line and less likely to rely on welfare compared with children with single mothers who used parent care or other relatives, or, again, used self-care. Children with single mothers receiving grandparent care had mothers who were different from other single mothers (except of those children whose single mother used school childcare programs) in that the former had the lowest rate of high school noncompletion compared with the latter. The significance for grandparents of Tables 1 and 2 is that they are crucial to parents' childcare decisions for school-aged children and their role as childcare providers for single mothers raising schoolchildren with disabilities is essential.

Table 3 examines childcare use by family structure and children's disability status. Children of single mothers are about twice as likely to use grandparent care compared with the children of married parents. But schoolchildren with disabilities of single mothers are the most likely among the groups of children to receive grandparent childcare. Table 3 shows that schoolchildren of single mothers are less likely to have mothers care for them, probably because single

Table 2. Patterns in Out-of-School Childcare Arrangements for Schoolchildren Aged 6 to 10 Years by Family Structure

| | Type of out-of-school care | | | | | | | | | | | |
| | Parent | | Self-care | | Grandparent | | Other relative | | Market[b] | | School | |
Variables of interest	Married mother	Single mother	Married mother	Single mother	Married mother	Single mother	Married mother	Single mother	Married mother	Single mother	Married mother	Single mother
Northeast	0.17	0.2	0.12	0.14	0.2	0.19	0.16	0.18	0.18	0.22	0.18	0.16
South	0.33	0.38	0.31	0.32	0.37	0.41	0.35	0.38	0.28	0.31	0.37	0.36
Midwest	0.26	0.23	0.35	0.3	0.2	0.2	0.27	0.22	0.31	0.26	0.23	0.2
West	0.24	0.2	0.22	0.23	0.23	0.2	0.23	0.21	0.23	0.21	0.22	0.27
Live in metro area	0.78	0.79	0.71	0.78	0.73	0.73	0.76	0.81	0.77	0.85	0.83	0.83
Working	0.6	0.57	0.7	0.75	0.91	0.89	0.7	0.74	0.88	0.9	0.78	0.92
Household income ($2001)[a]	$5,275	$1,867	$6,248	$2,062	$5,445	$2,575	$5,449	$2,018	$6,963	$2,352	$6,911	$2,497
At or below poverty line	0.14	0.54	0.07	0.4	0.08	0.32	0.12	0.46	0.06	0.33	0.05	0.26
Receive welfare	0.06	0.4	0.03	0.31	0.04	0.21	0.06	0.33	0.02	0.21	0.02	0.2
Mother's age	36.41	34.12	36.85	35.11	34.95	32.57	36.7	34.82	35.74	33.55	37.36	34.58
Mother has disability	0.16	0.34	0.14	0.3	0.14	0.24	0.18	0.33	0.15	0.21	0.14	0.25

Dropout	0.13	0.24	0.1	0.16	0.08	0.11	0.17	0.27	0.09	0.17	0.05	0.11
High school only	0.28	0.33	0.24	0.3	0.33	0.36	0.31	0.35	0.24	0.33	0.22	0.3
Some college	0.33	0.34	0.43	0.44	0.38	0.44	0.35	0.33	0.32	0.4	0.32	0.43
College plus	0.26	0.09	0.23	0.09	0.22	0.08	0.17	0.05	0.35	0.11	0.41	0.15
Child's age	7.75	7.72	8.64	8.55	7.6	7.74	7.94	7.84	7.41	7.61	7.64	7.58
Child has disability	0.12	0.17	0.14	0.17	0.12	0.22	0.11	0.18	0.1	0.2	0.13	0.16
Number of children	2.45	2.53	2.3	2.09	2.28	2.17	2.52	2.43	2.23	2.1	2.17	2.06
White	0.7	0.42	0.74	0.54	0.67	0.42	0.62	0.37	0.78	0.53	0.78	0.57
Black	0.07	0.34	0.09	0.32	0.12	0.36	0.11	0.38	0.06	0.29	0.08	0.3
Hispanic	0.17	0.19	0.11	0.11	0.15	0.16	0.2	0.2	0.13	0.15	0.09	0.09
Other race/ethnicity	0.06	0.05	0.06	0.03	0.06	0.06	0.07	0.05	0.03	0.02	0.05	0.04
Male child	0.5	0.53	0.58	0.49	0.52	0.52	0.49	0.49	0.44	0.53	0.5	0.54
N =	6,755	1,569	250	99	1,045	690	894	547	605	324	1,331	476

Source: SIPP 1996, 2001, 2004 panels.

[a] In $2001 monthly income.

[b] Market providers are nonrelatives, family daycare providers, and childcare centers with before- or after-school programs for school-aged children; Disability measures based on wave five topical modules.

Table 3. Utilization Patterns for Out-of-School Childcare Arrangements among Children Aged 6 to 10 Years by Family Structure and Disability Status

| | Child has a disability | | | |
| | Married mothers | | Single mothers | |
	No	Yes	No	Yes
Proportion using type of out-of-school care arrangement				
Parent	0.62	0.61	0.43	0.41
Self-care	0.02	0.03	0.03	0.03
Grandparent	0.1	0.1	0.18	0.21
Other relative	0.08	0.08	0.15	0.15
Market	0.06	0.05	0.08	0.1
School	0.12	0.14	0.13	0.11
Hours spent in out-of-school care arrangement per week				
Parent	7.35	8.17	7.26	5.33
Self-care	6.35	5.37	6.67	8.41
Grandparent	14.79	13.05	18.82	20.32
Other relative	11.21	9.85	15.94	15.8
Market	15.61	15.9	19.41	20.5
School	7.32	7.36	7.66	7.75
Cost of out-of-school care arrangement per week				
Grandparent	$3.38	$2.88	$4.25	$5.26
Other relative	$7.50	$7.45	$7.64	$6.10
School	$3.38	$2.15	$1.91	$2.21
Market	$46.07	$45.51	$39.64	$38.49
N =	9,602	1,278	3,038	667

Source: SIPP 1996, 2001, 2004 panels.

[a]In $2001.

[b]Market providers are nonrelatives, family daycare providers, and childcare centers with before- or after-school programs for school-aged children; Disability measures based on wave five topical modules.

mothers lack the flexibility to provide parental care like married parents can. Few children in this younger age range living with married parents or single mothers care for themselves, and those who do tend to be older (see Table 2).

Likewise, schoolchildren with disabilities of single mothers spend more hours each week in grandparent care before or after school than either schoolchildren without disabilities of single mothers or schoolchildren (nondisabled and disabled) of married parents. Schoolchildren with disabilities of single mothers spend nearly 50% more time in grandparent care outside of school hours compared with schoolchildren with and without disabilities of married parents. And Table 3 indicates that though schoolchildren with disabilities of single mothers spend slightly more time with grandparents than do schoolchildren without disabilities of single mothers, schoolchildren with disabilities of married parents spend less time with grandparents than do schoolchildren without disabilities of married parents. The costs per hour for out-of-school grandparent care within single-mother and married-parent households are equivalent, but costs per hour for grandparent care of a child with a disability living with a single mother approach double the costs per hour for grandparent care of a child with a disability living with a married parent. Consequently, patterns of childcare utilization and cost from Table 3 should reassure grandparents that when they provide childcare they are giving a major in-kind economic benefit for single mothers raising schoolchildren with disabilities.

Interesting similarities and differences among the childcare arrangements of school-aged children of married parents and single mothers are revealed in Tables 1, 2, and 3, however, the tables do not indicate whether employment status and economic disadvantage operate similarly on determining arrangements without controlling for these sorts of socioeconomic factors. Yet effects of employment status, economic disadvantage, and parental characteristics on childcare arrangements for schoolchildren with and without disabilities are issues foremost on the minds of those concerned with childcare for schoolchildren. The multivariate analyses address the issues by estimating the effects of childhood disabilities, economic disadvantage and employment status, controlling for parent and family characteristics, and while also modeling the related labor force participation decision.

Multivariate Regression Results by Family Structure

For brevity, Table 4 presents only estimates for the effects of disability status, disability conditions, and functional limitations on the odds of using grandparent care relative to parental care. See Table A.1 for all estimates from the bivariate regressions.

My main hypothesis was that children's disability status, given that that measure indicates more than a short-term health condition or temporary incapacitation, should have a positive association with the probability of using grandparent out-of-school childcare. The multivariate model for children living with single mothers confirms that hypothesis, but weakly. The variable "Has a disability" is statistically significant at conventional statistical levels, but at a significance level close to 0.10, the most reasonable inference is that the effect of disability status among school-aged children on the odds of using grandparent care is marginal.

Table 4. Estimated Coefficients for Measures of Disability Status, Disability Conditions, and Functional Limitations Based Upon Bivariate Probit Regressions by Family Structure and Type of Out-of-School Childcare Arrangement for Children Aged 6 to 10 Years

Measures of disability	Type of out-of-school care									
	Single mothers					Married mothers				
	Grand-parent	Self-care	Other relative	Market	School	Grand-parent	Self-care	Other relative	Market	School
Has a disability	0.12* [1.67]	-0.12 [-0.96]	0.03 [0.46]	0.17 [1.55]	-0.05 [-0.72]	0.01 [0.13]	0.01 [0.13]	-0.03 [-0.48]	-0.03 [-0.35]	0.12*** [2.62]
Functional limitation										
Cognitive only	0.1 [1.26]	-0.23 [-1.34]	0.02 [0.28]	0.18 [1.34]	0.04 [0.39]	0.02 [0.24]	0.08 [1.00]	-0.1 [-1.22]	0.02 [0.22]	0.11* [1.82]
Mobility only	0.36 [1.27]	-0.04 [-0.08]	-0.4 [-1.23]	0.56* [1.68]	-0.4 [-1.02]	0.15 [0.68]	0.09 [0.31]	0.14 [0.70]	-0.34 [-1.11]	-0.07 [-0.36]
Communication only	0.34* [1.62]	-0.54** [2.04]	0.21 [0.90]	-0.26 [-0.78]	-0.13 [-0.50]	-0.07 [-0.17]	-0.05 [-0.13]	-0.69* [-1.63]	0.19 [0.69]	0.28 [1.47]
A combination of types	0.05 [0.54]	-0.13 [-0.65]	0.08 [0.67]	0.13 [0.79]	-0.26 [-1.59]	-0.04 [-0.48]	-0.35 [-1.58]	0.16* [1.72]	-0.19 [-1.27]	0.15* [1.78]

Disability condition

Learning only	0.17* [1.67]	-0.18 [-0.90]	0.02 [0.18]	0.16 [1.08]	-0.11 [-1.15]	-0.04 [-0.50]	0.05 [0.43]	-0.07 [-0.87]	-0.09 [-0.80]	0.12 [1.60]
Development only	0.28 [0.81]	-3.42*** [-20.42]	0.05 [0.10]	0.21 [0.50]	0.16 [0.41]	0.01 [0.06]	-0.27 [-0.76]	-0.45 [-1.61]	-0.54 [-1.46]	-0.08 [-0.42]
Behavioral only	-0.1 [-0.50]	0.48 [1.49]	0.18 [0.71]	-0.11 [-0.32]	-0.04 [-0.13]	-0.28 [-1.22]	0.53** [2.40]	-0.12 [-0.50]	0.27 [0.91]	0.29 [1.40]
$N =$	3,705	3,705	3,705	3,705	3,705	10,880	10,880	10,880	10,880	10,880

Source: SIPP 1996, 2001, 2004 panels; *$p < 0.10$; **$p < 0.05$; ***$p < 0.01$; t statistics in brackets.

Notes: Comparison group for regressions is parent care. Three types of functional limitations and three types of disability conditions distinguished from wave-five topical modules on children's functional limitations and disabilities; regressions control for regional and within-state clustering, mothers' education levels, foreign-born status, children's race or ethnicity, monthly household income, number of children and children's age structure, poverty status, welfare use, metropolitan location, and state unemployment levels. See Appendix for full results for the childcare choice produced by the bivariate regressions.

My other hypotheses were driven by theorizing that the measure "disability status" is inadequate for understanding the effects of childhood disability conditions and functional limitations on the odds of using grandparent care. That is, what matters to increasing the odds of using grandparent care is the nature of the disability or limitation, not just having a disability. The model for children with single mothers offers some evidence supporting my theory that specifying the exact condition or limitation is better than the inexact measure of disability, but only for one limitation, "Communication only," and only one disability, "Learning only."

Multivariate results for measures of disabilities and functional limitations among schoolchildren on the odds of using grandparent and the other forms of nonparental, out-of-school care are overall unpersuasive and exhibit no obvious patterns, except for two notable trends. First, Table 4 reveals that if schoolchildren living with married mothers have disabilities or limitations, those factors appear to raise the chances of before- or after-school childcare while remaining unassociated with other forms of care, including relatives.

The model for use of out-of-school grandparent care also highlighted that demographic factors rather than economic disadvantage increase use of grandparent-provided care for schoolchildren. Minority children with single mothers as well as Black children with married parents were more likely than their respective White peers to use grandparent-provided out-of-school care. Likewise, children with more educated parents were more likely than children whose parents failed to complete high school to use grandparent-provided out-of-school care. As noted, poverty status (nor receipt of welfare for single mothers) did not increase the odds of grandparent childcare. But more children in households, increasing maternal age, and living in urban areas significantly lower the odds of using grandparents for all children.

Finally, I theorized that the maternal employment decision is positively correlated with the decision to use grandparent-provided out-of-school childcare. Each regression yielded a statically significant positive Rho coefficient, suggesting dependence between the decisions. Given the comparability between estimates for single and married mothers' labor force decisions, I was unsurprised that the effect of Rho on grandparent-provided childcare was similar for all mothers. Hence, mothers link use of out-of-school grandparent childcare decisions to work participation decisions. For married mothers, this joint decision is probably influenced by the availability of spouses, which brings added flexibility for organizing childcare. The import of Table 4 for grandparents is recognizing that their childcare provision for grandchildren outside of school hours is tied to their adult children's labor force decisions, the social and economic conditions of their adult children's families, and the presence of childhood disabilities within those families. Though unclear from Table 4, the type of disability may have an impact too.

Supplementary Results for the Work Decision, by Family Structure

Since the model distinguishes the work and childcare decisions, I examined factors that influence a mother's decision to work. Table 5 shows that single and married mothers' work decisions are influenced by the factors hypothesized to relate to their work decisions. Raising a child with a disability significantly lowered the probabilities of entering the workforce. While the effects of higher levels of education and greater economic advantage are to increase the chances of mothers working, the opposite effects are found for increasing maternal age and higher state unemployment rates. The married mothers of Black and Hispanic children were found more likely to work than White married mothers. Finally, increasing levels of household income had the parallel effect to economic advantage, that is, as household incomes rose, chances that children's single and married mothers would enter the workforce increased.

Discussion and Conclusions

Locating childcare during nonschool hours is critical for many parents of schoolchildren, especially working parents of schoolchildren with disabilities. With the exception of research on self-care, however, little is known about the childcare available for schoolchildren, importance of grandparents to childcare provision, factors influencing mothers' decisions about whether to work and what out-of-school childcare to use, and differences between the childcare decisions of married parents and single mothers. This dearth of knowledge persists despite theories and data suggesting the childcare can be conceptualized as either a market-supplied or family-supplied good, with the latter frequently supplied by grandparents as an intergenerational transfer of time. This study's findings on grandparent-provided childcare for children with disabilities help narrow gaps in our knowledge and bolster the notion that grandparents devote time to childcare.

The study finds that schoolchildren with disabilities from single-mother and two-parent families receive childcare during nonschool hours from a variety of providers, but principally from grandparents and parents. Thus, the choice of childcare for schoolchildren with disabilities is intertwined with intergenerational networks and indeed more complicated than any single dichotomous choice between any two types of childcare, for example, self-care and parent care. Rather, the choice involves deciding among several familial and nonfamilial types of childcare. The study shows that even single mothers have childcare options from which to choose, though parent care is a limited option for them.

Given the alternative out-of school childcare arrangements from which parents raising schoolchildren with disabilities can choose, future studies of childcare decision-making for school-aged children with disabilities should differentiate within family care, that is, parent, grandparent, older sibling, and other relative

Table 5. Determinants of Labor Force Participation Decision of Mothers
by Family Structure and Disability Status of Child

	Single mothers Work vs. No work	Married mothers Work vs. No work
Child disabled	−0.22 [−3.50]***	−0.09** [−2.47]
Male child	0.01 [0.30]	0.04* [1.67]
Children's ages	0.03* [1.83]	0.03*** [4.21]
Black	0.04 [0.57]	0.55*** [12.18]
Hispanic	0.06 [0.77]	0.15** [2.43]
Other race/ethnicity	0.11 [1.03]	0.08 [1.02]
Children in household	−0.02 [−0.56]	−0.09*** [−3.53]
Near poverty	0.30*** [3.86]	0.15** [2.38]
Not poor	0.51*** [5.39]	0.50*** [7.59]
Receives welfare	−0.77*** [−12.37]	−0.27*** [−3.20]
Log of monthly household income	0.11*** [4.98]	0.05*** [3.37]
Mother's age	−0.02*** [−5.82]	−0.01** [−2.05]
High school only	0.32*** [4.57]	0.30*** [6.87]
Some college	0.50*** [5.93]	0.40*** [8.55]
College plus	0.49*** [3.90]	0.39*** [8.12]
Mother foreign-born	−0.16 [1.58]	−0.19*** [−3.01]
Live in metro area	−0.01 [−0.18]	−0.18*** [−4.71]
State unemployment rate	−0.06** [−2.24]	−0.06*** [−3.23]
Constant	0.52 [1.89]	−0.15 [−0.69]
Log pseudo-likelihood	−3,000.42	−9,255.14
$N =$	3,704	10,879

Source: SIPP 1996, 2001, 2004 panels; *$p < 0.1075$; **$p < 0.05$; ***$p < 0.01$; t statistics in brackets.
Notes: Controls for regional and state differences.

care, from among the other childcare options available rather than maintain a broad, imprecise family childcare category. Specifying every type of childcare is impractical, but using explicit categories analogous to care by a grandparent, parent, other relative, at least more closely reflects possible familial alternatives from which parents raising schoolchildren with disabilities are choosing. Such categories then need comparison with school and market alternatives. Not only is isolating grandparent childcare from other types of familial care important, but explicitly incorporating the dependence between work and childcare decisions is essential. If future studies overlook the relationship, especially for single mothers, between deciding to work and deciding to use grandparent care for schoolchildren with disabilities, the risk of generating misleading results from miss-specified models is high. Growing numbers of schoolchildren with disabilities, their disproportionate numbers with single mothers, and the need of single mothers to work means that ignoring the methodological subtleties and complexities highlighted in this study is unwise.

The multivariate estimates for effects of types of disabilities and functional limitations among schoolchildren on use of grandparent childcare highlight the value of identifying childhood disabilities and limitations. The measure of disability status, though crude and not expected to register an effect on the probability of using grandparent care, did in fact indicate that single mothers raising children with disabilities were more likely to use grandparents. Hence, a disability, regardless of the type of disability or limitation, matters to single mothers' decisions about use of grandparent childcare.

When the disability status measure was replaced with functional limitations or disability condition measures, estimates suggested that specific types of limitations or conditions might matter more to the choice of grandparent childcare than disability status *per se*. I conjectured that limitations or disabilities might better reflect the confidence single mothers had about their children with disabilities being able to independently care for themselves or manage at childcare centers. Estimated effects for specific disability conditions or functional limitations were weak for single parents and undetectable for married parents, however. I argue that the specific nature of a disability or functional limitation among schoolchildren that drives parents' decisions about childcare, including grandparent care, is still worth testing, even if the SIPP data are inadequate for the task. Perhaps schoolchildren with communication limitations or learning disabilities were more likely to use grandparent care because these two barriers could prevent children from caring for themselves or integrating into after-school childcare. Future research should pursue this conjecture that parental childcare decisions depend upon the degree of autonomy that schoolchildren with disabilities can exercise.

The study also adds knowledge by documenting that the schoolchildren with disabilities who are most likely to receive grandparent-provided out-of-school childcare are those living with single mothers. Schoolchildren with disabilities in single-mother households also spend more hours under grandparent care and supervision than any other group of school-aged children. Though inconclusive, measures of disability conditions or functional limitations may matter more to use of grandparent childcare among single mothers than a measure of disability status.

No evidence suggests that single mothers are more prone than married mothers to leave schoolchildren in self-care. I infer that grandparent availability buffers against schoolchildren of single mothers, especially those with disabilities; being left home alone and spouse availability insures the same for schoolchildren of married parents. Surprisingly, school-based childcare is a function of parental preferences rather than economic need or employment status. In sum, my study reveals much about grandparent-provided childcare for school-age children with and without disabilities and much about the factors affecting parental out-of-school childcare decisions for children with disabilities.

(Appendix A.1 follows)

Table A.1. Bivariate Probit Regressions of Mothers' Out-of-School Grandparent Care, by Family Structure

	Disability status		Measures of functional limitations		Measures of limiting conditions	
	Single mothers	Married mothers	Single mothers	Married mothers	Single mothers	Married mothers
Male child	-0.04 [-0.95]	0.04 [1.43]	-0.03 [-0.75]	0.05 [1.57]	-0.03 [-0.80]	0.04 [1.43]
Children's ages	0.02 [0.99]	-0.02*** [-2.88]	0.02 [1.04]	-0.02*** [-2.83]	0.02 [0.99]	-0.02*** [-2.91]
Black	0.20*** [2.75]	0.28*** [3.95]	0.20*** [2.78]	0.28*** [3.92]	0.20*** [2.68]	0.28*** [3.97]
Hispanic	0.19*** [2.75]	0.12 [1.51]	0.19** [2.28]	0.12 [1.50]	0.18** [2.30]	0.12 [1.53]
Other race/ethnicity	0.34** [2.25]	0.13* [1.76]	0.33** [2.23]	0.13* [1.76]	0.34** [2.26]	0.13* [1.75]
Children in household	-0.07*** [-2.89]	-0.07** [-2.10]	-0.07*** [-2.85]	-0.07** [-2.12]	-0.07*** [-2.92]	-0.07** [-2.09]
Near poverty	0.23*** [3.25]	0.09 [1.14]	0.23*** [3.28]	0.09 [1.13]	0.23*** [3.16]	0.09 [1.14]
Not poor	0.22*** [2.68]	0.24*** [3.03]	0.22*** [2.65]	0.24*** [3.03]	0.22*** [2.68]	0.24*** [3.02]
Receives welfare	-0.33*** [-4.52]	-0.07 [-0.71]	-0.32*** [-4.40]	-0.07 [-0.68]	-0.32*** [-4.32]	-0.07 [-0.71]
Works full time	0.01 [0.08]	0.14*** [3.06]	0.00 [0.04]	0.14*** [3.07]	0.01 [0.12]	0.14*** [3.07]
Mother's age	-0.03*** [-7.82]	-0.03*** [-7.34]	-0.03*** [-8.02]	-0.03*** [-7.33]	-0.03*** [0.12]	-0.03*** [-7.38]
High school only	0.34*** [3.99]	0.24*** [3.73]	0.34*** [3.91]	0.24*** [3.75]	0.34*** [4.00]	0.24*** [3.69]
Some college	0.34*** [3.57]	0.22*** [3.23]	0.34*** [3.55]	0.22*** [3.22]	0.33*** [3.52]	0.22*** [3.23]
College plus	0.20 [1.51]	0.11 [1.16]	0.20 [1.44]	0.11 [1.16]	0.20 [1.51]	0.11 [1.16]
Mother foreign-born	-0.01 [-0.08]	-0.21*** [-3.26]	-0.01 [-0.13]	-0.21*** [-3.28]	-0.01 [-0.09]	-0.21*** [-3.27]
Live in metro area	-0.26*** [-3.36]	-0.16*** [-3.03]	-0.26*** [-3.38]	-0.16*** [-3.02]	-0.26*** [-3.34]	-0.16*** [-3.03]
Unemployment rate	-0.01 [-0.15]	-0.01 [-0.51]	-0.01 [-0.16]	-0.01 [-0.51]	-0.00 [-0.10]	-0.01 [-0.51]
Constant	0.12 [0.58]	-0.27 [-0.94]	0.13 [0.62]	-0.26 [-0.94]	0.11 [0.51]	-0.26 [-0.93]
Pseudo-loglikelihood	-3354.16	-9254.60	-3353.45	-9255.37	-3352.43	-9249.72
N =	3,705	10,880	3,705	10,880	3,705	10,880

Source: SIPP 1996, 2001, 2004 panels; *p < 0.1075; **p < 0.05; ***p < 0.01; t statistics in brackets.
Notes: Controls for regional and state differences.

References

Adler, M. 1995. Disability among children. *ASPE Research Notes: Information for Decision Makers.* Office of Disability, Aging & Long-Term Care Policy. Department of Health Services. Washington, DC: U.S. Government Printing Office. http://aspe.hhs.gov/daltcp/reports/1995/rn10.pdf

Agresti, A. 2010. *Analysis of ordinal categorical data.* New York, NY: Wiley.

Bianchi, S. M., Hotz, V. J., McGarry, K., and Seltzer, J. A. 2008. Intergenerational ties: Theories, trends, and challenges. In A. Booth et al. (Eds.), *Intergenerational caregiving* (pp. 3-44). Washington, DC: Urban Institute Press.

Bloom, B., Cohen, R. A., and Freeman, G. 2012. Summary health statistics for U.S. children: National Health Interview Survey, 2011. *Vital and Health Statistics,* 10(254). National Center for Health Statistics.

Brandon, P. D. and Hofferth, S. L. 2003. Determinants of out-of-school childcare arrangements among children in single-mother and two-parent families. *Social Science Research,* 32(1): 129-147.

Brault, M. W. 2011. School-aged children with disabilities in U.S. metropolitan statistical areas: 2010. *American Community Survey Briefs.* Washington, DC: U.S. Census Bureau. https://www.census.gov/prod/2011pubs/acsbr10-12.pdf

Cain, V. S. and Hofferth, S. L. 1989. Parental choice of self-care for school-age children. *Journal of Marriage and the Family,* 51: 65-77.

Caldwell, J. C. 2005. On net intergenerational flows: An update. *Population and Development Review,* 31: 721-740.

Cardia, E. and Ng, S. 2003. Intergenerational time transfers and childcare. *Review of Economic Dynamics,* 6(2): 431-454.

Fuller-Thomson, E. and Minkler, M. 2001. American grandparents providing extensive child care to their grandchildren: Prevalence and profile. *The Gerontologist,* 41(2): 201-209.

Hofferth, S. L., Brayfield, A. A., Deich, S. G., and Holcomb, P. A. 1991. *National Child Care Survey 1990.* Washington, DC: The Urban Institute.

Hogan, D. P., Msall, M. E., Rogers, M. L., and Avery, R. C. 1997. Improved disability population estimates of functional limitation among American children aged 5–17. *Maternal and Child Health Journal,* 1(4): 203-216.

Laird, R. D., Pettit, G. S., Dodge, K. A., and Bates, J. E. 1998. The social ecology of school-age child care. *Journal of Applied Developmental Psychology,* 19(3): 341-360.

Laughlin, L. 2013. Who's minding the kids? Child care arrangements: Spring 2011. *Current Population Reports* (pp. 70-135). Washington, DC: U.S. Census Bureau.

Long, J. S. 1997. *Regression models for categorical and limited dependent variables.* California: Sage.

Luo, Y., LaPierre, T. A., Hughes, M. E., and Waite, L. J. 2012. Grandparents providing care to grandchildren: A population-based study of continuity and change. *Journal of Family Issues,* 33(9): 1143-1167.

McNeil, J. M. 1997. Americans with disabilities: 1994-95. *Current Population Reports.* Washington, DC: U.S. Government Printing Office.

Presser, H. B. 1989. Some economic complexities of child care provided by grandmothers. *Journal of Marriage and the Family,* 51: 581-591.

Raftery, A. E. 1995. Bayesian model selection in social research. *Sociological Methodology,* 25: 111-163.

Seligson, M. 1983. *School-age child care: A policy report.* Massachusetts: Wellesley College Center for Research on Women.

Smith, K. E. and Casper, L. M. 1999. *Home alone: Reasons parents leave their children unsupervised.* Paper presented at the annual meetings of the Population Association of America, New York, March.

Soldo, B. J. and Hill, M. S. 1995. Family structure and transfer measures in the health and retirement study: Background and overview. *Journal of Human Resources,* 30: S109-S137.

Stein, R. E. K., Silver, E. J., and Bauman, L. J. 2001. Shortening the questionnaire for identifying children with chronic conditions: What is the consequence? *Pediatrics,* 107(4): e61.

U.S. Census Bureau. 2001. *Survey of income and program participation users' guide* (3rd ed.). Washington, DC. http://www.census.gov/content/dam/Census/programs-surveys/sipp/Methodology/SIPP_USERS_Guide_Third_Edition_2001.pdf

U.S. Bureau. 2011, August. Who's minding the kids? Child care arrangements. Spring 2010: Detailed tables. Retrieved July 18, 2014, from http://www.census.gov/hhes/childcare/data/sipp/2010/tables.htm

Wells, T. and Hogan, D. 2003. Developing concise measures of childhood activity limitations. *Journal of Maternal Child Health,* 7(2): 115-126.

World Health Organization. 2001. *International classification of functioning, disability and health.* Geneva: World Health Organization. http://www.who.int/classifications/icf/en/

PART 2

Co-residential and Custodial Grandparenting

http://dx.doi.org/10.2190/GITC6

CHAPTER 6

Portrait of American Grandparent Families

Lynne M. Casper, Sandra M. Florian,
C. Brady Potts, and Peter D. Brandon

While the style and amount of grandparent involvement with grandchildren varies considerably along a number of key demographic and structural lines, grandparenthood nevertheless continues to be a widespread and a hopeful aspiration for the majority of adults in the United States as they age. Survey respondents in one nationally representative sample report having increased their time with family; roughly one quarter of surveyed adults 65 years and older specifically mention time with grandchildren as one of the primary benefits of growing older (Taylor, Morin, Parker, Cohn, and Wang, 2009).

However, grandparenting has changed significantly in the past century, so much so that contemporary grandparent relationships bear only a partial resemblance to the intergenerational connections of the past (Uhlenberg, 2004). In the latter half of the 20th century, widespread and relatively rapid demographic changes in the United States began to reshape the contours of grandparenting. Decreases in family size, longer lifespans, falling birthrates, increases in non-marital births, high divorce rates and changing immigration rates and patterns have produced considerable variation in the experience and practice of grand-parenthood (Bengtson, 2001; Casper and Bianchi, 2002). Longer lifespans created more dynamic relationships over time: grandparent involvement changes significantly over the life course, from caring for infants to serving as a mentor for older grandchildren. Consequently, contemporary grandparent-grandchild relationships, and the highly varied social, economic, familial, and cultural contexts in which they are built, expressed, and practiced, have become more complex, diverse, and multifaceted. Given the projected increase in the elderly population in the decades to come, intergenerational relationships will likely become even more salient among families (Cherlin, 2010).

Many grandparents not only reside with their grandchildren, but also often assume the duties of primary caregiver of grandchildren. Given strong norms of expected support and obligations of grandparents toward grandchildren, the sacrifices and costs of grandparenting often go unacknowledged and even unrecognized (Ferguson, Douglas, Lowe, Murch, and Robinson, 2004). As in other blended families, grandparent families are incompletely institutionalized, often lacking structure and clearly defined roles; this is complicated by a widely held supposition that grandparents should not interfere with the parental authority of their children. The circumstances that lead to coresidence and custodial grandparenting are often such that custodial grandparents face significant challenges with relatively few resources. Consequently, grandparents tend to report not only lower satisfaction but also higher levels of stress in their roles as caregivers, in degrees that vary depending on familial circumstances, the amount and kind of care provided, and the health and prior situation of the grandparent (Musil and Ahmad, 2002). Thus, in contrast to traditional images of grandparenting as a jewel in the crown of a well-lived life, a more complicated (and less rosy) picture emerges of grandparents acting not just as ancillary support to parents but also as primary caregivers for grandchildren, often in familial, political, and economic contexts marked by poverty and a range of other disadvantaged situations that make custodial grandparent families one of the most vulnerable family types in the nation (Baker, Silverstein, and Putney, 2008).

In addition to changes in family structure and demographic trends, the last decades of the 20th century saw a variety of social and economic upheavals further altering the contexts in which grandparents and families operate. In an economy marked by growing disparities in income and wealth, and weakening social safety nets, families (and often grandparents) are forced to pick up the slack. As grandparents are increasingly sharing households with their children and grandchildren, multigenerational households have become more common (Cohen and Casper, 2002; Mutchler, Baker, and Lee, 2009; Uhlenberg, 2009). As of 2012, just over 7 million grandparents resided in a household with a grandchild under the age of 18, representing 4% of U.S. households, an increase of 22% from 2000 (Livingston, 2013).

State foster care and family services agencies have begun to adjust, if slowly and partially, to these new realities. However, participation in social welfare by custodial grandparents is low (Brandon, 2005). As some scholars have noted, stringent American social policy has contributed to the increased demand for grandparent caregiving while exacerbating the problems faced by disadvantaged grandparent caregivers (Copen, 2006; Seltzer and Bianchi, 2013; Smith and Beltran, 2003). Baker et al. (2008) argued that ideological preferences for traditional, and increasingly anachronistic, family forms in tandem with the disadvantaged structural position of custodial grandparents (most often female, poor, and disproportionately ethnic minorities) suggest that the political economy of grandparenting is profoundly shaped by race, class, and gender, perpetuating disadvantages among custodial grandparents.

State agencies, such as the State of Tennessee's foster agencies, have increasingly turned to family members, frequently grandparents, in order to place endangered children with relatives. In 2008, Tennessee's Upper Cumberland Development District won a $1.67 million federal grant from the department of Housing and Urban Development (HUD) selected from a group of over 80 applications to build Fiddler's Annex, the nation's first rural public housing project designed specifically for grandparents who act as primary caregivers for their grandchildren (Gonzales, 2013). The facility was built in response to a Congressional push for trial programs centered around intergenerational public housing and meant to serve low-income grandparent caregivers who are raising grandchildren. The complex offers not only subsidized housing, foster training, and other services, but also a sense of normalcy and support in a community in which skipped generation families are the norm. Owing to budget constraints, though, additional programs like Fiddler's Annex are unlikely to find federal funding. HUD has, instead, directed communities to find funding for such programs elsewhere. Given the retrenchment of social welfare programs and fraying social safety nets, grandparents are more important than ever for disadvantaged families within a society marked by widespread economic insecurity, high rates of unemployment, high rates of young parents' drug and alcohol abuse, incarceration, and an overburdened foster care system (Baker et al., 2008; Seltzer and Bianchi, 2013).

In this chapter, we review theoretical and demographic perspectives on intergenerational relationships and summarize recent research on the different roles and styles of grandparenting. Then we examine trends and characteristics of contemporary coresident grandparent families. We analyze recent data from the U.S. Census Bureau's American Community Survey on the structure and demographics of grandparent households and examine in more detail the differences in family structure of coresident grandparents by race/ethnicity, nativity, and socioeconomic characteristics, providing a context for the study of contemporary grandparent families.

Theoretical Perspectives on Intergenerational Support

Across disciplines such as economics, family studies, human development, gerontology, and sociology, theories on intergenerational investments have been rooted in either altruism and caring or exchange and reciprocity. More recently, evolutionary psychology has offered insights on genetic pressures of intergenerational support (Bianchi, Hotz, McGarry, and Seltzer, 2008). Studies of altruism and caring suggest multiple mechanisms toward caregiving and the provision of assistance rooted in socialization, norms, and roles, making untangling the bases for reciprocity and exchange difficult. Recent research has attempted to address this problem directly. Light and McGarry (2004) used direct reports by parents regarding resource transfers to children, while Hamoudi and Thomas (2006) conducted field experiments to estimate and measure altruism and other motivating factors for intergenerational support. The *wealth flow* perspective states that while wealth continues to flow, in large part, "down" the generations, care and resources flow up the generations as well, in a more or less reciprocal relationship (Caldwell, 2005). Resources, caregiving, and varied forms of assistance travel multiple paths within families and across generations.

Evolutionary psychologists argue that grandparents have a primary interest in propagating their genes that propels them to support grandchildren, even going as far as providing resources to adult children who may be delaying reproduction for economic reasons (Cox and Stark, 2005). Cox and Stark (2005) also have theorized a "demonstration effect," wherein parents model caregiving for their own children in the hopes that their children will support them in turn as they age. However, this model has remained largely untested and has failed to account for support proffered by childless adult children (Bianchi et al., 2008).

Shared among these perspectives is the recognition that familial ties, both within and between generations, serve as a resource and a bulwark against uncertainty, economic or otherwise. Theorists of exchange and reciprocity emphasize the way that family can serve as a form of insurance against unforeseen troubles, offering loans and other means of support (Cox, 1990). In this sense, gifts and transfers between generations can serve as a "support bank" throughout the life course (Antonucci, 1990). In contrast to the more impersonal and instrumental orientation of market-based relationships, familial ties offer not only care but also normative and moral obligations that often serve as a type of *enforceable trust* (Cherlin, 2004; see also Silverstein, 2005). Grandparents continue to anchor many of those familial ties of trust and moral obligation, and consequently they have increasingly come to serve as a source of significant intergenerational support, particularly in light of recent demographic, social, and political shifts.

Demographic Changes and Grandparenting

The availability of grandparents and the structure of intergenerational families are greatly shaped by demographic forces such as changes in mortality, fertility, marriage, divorce, and immigration. These forces affect individuals' roles in families as well as the time they spend as spouses, parents, and grandparents. Declines in mortality have extended life expectancy across successive cohorts, increasing the number of years of shared life across generations and the probability that children will have a greater number of living grandparents (Bengtson, 2001). Consequently, the rise in life expectancy has increased the probability of forming intergenerational families as individuals spend a greater proportion of their lives in the role of grandparents and adult children of older parents (Casper and Bianchi, 2002; Watkins, Menken, and Bongaarts, 1987). In the early 20th century, grandparents tended to be in fragile health and thus were less able to care for grandchildren. Less than a quarter of infants had four grandparents alive, and by the time they turned 30, only one-fifth of adults had any living grandparent. By the dawn of the next century, more than two-thirds of newborns had four grandparents alive, and by age 30, more than three-fourths still had at least one grandparent alive (Casper and Bianchi, 2002; Uhlenberg, 1996). The decline in mortality has been accompanied by health improvements; grandparents are not only living longer lives, but they are also living healthier lives in old age and thus are more likely to be able to care for grandchildren. Given these demographic shifts, intergenerational relations have become more salient for contemporary families, turning grandparents into valuable resources for adult children and grandchildren (Bengtson, 2001).

Over the last century, gains in mortality have been more rapidly achieved for women, generating a gender gap in life expectancy. Although the gap has slightly closed in recent years, women still live longer than men, and, hence, the vast majority of grandparents and great-grandparents are female; thus, the probability of having a grandmother alive is higher than that of having a grandfather alive (Casper and Bianchi, 2002; Uhlenberg and Kirby, 1998; Watkins et al., 1987). Delayed and forgone marriage, high levels of divorce, and nonmarital childbearing, coupled with the norms of female caregiving tend to lead to stronger relationships between grandchildren and maternal grandparents than paternal grandparents.

Changes in fertility patterns have also affected intergenerational families. As fertility declined, families became smaller in size. Since the 1970s, fertility in the United States has hovered around replacement level, which is slightly over 2 children per woman. The decline in fertility implies that grandparents have fewer grandchildren than they did in the last century. At the beginning of the 1900s, a woman aged 60–64 had on average 12 grandchildren; by the 1990s, a woman in the same age range had fewer than 6 grandchildren (Uhlenberg and Kirby, 1998). Moreover, since childlessness has also increased, a growing number of adults are aging without having any children or grandchildren (Watkins et al., 1987). The timing of fertility also affects intergenerational relations. In the early 1900s, it was not uncommon for parents to still be raising their children when they became grandparents. Fertility delays have increased the chronological distance between generations. Because couples are increasingly delaying childbearing, more adults become grandparents at a later stage of the life course. However, great variability exists by sociodemographic characteristics (Bengtson, 2001; Casper and Bianchi, 2002). Early childbearing is still prevalent among low-income and disadvantaged ethnic minorities, particularly African Americans, Native Americans, and Hispanics, thus, grandparents in these groups tend to be younger (Minkler and Fuller-Thomson, 2005). Having children at younger ages decreases the chronological distance between generations, causing parent and grandparent roles to be more likely to overlap.

Finally, immigration also shapes the incidence and patterns of grandparent families. The increase and diversification of immigration since the 1960s have altered the ethnic and demographic composition of families living in the United States. Before the 1960s, grandparents of immigrant children usually remained in their countries of origin, and thus contact between grandparent and grandchildren was very limited. Under family reunification laws, adult immigrants were able to bring their older parents with them. As a consequence, multigenerational families in the United States became more common among immigrants. Immigrant grandparents are more likely than their native-born counterparts to live in a home maintained by adult children (Florian and Casper, 2011). All these demographic changes have altered the prevalence of and variation among grandparent families.

Grandparenting Styles

Grandparent relationships take a number of forms, ranging from coresidential caregiving, the provision of material support, mentoring and affection, to more long-distance relationships. An important norm shaping intergenerational relations is that of noninterference: Americans believe that parents should have the final say in how their children are raised (Casper and Bianchi, 2002). Grandparent-grandchild relationships are varied and can be distinguished by the extent and type of connectedness between grandparents and grandchildren. Emotional closeness, shared values, assistance, level of interaction, roles and norms, and individual characteristics unite the generations to varying degrees and in distinctive, patterned ways.

Family sociologists Cherlin and Furstenberg (1985) proposed a typology based on the analysis of a nationally representative sample. The authors distinguished grandparent relationships by their levels of service exchange, exercise of parent-like authority, and frequency of contact between grandparent and grandchild. Cherlin and Furstenberg initially characterized grandparenting styles as *detached*, with low authority, contact, and some service exchange; *passive*, with frequent contact but otherwise minimal in authority or services; and *active*, with parent-like influence in their grandchildren's lives and frequent exchange of services. The authors further subdivided active grandparents into three groups: *supportive*, with a high degree of exchange; *authoritative*, with a high degree of authority; and *influential*, with a high degree of both exchange and parent-like authority. On the basis of their sample and typology, they then estimated that over 70% of grandparents do not assume parent-like roles, and while most are involved in their grandchildren's lives, the majority respects the norm of noninterference with parental authority. Grandparents with the more active grandparenting styles—supportive, authoritative, and influential—tended to be younger, live closer, and have more regular contact with grandchildren, with the most influential relationships reporting near daily contact. Finally, the style of grandparenting has been found to be related to the gender and ages of both grandparents and grandchildren, paternal or maternal lineage, family structure, and race/ethnicity (see Aldous, 1995 for a review).

Silverstein and Marenco (2001) found that the lifecourse stage of both grandparent and grandchild, along with the grandparents' gender, marital status, race, and education, shaped grandparents' roles in terms of the type of activities and degree of involvement. Younger grandparents provide more care to, and are in more regular contact with, younger grandchildren, while older grandparents provide more material support. Differences in the perception regarding the quality and type of relationship, and the intergenerational contexts in which those relationships occur, mattered as well. Harwood (2001) found that grandparents often described their relationships as closer than did grandchildren, who in turn saw the relationship as more active. In this way, grandparents and grandchildren often disagreed on their relationship type.

Coresidential Grandparent Household Structure

In this chapter, coresidential grandparent households are defined as those containing both grandparents and grandchildren, whether or not the grand-children's parents reside with them. We analyze data from the American Community Surveys collected by the U.S. Census Bureau to paint a broad picture of the growth and characteristics of multigenerational families and coresident grandparents.

Using Current Population Survey data, Bryson and Casper (1999) noted the importance of identifying homeownership in helping to deconstruct the direction of the flow of resources and support between generations, and in differentiating the socioeconomic and demographic characteristics of these households. They classified multigenerational households as either grandparent maintained or parent maintained based on who owns or rents the home. A parent-maintained household is one in which grandparents are hosted by their adult children. In this type of family, adult children support both their parents and their own children; thus, these households are sometimes referred to as *sandwich genera-tion* families (Bryson and Casper, 1999). Conversely, a grandparent-maintained household is one in which grandparents own or rent the home, hosting adult children and grandchildren (Bryson and Casper, 1999; Casper and Bianchi, 2002). Although this categorization aids in broadly classifying families, the reader is cautioned that it is difficult to determine precisely who benefits from multi-generational living, regardless of who owns the home, because coresidence often benefits both parties (Bianchi et al., 2008; Casper and Bianchi, 2002).

Figure 1 shows that the number of coresidential grandparent households increased substantially from slightly over 4 million in 2007 to 4.5 million in 2010, representing a 12% increase over this period. This tremendous growth is likely a response to the Great Recession of 2007–2009, which sent housing foreclosures

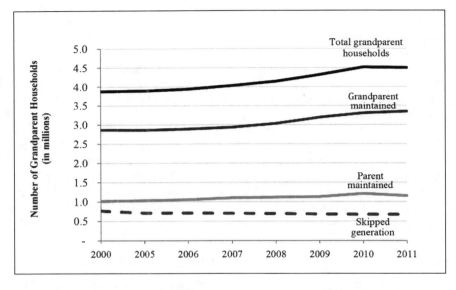

Figure 1. Growth in grandparent households: United States, 2000–2011.
Source: U.S. Census Bureau (2013), American Community Survey, 2011.

soaring, forcing some families out of their homes and into the homes of relatives. Because young families and those who recently purchased homes were hit the hardest by the Great Recession, it is unsurprising that the increase in grandparent households since the recession was driven primarily by grandparent-maintained households. As Figure 2 shows, in 2011, 74% of coresidential grandparent households were maintained by grandparents compared with only 25% maintained by parents. The large proportion of grandparent-maintained households is partially explained by the relatively high divorce rates in the United States and by the large proportion of births that occur to unmarried women—nearly 40%. Following a divorce or a nonmarital birth, mothers—who usually retain custody of their children—often move to their parents' homes with their children. Although this living arrangement may be temporary, it increases the number of grandparent-maintained families at any single time.

Coresidential grandparent households can be further classified by examining whether or not the parents of the grandchildren reside in the home. A three-generation household is one in which at least one of the child's parents is present. These households can be maintained by either a parent or grandparent. A skipped-generation household has no parents present and is usually maintained by a grandparent (Bryson and Casper, 1999). According to our calculations using data from the American Community Survey (U.S. Census Bureau, 2013), 85% of the 4.5 million grandparent households in the United States were three-generation households, and nearly 15% were skipped-generation households. When parents are absent, grandparents often assume primary responsibility for the care of grandchildren (Biblarz, Casper, and Jayasundera, 2009). However, in some of these households, aunts, uncles, and other relatives become primary caregivers (Jayasundera and Casper, 2010). Skipped-generation households are generally formed when parents are unable to care for their children for various reasons. Sometimes parents work or attend school in a distant area and may be unable to bring their children with them. Other times social services place children with a grandparent due to child abuse or neglect, or because of drug abuse, incarceration, or illness of the parents.

An important factor shaping the need for grandparent caregiving is the relatively high level of maternal labor force participation, especially where younger children are concerned. Mother's labor force participation significantly rose from the mid-1960s through the mid-1990s, creating a great demand for childcare. Overall, childcare arrangements have been varied and clear trends are difficult to discern, but grandparents continue to play important roles in the provision of childcare.

Nativity and Race/Ethnicity

The structure of coresidential grandparent households varies greatly by immigrant status. In 2011 in the United States, 3.3 million (73%) coresidential grandparent households were native born, and 1.2 million (27%) were foreign born. Figure 2 highlights some of the major differences in the structure of grandparent families by nativity. Among the native born, grandparents maintained almost 80% of households, parents maintained nearly 20%, and less than 1% were maintained by someone else. By contrast, among the foreign born, only 59% of coresidential grandparent households were maintained by grandparents, whereas 41% were maintained by parents. This difference is partly explained by patterns of immigration; immigrants often send for their parents after they move to the United States. Some scholars have argued that the nativity difference in family structure is also due to variations in cultural norms and the often difficult economic circumstances of immigrant families that force them to share homes with extended family members (Florian and Casper, 2011; Glick and Van Hook, 2002). Still, the majority of coresidential grandparent households, either native born or immigrant, are maintained by grandparents, revealing the importance of grandparents for contemporary families with children.

The structure of coresidential grandparent families also varies by race/ethnicity. As Figure 3 shows, grandparent-maintained households are more common among Native American and African American families. In 2011, 87% of Native American and 85% of African American grandparent households were maintained by grandparents, compared with 78% of White grandparent households. This

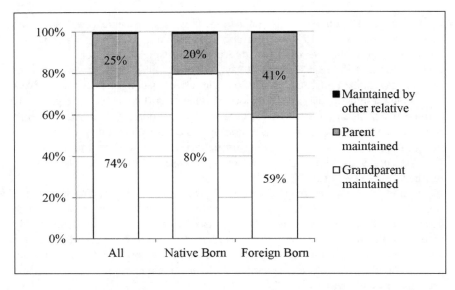

Figure 2. Grandparent households by nativity;[a] United States, 2011.[b]
Source: U.S. Census Bureau (2013), American Community Survey, 2011.
[a]Nativity of the household based on the householder's place of birth.
Puerto Ricans are officially native-born U.S. citizens. However,
given their distinctive migration patterns to and from
the U.S. mainland, we classify them as foreign born.
[b]Weighted by household weight.

percentage was much lower for Hispanics, 67%, and especially low for Asians, 37%, who are more likely to be foreign born and practice filial piety—a cultural norm "requiring" respect and care for elders.

The proportion of skipped-generation households follows a similar gradient by race/ethnicity. In 2011, nearly 27% of Native American and African American grandparent-maintained households were skipped-generation families compared with 22% of White, but only 10% of Hispanic, and 9% of Asian grandparent-maintained households. The high rates of skipped-generation families among Native Americans and African Americans are partly explained by their relative low marriage rates, high rates of divorce and nonmarital childbearing, and their disadvantaged economic positions. It is not uncommon for young Native American and African American women to start families with a nonmarital birth and rely on extended family networks, especially grandmothers, to raise their children (Dunifon and Kowaleski-Jones, 2007; Fuller-Thomson and Minkler,

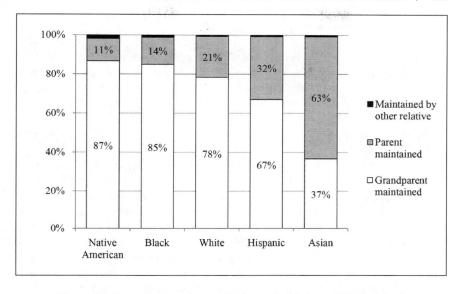

Figure 3. Coresident grandparent households by race/ethnicity;[a]
United States, 2011.[b]
Source: U.S. Census Bureau (2013), American Community Survey, 2011.
[a]Mutually exclusive race/ethnic categories (i.e., White means
non-Hispanic White).
[b]Weighted by household weight.

2005; Mutchler and Baker, 2009). Although Hispanics are also likely to start families this way, they are more likely to marry or enter cohabiting relationships.

Besides economic circumstances, expectations of kin support and other cultural norms may also explain some of the racial/ethnic differences in grandparent family structure. Some studies have found that African Americans are more likely to provide practical support including childcare and household work, whereas Whites more often provide economic and emotional support. Although Hispanics are also more likely to provide household and childcare help than Whites, this difference seems to be explained mostly by socioeconomic factors (Sarkisian, Gerena, and Gerstel, 2007; Sarkisian and Gerstel, 2004). The lower proportion of grandparent-maintained and skipped-generation households among Hispanic and Asian families in part reflects the higher economic standing of adult parents relative to grandparents and the fact that many of these grandparents are brought to the United States by their adult children (Glick and Van Hook, 2002).

Single Parenthood and Grandparenting

The vast majority of single parents are single mothers. Between 1960 and 2011, the number of single mothers in the United States who maintained their own residences increased from 2 million to 8.7 million. An additional 1.4 million single mothers lived in someone else's house, usually in grandparents' homes. Overall an estimated 36% of single mothers live in their parents home at some point while raising their children (Casper and Bianchi, 2002; U.S. Census Bureau, 2011a, 2011b).

Changing the unit of analysis to children, 16% of children in single-parent families have a grandparent living in their home (Livingston, 2013). Children in mother-only families tend to be greatly disadvantaged, not only because they often lack the emotional, social, and economic support of their fathers, but also because their mothers tend to be less educated and have lower incomes than married mothers. Thus, children in single-mother families are more likely to be poor—in 2011, 22% of U.S. children were living in poverty, but children in mother-only families were twice as likely (44%) to be living in poverty (U.S. Census Bureau, 2011c). Grandparents, especially grandmothers, represent valuable resources for these families, often providing childcare, emotional, and economic support for single mothers and their children. Mutchler and Baker (2009) found that children of single mothers who live with a grandparent are significantly less likely to be poor than children of single mothers who do not live with a grandparent, partly due to the economic contributions of coresident grandparents. Previous research has found that grandparents in single-mother families can also buffer against other types of disadvantages that children may face. For example, adolescents in single-mother families with coresident grandparents exhibit similar or better developmental outcomes, such as being enrolled in college, lower smoking and drinking rates, and older ages at sexual initiation, when compared with adolescents in married-couple families (DeLeire and Kalil, 2002).

Nonetheless, other studies have found some negative outcomes associated with the presence of grandparents for children in single-mother families. One study found that adolescents raised by single mothers and a coresident grandparent were more likely to drop out of high school than children of single mothers with no grandparent present (McLanahan and Sandefur, 1994). Another study found that the presence of grandparents in mother-only families was associated with improved cognitive outcomes for White children only, but not for African American children (Dunifon and Kowaleski-Jones, 2007). These results suggest that selectivity factors may play a role; that is, children who have more disadvantaged backgrounds or exhibit characteristics associated with negative child outcomes may be the ones more likely to live in single-mother, multigenerational households. Thus, the negative outcomes observed may not be a causal effect of grandparent's presence but a result of unobserved charac- teristics of children and their social contexts. It is worth noting that living with a grandparent is frequently a temporary situation, since single mothers often transition into other types of living arrangements as they marry or enter cohabitating relationships.

Characteristics of Coresident Grandparents in Multigenerational Households

Coresident grandparents differ in their socioeconomic and demographic characteristics, such as gender, race, education, income, and family structure. Coresident grandmothers outnumber coresident grandfathers. In 2011, of the nearly 7 million grandparents who were living with their grandchildren in the United States, 4.5 million were grandmothers and 2.5 million were grandfathers, that is, almost two-thirds of coresident grandparents were grandmothers. Grandmothers are more common in part because men have higher mortality rates, thus, wives often outlive their husbands. Widowed women are less likely to remarry at older ages and frequently move into their adult children's homes for companionship, economic support, and help with personal care. The high rates of poverty among unmarried older women compared with older couples or unmarried older men also help explain why older women tend to share homes with extended family, usually with their adult children and their families. These factors, coupled with higher expectations that women should provide care, result in a higher number of grandmothers coresiding with grandchildren (Bianchi et al., 2008; Casper and Bianchi, 2002).

Table 1 provides a description of grandparents by family structure, gender, and sociodemographic characteristics. The first panel depicts grandmothers and the lower panel, grandfathers. Overall, ethnic minority grandparents are more likely to coreside with grandchildren. For example, although in 2011 African Americans constituted 9% of the U.S. female population age 30 and older, they represented 18% of all coresident grandmothers. Similarly, Hispanics composed 13% of the U.S. female population age 30 and older, but 25% of coresident grandmothers (U.S. Census Bureau, 2013). By contrast, Whites represented 70% of the female population 30 and over, but only 46% of all coresident grandmothers, partly due to White women's relatively high socioeconomic standing, which allows them to live independently at older ages. As a recent study revealed, grandparents with more economic resources, particularly Whites, more often provide nonresidential care, whereas ethnic minorities are more likely to provide residential care (Luo, LaPierre, Hughes, and Waite, 2012). The racial/ethnic composition is more balanced among coresident grandfathers.

By family type, grandmother-maintained households, with or without parents present, exhibit the highest poverty rates, 29% and 44%, respectively. Note that they are also more likely to be headed by African Americans; African American grandmothers composed 30% of all grandmother-maintained households with

Table 1. Characteristics of Grandparents in Multigenerational Households: U.S. 2011 (Number and percent distribution)

	All coresident grandparents	Grandparent-maintained households						Parent-maintained households				
		Total	Both grand-parents, some parents	Both grand-parents, no parents	Grand-mother only, some parents	Grand-mother only, no parents	Grand-father only	Total	Both grand-parents, some parents	Grand-mother only, some parents	Grand-father only, some parents	Other
All grandparents	**7,060,659**	**6,020,263**	**2,669,467**	**664,663**	**1,141,921**	**295,317**	**248,895**	**1,911,115**	**602,981**	**1,049,761**	**258,383**	**129,291**
Grandmothers	**4,533,209**	**3,094,113**	**1,327,746**	**329,129**	**1,141,921**	**295,317**	(X)	**1,349,710**	**299,959**	**1,049,761**	(X)	**89,386**
Race/Ethnicity												
White	45.5	48.7	52.1	64.4	41.8	42.9	(X)	38.3	28.1	41.2	(X)	44.1
Black	18.2	21.6	11.5	17.7	29.6	40.7	(X)	10.1	2.8	12.2	(X)	21.6
Hispanic	25.3	22.5	27.8	11.7	22.5	10.9	(X)	31.8	34.3	31.0	(X)	24.5
Asian	7.7	3.6	5.5	2.5	2.4	1.0	(X)	17.2	32.6	12.8	(X)	5.0
Native American	1.4	1.7	1.3	2.0	1.8	2.1	(X)	0.6	0.3	0.8	(X)	2.6
Other	1.9	1.8	1.6	1.7	1.9	2.3	(X)	2.0	2.1	1.9	(X)	2.2
Age												
Less than 45	9.8	12.7	13.5	3.0	16.8	4.0	(X)	2.8	2.3	2.9	(X)	16.7
45–54	28.7	33.8	39.1	29.2	31.2	25.1	(X)	15.8	17.6	15.3	(X)	45.3
55–64	33.7	34.3	34.6	44.7	30.3	36.6	(X)	33.1	35.7	32.4	(X)	23.9
65+	27.8	19.2	12.8	23.0	21.7	34.2	(X)	48.3	44.1	49.5	(X)	14.1
Education												
Less than HS	27.6	23.2	23.2	18.9	23.2	27.2	(X)	37.6	42.7	36.1	(X)	30.5
High school	42.5	43.7	44.5	48.8	41.6	42.6	(X)	39.7	36.9	40.5	(X)	44.6
Some college+	29.9	33.1	32.3	32.2	35.2	30.2	(X)	22.7	20.4	23.4	(X)	24.9
Employment status												
Employed	41.9	50.5	52.7	43.1	53.3	38.2	(X)	22.4	20.9	22.6	(X)	38.4
Not employed	58.1	49.5	47.3	56.9	46.7	61.8	(X)	77.6	79.1	77.2	(X)	61.6

Responsibility for grandchildren												
Primary caretaker	37.6	50.3	42.4	86.2	42.3	76.8	(X)	8.0	8.1	8.0	(X)	47.2
Not primary caretaker	62.4	49.7	57.6	13.8	57.7	23.2	(X)	92.0	91.9	92.0	(X)	52.8
Self-care difficulty												
Difficulty	6.7	5.0	3.6	4.5	6.1	7.5	(X)	10.7	6.3	12.0	(X)	7.7
No difficulty	93.3	95.0	96.4	95.5	93.9	92.5	(X)	89.3	93.7	88.0	(X)	92.3
Poverty status												
Poor	19.4	21.0	10.8	13.3	29.0	44.2	(X)	14.4	9.7	15.8	(X)	41.0
Not poor	80.6	79.0	89.2	86.7	71.0	55.8	(X)	85.6	90.3	84.2	(X)	59.0
Welfare recipient												
Yes	3.7	4.1	1.5	4.0	5.0	12.4	(X)	2.9	1.9	3.1	(X)	5.2
No	96.3	95.9	98.5	96.0	95.0	87.6	(X)	97.1	98.1	96.9	(X)	94.8
Grandfathers	**2,527,450**	**1,926,140**	**1,341,721**	**335.524**	**(X)**	**(X)**	**248.895**	**561,405**	**303.022**	**(X)**	**258.383**	**39,905**
Race/Ethnicity												
White	49.6	54.2	51.6	64.3	(X)	(X)	55.1	34.6	27.9	(X)	43.0	36.5
Black	12.2	13.9	12.1	18.7	(X)	(X)	17.3	5.8	3.0	(X)	9.0	22.4
Hispanic	26.6	24.7	28.7	12.2	(X)	(X)	20.2	32.7	35.2	(X)	29.8	31.1
Asian	8.7	4.3	5.0	1.8	(X)	(X)	3.5	24.0	31.7	(X)	15.0	6.7
Native American	1.3	1.5	1.2	1.9	(X)	(X)	2.0	0.8	0.3	(X)	1.4	1.8
Other	1.5	1.4	1.4	1.1	(X)	(X)	1.9	1.8	1.9	(X)	1.7	1.4
Age												
Less than 45	6.7	7.9	9.3	2.6	(X)	(X)	7.1	1.7	1.6	(X)	1.7	20.7
45–54	26.3	30.1	33.0	21.7	(X)	(X)	25.9	12.6	12.4	(X)	12.9	36.1
55–64	36.0	38.0	37.5	43.2	(X)	(X)	33.5	29.8	30.1	(X)	29.4	25.7
65+	31.0	24.1	20.2	32.5	(X)	(X)	33.5	56.0	55.9	(X)	56.0	17.5
Education												
Less than HS	27.9	24.9	25.3	22.8	(X)	(X)	25.8	37.8	39.3	(X)	36.1	33.0
High school	40.8	42.1	41.7	43.9	(X)	(X)	41.8	35.6	32.7	(X)	39.1	48.0
Some college+	31.3	32.9	32.9	33.3	(X)	(X)	32.3	26.6	28.0	(X)	24.8	19.1

Table 1. (Con't.d)

	All coresident grandparents	Grandparent-maintained households						Parent-maintained households				
		Total	Both grand-parents, some parents	Both grand-parents, no parents	Grand-mother only, some parents	Grand-mother only, no parents	Grand-father only	Total	Both grand-parents, some parents	Grand-mother only, some parents	Grand-father only, some parents	Other
Employment status												
Employed	52.7	60.6	64.5	53.0	(X)	(X)	50.2	25.3	28.1	(X)	22.0	54.0
Not employed	47.3	39.4	35.5	47.0	(X)	(X)	49.8	74.7	71.9	(X)	78.0	46.0
Responsibility for grandchildren												
Primary caretaker	40.1	49.7	43.2	81.8	(X)	(X)	41.6	7.2	8.4	(X)	5.9	41.3
Not primary caretaker	59.9	50.3	56.8	18.2	(X)	(X)	58.4	92.8	91.6	(X)	94.1	58.7
Self-care difficulty												
Difficulty	5.6	4.6	4.2	5.8	(X)	(X)	5.1	9.3	6.7	(X)	12.4	5.2
No difficulty	94.4	95.4	95.8	94.2	(X)	(X)	94.9	90.7	93.3	(X)	87.6	94.8
Poverty status												
Poor	12.5	12.4	10.7	13.4	(X)	(X)	20.3	11.6	9.7	(X)	13.8	31.2
Not poor	87.5	87.6	89.3	86.6	(X)	(X)	79.7	88.4	90.3	(X)	86.2	68.8
Welfare recipient												
Yes	1.5	1.1	0.6	1.3	(X)	(X)	2.5	2.7	2.9	(X)	2.4	3.9
No	98.5	98.9	99.2	98.7	(X)	(X)	97.5	97.3	97.1	(X)	97.6	96.1

(X) = Not applicable.
Source: U.S. Census Bureau, American Community Survey, 2011.

some parents present, and 41% of all skipped-generation, grandmother-only households. As Table 1 shows, grandmothers in these types of families are a particularly vulnerable population as they tend to have low levels of education, be out of the labor force, exhibit high levels of functional limitations, and are more likely to live in poverty.

Figure 4 highlights some of the major differences in the characteristics of grandparents by gender and household structure. Overall, coresident grandparents who maintain their households tend to be younger and better educated. Only 19% of grandmothers and 24% of grandfathers in grandparent-maintained households were age 65 or older, but nearly half were age 65 or older in parent-maintained households, 48% of grandmothers and 56% of grandfathers. Grandparents in grandparent-maintained households are slightly more educated than those in parent-maintained households; three-fourths of grandparents who maintain their homes graduated from high school—77% of grandmothers and 75% of grandfathers—compared with 62% of grandparents living in their adult children's homes.

Grandparents who maintain their households exhibit higher employment rates; at least half of them were employed—51% of grandmothers and 61% of grandfathers. By contrast, only about a quarter of grandparents in parent-maintained households were employed—22% of grandmothers and 25% of grandfathers. Coresident grandparents often experience financial hardship, especially

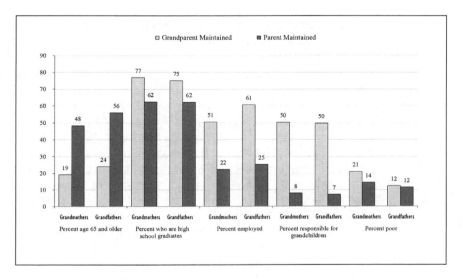

Figure 4. Characteristics of coresident grandparents, percentage distribution: United States, 2011.
Source: U.S. Census Bureau (2013), American Community Survey, 2011.

grandmothers (Luo et al., 2012). In 2011, the official poverty rate in the United States for all adults was 14% (Edwards, 2014); however, 21% of grandmothers in grandparent-maintained households were below the poverty line, compared with only 12% of grandfathers. The poverty rate is lower for grandmothers who live in their adult children homes (14%). Poverty is even more severe among African American and Native American coresidential grandmothers, many of whom rely on welfare and other types of public assistance for their own sustenance and that of their grandchildren (Fuller-Thomson and Minkler, 2005; Haxton and Harknett, 2009; Mutchler and Baker, 2009). Poverty rates are especially high for grandmothers in skipped-generation houses (44%) and for lone-grandmother, lone-parent households (29%).

Grandparents in grandparent-maintained households are also more likely to assume primary responsibility for the care of grandchildren compared with grandparents who live in parent-maintained households. Whereas half of grandparents in grandparent-maintained households claim primary responsibility for the care of grandchildren, only 8% or less do so among grandparents living in parent-maintained households. Custodial grandparents have captured the interest of family sociologists not only because of the important role they fulfill as caregivers, but also because of their particular characteristics. In the next section, we examine more closely the characteristics of grandparents who assume the primary responsibility of caring for grandchildren.

Grandparents as Childcare Providers and "Custodial" Grandparents

Grandparents play important roles in contemporary families, often providing childcare while parents work and, at times, assuming the primary care of grandchildren who reside with them (Biblarz et al., 2009; Fuller-Thomson, Hayslip, and Patrick, 2005; Wichinsky, Testa, and Thomas, 2013). According to the Census Bureau's Survey of Income and Program Participation (SIPP), in 2011, 4.8 million (24%) preschool children, under the age of five, received regular childcare from a grandparent (Laughlin, 2013). Preschool children of employed mothers are significantly more likely to spend time in the care of a grandparent than are preschoolers whose mothers do not work. Nearly 30% of children of non-Hispanic, White employed mothers were cared for by grandparents, as were 34% of children of Hispanic mothers. In both groups, grandparents and fathers were about as likely to be caregivers. However, among the children of African American employed mothers, grandparents were more likely to act as caregivers than fathers. Given the high cost of nonfamilial childcare, poor children with an employed mother rely more heavily on grandparents than on daycare. Even among children whose mothers do not work, grandparent care remains the most common childcare arrangement (Laughlin, 2013).

The American Community Surveys (ACS) (U.S. Census Bureau, 2013) ask grandparents in coresidential households whether they are responsible for the primary care of each grandchild in their household. For simplicity we refer to grandparents who claim to be providing primary care as "custodial" grandparents, however, we acknowledge that these grandparents may or may not have legal or physical custody of their grandchildren. Grandparents often gradually become primary caretakers of grandchildren over extended periods of time. According to our analysis of ACS data, in 2011, nearly 4 in 10 coresident grandparents claimed to be primary caregivers of grandchildren and many more of them may be informally acting like custodial grandparents, even when the parents are present in the home. A recent study found that over 70% of grandparents provided primary care for at least 2 years or more, and 60% did so for more than 10 years (Luo et al., 2012).

Caring for grandchildren can be costly and stressful to grandparents, but the likelihood and types of hardship vary depending on family structure, family situation, and the degree and kind of grandparent involvement. Goodman and Silverstein (2001) found that caregiving grandmothers who play a linking role between grandchildren and parents report greater satisfaction with their role. By contrast, custodial grandparents often report greater stress and disadvantages, particularly those who lack social support (Hayslip and Kaminski, 2005; Musil and Ahmad, 2002). Large-scale studies of a range of grandparenting styles have found that although a minority of custodial grandparents may experience a decline in health while assuming custody and care of grandchildren, these health disadvantages often can be attributed to grandparent's social characteristics and prior living situations more so than to the provision of care (Hughes, Waite, LaPierre, and Luo, 2007).

Class and ethnicity also interact with stress, mediating the effect of custodial grandparenting roles. A nationally representative study of over 500,000 African American grandparents age 45 and older found that grandparents raising grandchildren were disproportionally more likely to be living in poverty and to suffer from serious health problems compared with their noncaregiving peers (Minkler and Fuller-Thomson, 2005). According to this study, four-fifths of grandparent caregivers living below the poverty line were not receiving public assistance, suggesting a need for more responsive social policy to help impoverished custodial grandparents. Custodial grandparents in low-income neighborhoods also report more health problems (Bachman and Chase-Lansdale, 2005). But another study of coparenting and custodial grandmother households in Los Angeles found that the tradition of intergenerational living in Latino families was associated with higher levels of well-being among custodial Latino grandmothers. Similarly, African American grandmothers in the same study fared better in custodial arrangements once the stress caused by parent's situation was parceled out. By contrast, White custodial grandmothers were not different in their levels of well-being compared with their noncustodial counterparts (Goodman and Silverstein, 2001).

Conclusions

In this chapter we painted a portrait of contemporary grandparent families highlighting changes over time and variation among families. Our findings point to the important role played by grandparents in their adult children's and grandchildren's lives, from providing companionship and care to assisting with financial resources and a place to live, to acting as surrogate parents assuming primary responsibility for raising their grandchildren.

Changing demographic, economic, and sociopolitical factors have increased the potential for and longevity of grandparent-grandchild relationships and have changed the context in which they are experienced. Individuals today are likely to have more grandparents alive for a longer span of time compared with generations past. Given the widening income inequality in the country and the far-reaching effects of the recent Great Recession, many more people are living in coresident grandparent-grandchildren households, with the most recent growth driven by the increase in households maintained by grandparents.

Grandparent families differ in their structure. Grandparents maintain the vast majority of multigenerational households (74%), while only 25% are maintained by parents. Compared with native-born White, Black and Native American coresidential grandparent households are more likely to be grandparent maintained, whereas immigrant, Asian, and Hispanic grandparent households are more likely to be parent maintained. Adult children in these households provide a residence for their parents and children and are sometimes referred to as "sandwich generation families." Nearly two thirds of coresident grandparents are women, reflecting women's longer lifespan and greater likelihood of providing care for family members.

Coresident grandparents are not a monolithic group; our results demonstrate the vast variation among them. On the one hand, some grandparents experience increased levels of stress, economic hardship, and poor health. Coresident grandparents, especially grandmothers, are more likely to live in poverty than other adults. On the other hand, coresident grandparents who own or rent their homes are more likely to be relatively young, employed, and have no physical impairments. In 2011, nearly 4 in 10 coresident grandparents claimed they acted as surrogate parents, assuming primary caregiving responsibilities for their grandchildren.

References

Aldous, J. 1995. New views of grandparents in intergenerational context. *Journal of Family Issues*, 16: 104-122.

Antonucci, T. C. 1990. Social supports and social relationships. In R. H. Binstock and K. George (Eds.), *Handbook of Aging and the Social Sciences* (pp. 205-226). New York, NY: Academic Press.

Bachman, H. J. and Chase-Lansdale, P. L. 2005. Custodial grandmothers' physical, mental, and economic well being: Comparisons of primary caregivers from low-income neighborhoods. *Family Relations*, 54: 475-487.

Baker, L. A., Silverstein, M., and Putney, N. M. 2008. Grandparents raising grandchildren in the United States: Changing family forms, stagnant social policies. *Journal of Sociology and Social Policy*, 28: 53-69.

Bengtson, V. L. 2001. The Burgess Award Lecture: Beyond the nuclear family: The increasing importance of multigenerational bonds. *Journal of Marriage and Family*, 63: 1-16.

Bianchi, S. M., Hotz, V. J., McGarry, K., and Seltzer, J. A. 2008. Intergenerational ties: Theories, trends, and challenges. In A. Booth et al. (Eds.), *Intergenerational caregiving* (pp. 3-44). Washington, DC: Urban Institute Press.

Biblarz, T. J., Casper, L. M., and Jayasundera, R. 2009. *Co-resident grandparents and their grandchildren: Family structure matters*. Paper presented at the Annual Meeting of the Population Association of America, Detroit, MI, May 2009.

Brandon, P. D. 2005. Welfare receipt among children living with grandparents. *Population Research and Policy Review*, 24: 411-429.

Bryson, K. and Casper, L. M. 1999. Co-resident grandparents and their grandchildren: Grandparent maintained families. *Current Population Reports*, Report No. P-23. Washington, DC: U.S. Bureau of the Census.

Caldwell, J. C. 2005. On net intergenerational flows: An update. *Population and Development Review*, 31: 721-740.

Casper, L. M. and Bianchi, S. M. 2002. *Continuity and change in the American family*. Thousand Oaks, CA: Sage.

Cherlin, A. J. 2004. The deinstitutionalization of American marriage. *Journal of Marriage and Family*, 66: 848-861.

Cherlin, A. J. 2010. Demographic trends in the United States: A review of research in the 2000s. *Journal of Marriage and Family*, 72: 403-419.

Cherlin, A. J. and Furstenberg, F. F. 1985. Styles and strategies of grandparenting. In V. L. Bengtson & J. F. Robertson (Eds.), *Grandparenthood* (pp. 97-116). Beverly Hills, CA: Sage.

Cohen, P. N. and Casper, L. M. 2002. In whose home? Multigenerational families in the United States, 1998-2000. *Sociological Perspectives*, 45: 1-20.

Copen, C. 2006. Welfare reform: Challenges for grandparents raising grandchildren. *Journal of Aging and Social Policy*, 18: 193-209.

Cox, D. 1990. Intergenerational transfers and liquidity constraints. *The Quarterly Journal of Economics*, 105: 187-217.

Cox, D. and Stark, O. 2005. On the demand for grandchildren: Tied transfers and the demonstration effect. *Journal of Public Economics*, 89: 1665-1697.

DeLeire, T. and Kalil, A. 2002. Good things come in 3's: Multigenerational coresidence and adolescent adjustment. *Demography*, 39: 393-413.

Dunifon, R. and Kowaleski-Jones, L. 2007. The influence of grandparents in single-mother families. *Journal of Marriage and Family*, 69: 465-481.

Edwards, A. 2014. Dynamics of economic well-being: Poverty, 2009–2011. *Household Economic Studies*, Report No. P70-137. Washington, DC: U.S. Bureau of the Census. Retrieved March 14, 2014 from http://www.census.gov.libproxy.usc.edu/hhes/www/poverty/

Ferguson, N., Douglas, G., Lowe, N., Murch, M., and Robinson, M. 2004. *Grandparenting in divorced families.* Bristol, UK: Policy Press.

Florian, S. M. and Casper, L. M. 2011. *Structural differences in native-born and immigrant intergenerational families in the U.S.* Paper presented at the American Sociological Association 2011 Annual Meeting, Las Vegas, NV.

Fuller-Thomson, E. and Minkler, M. 2005. American Indian/Alaskan native grandparents raising grandchildren: Findings from the Census 2000 Supplementary Survey. *Social Work,* 50: 131-139.

Fuller-Thomson, E., Hayslip, Jr., B., and Patrick, J. H. 2005. Introduction to the special issue: Diversity among grandparent caregivers. *The International Journal of Aging and Human Development,* 60: 269-356.

Glick, J. E. and Van Hook, J. 2002. Parents' coresidence with adult children: Can immigration explain racial and ethnic variation? *Journal of Marriage and Family,* 64: 240-253.

Goodman, C. and Silverstein, M. 2001. Grandmothers who parent their grandchildren: Affective relations across three generations and implications for psychological well-being. *Journal of Family Issues,* 22: 557-578.

Gonzalez, T. 2013, July 1. Smithville facility creates home for grandparents raising kids. *The Tennessean.* Retrieved November 1, 2013 from www.tennessean.com/article/20130701/NEWS21/307010035

Hamoudi, A. and Thomas, D. 2006. *Do you care? Altruism and inter-generational exchanges in Mexico.* Online Working Paper Series, California Center for Population Research, University of California-Los Angeles. Retrieved March 11, 2014 from http://escholarship.org/uc/item/03s0k54t

Harwood, J. 2001. Comparing grandchildren's and grandparent's stake in their relationship. *International Journal of Aging and Human Development,* 53: 195-210.

Haxton, C. and Harknett, K. 2009. Racial and gender differences in kin support: A mixed-methods study of African American and Hispanic couples. *Journal of Family Issues,* 30: 1019-1040.

Hayslip, B. and Kaminski, P. L. 2005. Grandparents raising their grandchildren: A review of the literature and suggestions for practice. *The Gerontologist,* 45: 262-269.

Hughes, M. E., Waite, L. J., LaPierre, T. A., and Luo, Y. 2007. All in the family: The impact of caring for grandchildren on grandparents' health. *The Journals of Gerontology Series B: Psychological Sciences and Social Sciences,* 62: S108-119.

Jayasundera, R. R. and Casper, L. M. 2010. *Why don't grandparents claim responsibility for grandchildren in skipped generation households?* Paper presented at the Pacific Sociological Association 2010 Annual Meeting, Oakland, CA.

Laughlin, L. 2013. Who's minding the kids? Child care arrangements: Spring 2011. *Current Population Reports.* Report No. P70-135. Washington, DC: U.S. Bureau of the Census.

Light, A. and McGarry, K. M. 2004. Why parents play favorites: Explanations for unequal bequests. *American Economic Review,* 94: 1669-1681.

Livingston, G. 2013. At grandmother's house we stay: One-in-ten children are living with a grandparent. Pew Research Center. Retrieved March 11, 2014 from http://www.pewsocialtrends.org/files/2013/09/grandparents_report_final_2013.pdf

Luo, Y., LaPierre, T. A., Hughes, M. E., and Waite, L. J. 2012. Grandparents providing care to grandchildren: A population-based study of continuity and change. *Journal of Family Issues,* 33: 1143-1167.

McLanahan, S. and Sandefur. G. 1994. *Growing up with a single parent: What helps, what hurts.* Cambridge, MA: Harvard University Press.

Minkler, M. and Fuller-Thomson, E. 2005. African American grandparents raising grandchildren: A national study using the Census 2000 American Community Survey. *The Journals of Gerontology Series B: Psychological Sciences and Social Sciences,* 60: S82-S92.

Musil, C. M. and Ahmad, M. 2002. Health of grandmothers: A comparison by caregiver status. *Journal of Aging and Health,* 14: 96-121.

Mutchler, J. E. and Baker, L. A. 2009. The implications of grandparent coresidence for economic hardship among children in mother-only families. *Journal of Family Issues,* 30: 1576-1597.

Mutchler, J. E., Baker, L. A., and Lee, S. 2007. Grandparents responsible for grandchildren in Native-American families. *Social Science Quarterly,* 88: 990-1009.

Sarkisian, N. and Gerstel, N. 2004. Kin support among blacks & whites: Race and family organization. *American Sociological Review,* 69: 812-837.

Sarkisian, N., Gerena, M., and Gerstel, N. 2007. Extended family integration among Euro and Mexican Americans: Ethnicity, gender, and class. *Journal of Marriage and Family,* 69: 40-54.

Seltzer, J. A. and Bianchi, S. M. 2013. Demographic change and parent-child relationships in adulthood. *Annual Review of Sociology,* 39: 275-290.

Silverstein, M. 2005. Intergenerational family transfers in social context. In R. Binstock, L. George, and J. Hendricks (Eds.), *Handbook of Aging and the Social Sciences* (pp. 166-181). San Diego, CA: Academic Press.

Silverstein, M. and Marenco, A. 2001. How Americans enact the grandparent role. *Journal of Family Issues,* 22: 493-522.

Smith, C. J. and Beltran, A. 2003. Role of federal policies in supporting grandparents raising grandchildren. *Journal of Intergenerational Relationships,* 1: 5-20.

Taylor, P., Morin, R., Parker, K., Cohn, D., and Wang, W. 2009. *Growing old in America: Expectations vs. reality.* Pew Research Center. Retrieved March 11, 2014 from http://www.pewsocialtrends.org/files/2010/10/Getting-Old-in-America.pdf

Uhlenberg, P. 1996. Mortality decline in the twentieth century and supply of kin over the life course. *The Gerontologist,* 36: 681-685.

Uhlenberg, P. 2004. Historical forces shaping grandparent-grandchild relationships: Demography and beyond. *Annual Review of Gerontology and Geriatrics,* 24: 77-97.

Uhlenberg, P. 2009. Children in an aging society. *Journals of Gerontology Series B: Psychological Sciences and Social Sciences,* 64: 489-496.

Uhlenberg, P. and Kirby, J. B. 1998. Grandparenthood over time: Historical and demographic trends. In M. Szinovacz (Ed.), *Handbook of grandparenthood* (pp. 23-39). Westport, CT: Greenwood Press.

U.S. Census Bureau. 2011a. *Unmarried partners of the opposite sex, by presence of children: 1960 to present* (Table UC-1). Retrieved October 24, 2012 from http://www.census.gov/population/socdemo/hh-fam/uc1.xls

U.S. Census Bureau. 2011b. *Family status and household relationship of people 15 years and over, by marital status, age, and sex: 2011* (Table A2). Retrieved March 11, 2014 from http://www.census.gov/hhes/families/data/cps2011.html

U.S. Census Bureau. 2011c. *Living arrangements of children under 18 years/1 and marital status of parents, by age, sex, race, and Hispanic origin/2 and selected characteristics of the child for all children: 2011* (Table C3). Retrieved March 11, 2014 from http://www.census.gov/hhes/families/data/cps2011.html

U.S. Census Bureau. 2013. American Community Survey, 2000, 2005, 2006, 2007, 2008, 2009, 2010, 2011. In S. J. Ruggles, A. Trent, K. Genadek, R. Goeken, M. B. Schroeder, and M. Sobek. *Integrated Public Use Microdata Series: Version 5.0* [Machine-readable database]. Minneapolis. MN: University of Minnesota, 2010. Retrieved March 11, 2014 from https://usa.ipums.org/usa/sda/

Watkins, S. C., Menken, J. A., and Bongaarts, J. 1987. Demographic foundations of family change. *American Sociological Review,* 52: 346-358.

Wichinsky, L., Testa, M., and Thomas, J. (Eds.). 2013. Understanding kinship care: Implications for policy and practice. Special issue of the *Journal of Family Social Work,* 16: 349-479.

http://dx.doi.org/10.2190/GITC7

CHAPTER 7

Multigenerational Relationships in Families with Custodial Grandparents*

Rachel Dunifon, Kimberly Kopko, P. Lindsay Chase-Lansdale, and Lauren Wakschlag

This chapter examines patterns of parent-child relationships among youth in custodial grandparent households. We do so using unique, multimethod data gathered from custodial grandparents and their teenaged grandchildren in New York State. Our analysis reveals several themes: in some instances the parent takes a friend-like role in the child's life, while in others the parent can be unreliable or even destructive. Adolescents' feelings toward their parents include anger, ambivalence, and longing. Finally, grandparents play key roles in moderating the youth-parent relationship, oftentimes working hard to build ties between the grandchildren they are raising and their nonresidential parents.

Multigenerational Relationships in Families with Custodial Grandparents

Researchers, practitioners, and policymakers alike increasingly seek to better understand a unique family type: those in which grandparents are raising their grandchildren with no parent present in the home. Currently, 2% of all U.S. children live in such households, in what are commonly called custodial grandparent families (U.S. Census Bureau, 2011). Most custodial grandparent arrangements came about informally, meaning that they are outside of the reach of

*We are grateful for support from the William T. Grant Foundation Scholars Program, the Cornell Institute for Social Sciences, and USDA Hatch and Smith-Lever Funds. We gratefully acknowledge helpful comments and feedback from Megan Dolbin-MacNab, Kevin Roy, Sharon Sassler, Laura Tach, and Maureen Waller.

many social service agencies and oftentimes do not access the limited services for which they are eligible (Macomber, Geen, and Clark, 2001). Previous research shows that there are a variety of potentially co-occurring reasons why children leave their parental home to live with their grandparents, primarily due to parental problems and events, including substance use, abuse and neglect, incarceration, mental health issues, young age, and death (Gleeson, Wesley, Ellis, Seryak, Talley, and Robinson, 2009; McKlindon et al., 2007). New research highlights that the most common reason for children to enter custodial grandparent arrangements is that their parent voluntarily gave them up to the grandparent (Dunifon, Ziol-Guest, and Kopko, 2014).

Despite their absence from the households, parents have the potential to play key roles in custodial grandparent families. Approximately two-thirds of children raised by grandparents have regular, ongoing contact with their mothers, and around 40% have regular contact with their fathers (Dunifon et al., 2014). Despite this, little is known about the perceptions that youth in custodial grandparent households have regarding their relationships with their own parents or the ways in which these relationships spill over to influence the larger family system. Using a unique multimethod design, including youth perspectives on their relationships with their parents and videotaped observations of grandparent-grandchild interactions, this study seeks to fill that gap. Specifically, the goal of this chapter is to examine patterns of parent-child relationships among youth in custodial grandparent households. We then examine how these patterns vary by dimensions of youth well-being, the grandparent-grandchild relationship quality, and the child's experience before leaving the parental home.

Theoretical Perspectives

This study is motivated by lifecourse theory, which emphasizes the interconnected lives of family members. Stack and Burton's (1993) notion of "kinscripts" describes families as a collection of individuals spanning multiple generations, each of whom has complex obligations to the other. This builds upon the key lifecourse concept of "linked lives," in which intergenerational relationships evolve over time and within social contexts, and family members influence each other reciprocally (Crosnoe and Elder, 2002). In terms of custodial grandparent families, the actions of one family member (the parent) cause another member (the grandparent) to take on the responsibility of raising a third (the grandchild). Additionally, given the ongoing interactions between parents, grandparents, and grandchildren in such families, the parent can continue to play a central role in the dynamics of custodial grandparent households. In the case of grandparent-headed households, the role of the biological parent can range from absence to being present in various degrees. Variability of parental proximity may not only influence the relationship youth have with their parents but also the relationship between the custodial grandparent and the grandchild. For example, the potential exists for teens to transfer feelings of anger and loss about their circumstances directed at the parent to the grandparent.

A second theory guiding this chapter is family systems theory (Cox and Paley, 2003), which poses that families are a large system composed of smaller sub-systems that affect one another and the system as a whole. In the present investigation, the whole family system is composed of custodial grandparents, grand-children, and that grandchild's parents. Three subsystems are operating and affect one another: grandmother-grandchild; grandmother-parent (her child); and parent-child (custodial grandchild). The quality of each subsystem or relationship (e.g., closeness, warmth, conflict, respect, and clarity of communication) affects the quality of the other subsystems and the functioning of the family system as a whole.

The goal of this chapter, then, is to examine patterns of parent-child relation-ships among youth in custodial grandparent households. We do so using unique, multimethod data, including videotaped observational data on the nature of the grandparent-grandchild relationship and on dimensions of youth well-being. The relationship between parents, grandparents, and grandchildren in custodial grandparent families may be particularly salient in the teenage years (Dolbin-MacNab and Keiley, 2009). It is during this period that adolescents address the tasks of identity formation and autonomy development (Graber and Brooks-Gunn, 1996). This identity-formation process is smoothest when it occurs within emotionally close and supportive family relationships, as it is in this context that caregivers and teens are best able to communicate about the teen's increased need for autonomy and navigate changing family relationship patterns (Steinberg and Silk, 2008). Literature on divorce highlights that navigating the complex developmental tasks of adolescence is particularly challenging for adolescents who may be separated from a parent due to divorce; oftentimes adjustment problems may resurface during adolescence, even if the divorce occurred many years earlier (Hetherington, Bridges, and Insabella, 1998). Similar challenges are likely the case for teenagers in custodial grandparent families, particularly if the nature of their relationships with the two key adults in that teen's life—the parent and the grandparent—are unsettled or in flux. This highlights the need for greater research on family relationships among adolescents being raised by grandparents.

Literature Review

The structure and functioning of custodial grandparent families are similar to and distinct from other custodial families, for example, those in which one parent (typically the mother) has primary residential custody while the other parent (usually the father) is nonresidential. This type of family structure typically occurs after divorce or in never-married families (McLanahan, 2004). The extensive research on these families demonstrates that the noncustodial parent has the potential to play an important role in the development and well-being of the child, both because of their ongoing contact and the primacy of parent-child relationships (Davies and Cummings, 1994). This same phenomenon is also prevalent in custodial grandmother families. Indeed, several studies document that the vast majority of youth being raised by grandparents have regular contact with at least one of their parents (Dolbin-MacNab and Keiley, 2009; Dunifon 2014; Messing, 2006). A second similarity between previous research on non-custodial parents and custodial grandparent families is that the absence of the noncustodial parent often occurs because of problems such as conflict, mental illness, incarceration, and the like. As with mother-father noncustodial families, the implications of parent-child contact likely depend on the nature of the parent-child relationship, which itself is influenced by a host of factors, including the reasons why the two parents are not in a committed partnership, the parent's characteristics, and the involvement of partners, spouses, or other children of each separated parent. These factors also apply to custodial grandparent families and in addition include the reasons why the parent rejected the child from the parental home as well as the quality of the grandparents' relationship with the parent. We therefore frame our literature review around the larger body of research related to noncustodial families, highlighting its implications for our study of family relationships in custodial grandparent families.

Just as the majority of children in custodial grandparent households have some kind of regular contact with their nonresident parent, studies show that the majority of children living with divorced or never-married mothers have regular contact with their nonresident fathers, although such contact decreases over time (Berger and Langton, 2011). Evidence suggests that it is not simply the frequency of contact between nonresident fathers and their children that matters for child well-being but rather the quality of that contact. Oftentimes, nonresident fathers assume a friend-like role when interacting with their child and do not engage in parent-like activities such as discipline or teaching (Berger and Langton, 2011; Hetherington et al., 1998). Similarly, among children in custodial grandparent households, many describe their relationship with the parent as one of com-panionship and fun (Dolbin-MacNab and Keiley, 2009) or more sibling-like rather than parental (Messing, 2006). However, when nonresident parents do take on an active, authoritative parenting role (e.g., providing emotional support and discipline), doing so is linked to children's improved academic outcomes and decreased behavior problems (Amato and Gilbreth, 1999).

Behavioral or emotional issues on the part of the nonresident parent can influence parent-child interactions. Compared to resident fathers, nonresident fathers are more likely to exhibit negative emotionality, poor mental health, substance use, and antisocial behavior (such as criminal activity) (Jaffee, Caspi, Moffitt, Taylor, and Dickson, 2001). Mental health problems, substance use, and incarceration often co-occur, especially in economically disadvantaged families (Braman, 2004). This constellation of issues can have negative repercussions for parent-child interactions, as children and their resident parents express fear of the nonresident parent, frustration at his unreliable behavior, and experience long periods of absence, either due to incarceration or behavioral issues. Additionally, there is evidence that contact with nonresident parents exhibiting such problems may not be in the child's best interest; when fathers exhibit high levels of problematic behavior, children fare best when they are not living in the household (Jaffee, Moffitt, Caspi, and Taylor, 2003), due at least in part to poor father-child interactions among nonresidential fathers with antisocial tendencies. Similarly, the child's parents can be a stressor in custodial grandparent households, with issues revolving around the parents' inconsistent involvement with their child and parents' behavioral and mental health problems, including substance abuse (Musil, Warner, McNamara, Rokoff, and Turek, 2008). Teenagers being raised by grandparents often describe their relationship with their parents as characterized by distrust, anger, and loss, highlighting their parents' unreliability, lack of attention, and inability to keep them safe (Dolbin-MacNab and Keiley, 2009).

The literature on parent-child attachment as it relates to divorce and remarriage is also relevant when thinking about noncustodial parents and custodial grandmother families. Attachment is the emotional bond between parents and children and is developed through warm, responsive, stable parent-child interactions (Davies and Cummings, 1994). When a child is separated from his or her attachment figure (usually the mother), a variety of negative responses may occur, including anger, avoidance, ambivalent behavior (simultaneously wanting and avoiding the parent) or longing (Bowlby, 1982; Sroufe, 2002). Conflict within the family can adversely influence children's secure attachment (Davies and Cummings, 1994), and how children respond to such changes may differ by developmental period. Studies of divorce and remarriage find that experiencing such family change in the preschool period is particularly linked to long-term negative outcomes (Hetherington et al., 1998). The pain at separation from a parent is evident when considering adolescents being raised by grandparents. In one study, 20% of teenagers refused to talk about their parents in the interview, primarily because it was too distressing (Dolbin-MacNab and Keiley, 2009).

Finally, the literature on coparenting is pertinent when thinking about relationships among children, parents, and grandparents in custodial grandparent households. Children benefit when parents, despite living apart, can work together in the best interests of the child, providing a consistent set of rules and a safe family context (McHale, Salman, Strozier, and Cecil, 2013). The key concepts of effective coparenting include avoiding conflict and cooperating together (Maccoby and Mnookin, 1992); in contrast, when coparents battle for authority, the child can get caught in the middle (McHale, Khazan, Erera, Rotman, DeCourcey, and McConnell, 2008). The custodial parent (usually the mother) often can have a key influence on coparenting behaviors, taking on a gatekeeper role, either promoting or hindering the involvement of the nonresident parent in the child's life (Carlson and Magnuson, 2011; Tach and Edin, 2011).

Much of the coparenting literature assumes that the child is living with the mother, who is seeking to coparent with the father. In custodial grandparent households, a child is living with the grandparent, and it is the nonresident mother with whom the grandparent often seeks to coparent. A series of studies has examined coparenting relationships focusing specifically on incarcerated mothers and the grandparents raising their grandchildren (Cecil, McHale, Strozier, and Pietsch, 2008; McHale et al., 2013; Strozier, Armstrong, Skuza, Cecil, and McHale, 2011). Findings indicate that antagonism, detachment, and disparagement between mothers and grandmothers were negatively related to effective coparenting, while shared parenting ideology, cooperation, and support positively predicted coparenting. Additionally, effective coparenting was associated with improved child behavior.

We know from family systems theory as well as from extensive empirical work on other child custody families that there is considerable variability and complexity in the quality of the relationships among children, parents, and grandparents in custodial grandparent households. However, little research has taken a "linked lives" or family systems approach to custodial grandmother families. Evidence from some studies that are exceptions suggest that conflict between the grandparent and parent are linked to lower grandparent well-being (Goodman, 2003; Goodman and Silverstein, 2001; Smith, Palmieri, Hancock, and Richardson, 2008), and worse child behavioral outcomes (Goodman, 2003; Smith et al., 2008). These studies relied on survey-based grandparent reports of the relationships between grandparents, parents, and children.

Even fewer studies have used videotaped observational data to measure the quality of the relations among parents, grandparents, and grandchildren. Two key exceptions examined African American multigenerational families with young children, focusing on ways in which the relationship between mothers and grandmothers influenced each woman's relationship with the child (Chase-Lansdale, Gordon, Coley, Wakschlag, and Brooks-Gunn, 1999; Wakschlag, Chase-Lansdale, and Brooks-Gunn, 1996). Findings indicate that the grandparent-parent relationship quality predicted the quality of the mother-child relationship, highlighting the importance of considering the inter-connected nature of the grandparent-parent-child system in alternative family structures.

Thus, extensive research on noncustodial parents highlights several themes relevant to custodial grandparent families: (a) the nature of the contact between nonresident parents and children; (b) the role of parents' emotional and behavioral issues in such relationships; (c) how children respond to their separation from their parents; and (d) the coparenting relationship between parents and grand-parents in custodial grandparent households. Additionally, family systems theory and lifecourse theory emphasize the importance of considering the intercon-nected relationships among the key figures in the lives of children in custodial grandparent households: the grandparents, parents, and grandchild.

Data and Methods

Participants

A purposive sample of 59 pairs of grandparents and adolescent grandchildren in custodial grandparent families was recruited through community agencies in New York State. Some families ($n = 26$) were recruited through Cornell Cooperative Extension offices offering programs for grandparents raising their grandchildren. The remaining families were recruited through an email sent to a statewide network of providers of programming for grandparents raising their grandchildren and through the New York City Department for the Aging Grandparent Resource Center. The sample came from a diverse range of locations across the state, including New York City, two distant suburbs of New York City, a midsized city and surrounding areas, and a rural county.

At each agency, someone working directly with grandparents raising grandchildren recruited participants, focusing on families containing one or more grandparents raising a teenager between the ages of 12 and 18 with no parent living in the household. They were also asked to limit their recruitment to families able to read and speak English and in which both the teenager and grandparent were mentally competent to take part in the study. Only one grandparent and one teenager per household were eligible to participate. The sample in this study, therefore, consists of families who had some connection to a community agency. However, the level of contact between the families and the agency varied widely—some families attended monthly support group meetings while others had not taken part in any activities organized by the agency in over a year.

Table 1 presents information on the characteristics of sample families. When possible, these characteristics are compared to those of a national sample of custodial grandparents. The vast majority of grandparents interviewed were grandmothers—47% of the sample consisted of maternal grandmothers and 34% consisted of paternal grandmothers. The average age of the grandparents was 63 years, and for youth, 15 years. The sample was relatively diverse: 26% of youth were African American, 15% were Hispanic, and 42% were White. The youth had, on average, lived with their grandparent(s) for 10 years; only 7% had lived there less than a year. Almost half (47%) of the grandparents were married, and the average grandparent had completed high school, but had no further education. Only 24% of the grandparents were employed; the most common reason for not being employed was that the grandparent was retired, while 34% of grandparents reported that they did not work due to a disability. Illustrating the complexity of family living arrangements, 80% of the youth had a sibling living outside of their current household.

Procedure

A total of 59 grandparent/teen pairs were interviewed in person between February and August of 2009. The first two authors performed 51 of these

Table 1. Sample Description

Variable	Mean (SD) or percentage	Comparison to national samples
Grandparent age	63 (7.44)	
Grandparents aged 65+	47%	15%[a]
Youth age	15.00 (1.91)	
Youth is a male	33%	
Caregiver is African American, non-Hispanic	28.81	
Caregiver is Hispanic	7%	
Caregiver is White, non-Hispanic	64%	
Youth is African American, non-Hispanic	26%	32%[b]
Youth is Hispanic	15%	21%[b]
Youth is White, non-Hispanic	42%	42%[b]
Youth is Other race	13%	
Years youth has lived with GP	9.98 (5.72)	
Youth has lived with GP for 10 or more years	56%	
Age youth arrived in GP household	5.27 (5.02)	
Youth has siblings outside of HH	80%	
Number of children in HH	.83 (1.05)	
Grandparent married	47%	48%[a]
Grandparent has less than HS education	19%	33%[a]
Grandparent has HS degree	41%	29%[a]
Grandparent has some college	31%	26%[a]
Grandparent is college graduate	9%	12%[a]
Grandparent employed	24%	
Grandparent has a disability	32%	
Youth has a health condition ($n = 41$)	51%	19%[a]
Average income of Census Tract (1,000s)	34.90 (18.39)	
Grandparent is maternal grandmother	47%	
Grandparent is paternal grandmother	34%	
Grandparent is maternal grandfather	7%	
Grandparent is other (great-grandmother or step-grandfather)	12%	

[a]Indicates data is drawn from the 1999 National Survey of America's Families, cited in Scarcella, Ehrle, and Geen (2003).
[b]Indicates data is drawn from the 2011 American Community Survey.

interviews, and a graduate student assistant performed those remaining. The interviews took place at the local community agency and lasted on average 1.5 hours. Informed consent was obtained from the grandparent and written assent was obtained from the teenager. The grandparent and teen also signed performance consent forms agreeing to be video- and audiotaped. Both the teenager and grandparent received $30.

Surveys

First, both the grandparent and the youth were given a survey. The grandparent survey was read aloud and filled in by the interviewer. The youth survey was administered via computer using an online survey tool. Many items were drawn from existing surveys such as the National Longitudinal Survey of Youth 1997 sample, the Three Cities Study, and the National Survey of Adolescent Health. Items were drawn to capture key items of interest in the overall study, such as the parenting behaviors of the grandparents, the relationship quality and family life of youth and grandparents, youth behavioral and academic adjustment, grandparent mental health, and demographic characteristics.

Videotaped Data Collection

After both the grandparent and youth completed their surveys, they took part in a 20-minute videotaped discussion. Families were given a series of four flip cards, were asked to discuss each card in order for 5 minutes, and in doing so were encouraged to have a typical conversation, "such as you would have at home." The cards were designed to probe for the key issues of family processes and the narrative told by each family member about their living situation. The first card asked the grandparent to take the lead in discussing the following question: "What is it like for families like ours with a grandparent raising a teenager? What is the best thing and what is the hardest thing?" The next card asked the teenager to discuss same question from his or her perspective. These first two cards, composing 5 minutes of discussion each for a total of 10 minutes, composed the first segment of observational data.[1]

The next set of cards consisted of a disagreement task (Wakschlag et al., 1996). First, the youth was asked to name a topic on which he or she disagreed with the grandparent and to lead a discussion with the grandparent on that topic, trying to resolve it. For the fourth and final card, the grandparent was asked to do the same. These last two cards, each composed of 5 minutes of discussion,

---

[1] It should be noted that for the first six interviews, which constituted a pilot study, the first youth discussion topics differed from those of the subsequent interviews. For these first six interviews, the youth was asked to discuss "What would we do if we had the whole afternoon to spend together doing whatever we wanted." The first grandparent discussion card was the same as in the rest of the study, as were the disagreement tasks (described below).

composed the second segment of the videotaped data collection. After turning on the camera, the interviewer left the room, returning after the 5 minutes was up in order to transition the dyad to the next card.[2]

Open-Ended Interviews

After the videotaped discussions were completed, the youth was paid and left the room. The grandparent remained for a brief (10–20 minute) open-ended audiotaped discussion. First they were asked, "Can you tell me more about how [youth] came to live with you?" Next, the grandparent was asked, "What can you tell me about [youth's] parents?" If relevant, the grandparent was asked how often they and the youth see each parent, as well as how they and the youth feel about those visits. Finally, the grandparent was asked, "Do you look at raising children differently this time than you did the first time, when you were raising your own children?"[3]

Measures and Analysis

Survey Data

Survey data from the grandparent and youth was matched on a unique family ID, input into a statistical software program (STATA) and coded to create variables capturing demographic and other information (see Table 1). Key measures used in this analysis were the length of time the youth had lived with the grandparent and age at which the youth came to live with the grandparent, reported by the grandparent. We also used a youth-reported measure of behavior problems, based on responses to 27 questions asked about specific feelings and behaviors, such as destroying things or feeling unhappy, in which answers of "not true" were given a score of 0, and responses of "sometimes" or "often" true were given a score of 1, with all responses summed to create a scale ranging from 1 to 27. These items were taken from the 1997 National Longitudinal Survey of Youth.

---

[2] One dyad was not able to take part in the videotaped data collection due to confusion and advanced age among the grandmother. Another dyad's video data was not usable because of technical difficulties. Two dyads could not take part in the videotape data collection due to language difficulties, and three additional dyads chose to only take part in the first 10-minute segment. Thus, 55 families contributed videotaped data for the first segment (discussing "what it is like for families like ours"), and 52 families took part in the second segment (the disagreement task). The majority of the missing videotaped data (2 out of 4 on the first segment and 5 out of 7 on the second segment) came from the New York City sample.

[3] One grandparent did not take part in the audiotaped interview due to confusion and advanced age.

Coded Videotaped Data

Three researchers (the two first authors and a graduate student) viewed and coded the videotaped data. Tapes were randomly assigned. Each 10-minute video segment was assigned and coded separately. The researchers watched each tape at least two times—once to code for the teen and another to code the grandparent, with the order chosen randomly. Items coded for the grandparent were anger, communication, depression, dominance, inductive reasoning, listener responsiveness, monitoring, parental influence, validation, and warmth. Items coded for the teen were anger, communication, defiance, depression, dominance, emotional maturity, listener responsiveness and warmth. Finally, researchers coded a dyad-based code of overall relationship quality.

The codes were adapted from three sources. First was the Scale of Intergenerational Relationship Quality (SIRQ) (Wakschlag et al., 1991), which has been used to measure the relationship between teen mothers and their mothers in lower-income, diverse samples. The second source was the Iowa Family Interaction Rating Scales (IFIRS) (Melby, Conger, Book, Rueter, Lucy, Repinski, Rogers, Rogers, and Scaramella, 1998), which were developed to measure the verbal and nonverbal behaviors and communications of individuals and groups of people. All measures were coded on a scale of 1 to 9 (in which 1 = highly uncharacteristic and 9 = highly characteristic). The first two authors double-coded a random set of tapes until consensus was reached (defined as when the average discrepancy across five segments was 1 point or less, representing 80% reliability). Once the first two authors reached consensus, the first author became reliable with the third coder. The three researchers then coded the remaining segments. A total of 30% of all segments were double-coded and consensus was reached in instances in which the two coders were greater than 1 point apart or when one coder had a 1 and the other had a 2 on any scale.

The 1–9 rating of relationship quality across the two 10-minute tasks were correlated at .71 and were averaged into a single item of overall relationship quality. We also used a measure of youth anger consisting of the average ratings across the two videotaped tasks (correlation of .55). Finally, we used a measure of youth depression, again averaged across the two videotaped tasks (correlation of .52).

Qualitative Data

The transcribed video- and audiotapes were coded to capture the grandparent and youth perception of the relationship the child had with his or her parent, using Dedoose mixed-method software. In order to determine the concepts for which these transcripts would be coded, the team undertook a detailed process, with a focus on the themes key to this study—relationship quality and parenting in grandparent-headed families. First, a thorough literature review was used to identify concepts. Next, the first two authors met with a group of community educators who worked regularly with grandparent-headed families to further identify concepts of interest to them and the families they served. A research team of five people (the first two authors, as well as three others who did not conduct the interviews) then read a random selection of transcripts in order to identify any new concepts and to compare these against those that had already been identified. The team then came up with a preliminary list of concepts and read through two random transcripts to classify overarching categories. The list of concepts was then modified and a codebook was developed. This codebook was used to code two more randomly chosen transcripts, the team met and came to consensus on coding those transcripts, and the codebook was finalized. Each member of the five-person team coded randomly assigned transcripts and then met with the first author to reach consensus for 20% of the transcripts.

The transcribed video- and audiotape transcripts were analyzed for themes related to perceptions of the parent-grandchild relationship. Specifically, we looked at excerpts that had been coded to reflect both the youth and the grand-parents' discussion of the view of the role of the parent in the child's life, the parents' priorities, youth reactions to spending time with the parent, and youth longing for the parent. These codes were applied separately for both grandparents and youth. We then integrated the concepts into the findings described below and chose illustrative quotes for those concepts. A total of 8 families did not discuss the child's relationship with the parent due to the fact that both parents were either dead or had had no contact with the child since infancy. An additional seven families briefly discussed the child's parent but did not go into enough detail to allow for further analysis. The findings discussed below are based on the remaining 44 families.

The transcribed video- and audiotape transcripts were also read and classified into categories representing the reasons why the youth was not living with their parent. Reading through the open-ended questions on this topic asked of the grandparent, we inductively coded several nonmutually exclusive reasons, shown in Table 2. The most common reason youth were not living with their mother or father was that the parent had voluntarily given the child to the grandparent. This reason encapsulated situations in which the parent was not forced to give up the child but rather made an active choice to give the child up. Below is a quote illustrating this reason:

> His birth mother really signed off on him when he was four . . . after she and my son divorced. . . . He went with my son for 8 years and that was just horrible. My son didn't take care of him. . . . They had two more children. . . . And they were the precious little girls. . . . And Max just got shoved by the wayside. . . . And then when he was 13, they just called us one Saturday night and said Max's not going to live here anymore, come and get him, he's out.

Other reasons for children not living with their parent include parental substance abuse problems, abuse and neglect, parental death and parental incarceration

Table 2. Reasons Not Living with Parents
(not Mutually-Exclusive)

	Reason not living with mother	Reason not living with father
Voluntarily gave up child	40%	34%
Substance abuse	26%	12%
Abuse/neglect of child	26%	10%
Partner had issues with child	16%	3%
Deceased	10%	12%
Incarcerated	10%	21%
Too young	10%	2%
Mental health problems	7%	—
Left child alone/abandoned	7%	10%
In gang/violent	2%	3%

(more common for fathers), and that the parent's new partner or spouse did not want to live with the child or was abusive of the child.

Findings

Analyses of the 44 families in which perceptions of the youth's relationship with the parent were discussed revealed seven themes. These themes were not mutually exclusive; families could be represented in more than one theme. Below we discuss the themes, utilizing quotes to highlight each theme, as well as incorporating other data to further shed light on the characteristics of families in each of the themes. The themes, illustrative quotes, and characteristics of families in each theme are presented in Table 3.

Parent is Like a Friend

Out of 44 families, 5 (11%) described their relationship with the teen's parent as being more like that of a friend rather than a typical parent. One grand-parent described the type of relationship that the youth has with his father in this way: "He [dad] interacts with them and he's pretty good. I would say his behavior is more like a favorite uncle than a dad . . . kind of a warm relationship, but it's not real close."

Sometimes the friend-like interactions that youth have with their parents can create problems for the grandparent if, for example, the parent models behaviors or encourages activities that are inconsistent with the values and behaviors the

Table 3. Perceptions of Youth Relationships with Parent

	Number of families	Observed grandparent-grandchild relationship quality (range 1-9)	Observed youth anger (range 1-)	Observed youth depression (range 1-9)	Youth reported behavior problems (range 0-27)	Whether youth was given up voluntarily by mother	Whether welfare agency involved in youth leaving parental home	Length of time youth living with GP (years)	Age youth arrived to live with GP (years)
Parent is like Friend: His [dad's] behavior is more like a favorite uncle than a dad.	5	5	4.8	1.5	14.0	.40	.40	10.75	4.83
Parent is Unreliable: He [dad] makes all kinds of promises to him and never carries through.	14	6.58	1.75	1.54	12.69	.38	.46	8.63	6.23
Longing for Parent: I love my mom. I miss my mom. Just thinking about her makes me want to cry!	6	6.25	2.17	1.75	15.83	.17	.33	7.21	7.46
GM Bonds Parent and Child Together: She wasn't talking to her mother and the mother wasn't talking. . . . But I bonded them back. It took twice, but I did it. I bonded them together.	13	5.54	2.46	1.42	11.67	.58	.33	8.97	5.79

GM Points Out Parental Faults: I told her . . . go live with your father then. You know, call him up and see. He's always telling you how he's always there and all this good stuff.	2	5.25	2.5	1.0	18.5	0	1.00	5.92	9.08
Anger Toward Parent: When he got to be a teenager . . . then it started to get bad with him. He was just so angry at both of [his parents].	8	5.63	3.19	1.38	11.63	.63	.38	8.54	6.46
Ambivalence Toward Parent: She wants to be with her mother, but when her mother's there she doesn't interact with her.	4	4.25	4.63	3.13	7.67	.50	.50	9.43	5.25
Sample Mean		5.35	3.03	1.69	12.59	.40	.40	9.98	5.27

grandparent wishes to impart. One grandmother mentioned that, when the grand-daughter spent the night at her mother's house, the mother allowed her to have her boyfriend sleep over, in direct conflict with the rules that the grandparent had established. Another grandmother stated,

> It's a very good relationship for Natalie [with the mom]. . . . It's a very difficult relationship for us . . . because there's been times when her mother has given her poor advice. . . . I mean Natalie's very immature and so is her mother, so I think that on a level of, mature level they're about at the same level.

It is possible that the ambiguous role that parents play in the lives of youth in this group has negative repercussions for the youth themselves. As noted by Carroll, Olson, and Buckmiller's (2007) review on family boundary ambiguity, unclear boundaries regarding who is performing which roles within a family can lead to poor functioning of its members. In this case, youth may be reacting negatively to the nonparent-like behavior on the part of their parents. Youth in these families had higher-than-average scores on the measure of anger based on the videotaped interaction.

Youth in these families had also been living with their grandparent longer than other youth, on average almost 11 years, arriving in the grandparental household when they were less than 5 years old. Perhaps the friend-like role of the parent in such families reflects the long time that the grandparent had been taking care of the child, suggesting that while the grandparent was able to evolve into a parental role over this extended period, the nonresident parent found an alternate role that was more friend-like than parental.

Parent is Unreliable

A total of 14 families (32%) reported that the parent-child relationship was hindered by the parent's unreliable behavior. As one grandparent described, "When [dad] feels like seeing him, then he sees him, and he makes all kinds of promises to him and never carries through." Grandparents mentioned how hurtful it was for the youth to experience their parents' changing and unreliable attentions and affections, and oftentimes described parents who sporadically decided to "play mom" for a short period of time, before losing contact again.

Several youth themselves had clear-eyed views of their parents' limitations and explicitly highlighted that they were better off living with their grandparent than they would be if they had remained with their unreliable parent. Youth mentioned that they appreciated the fact that, in contrast to their parent, their grandparent provided consistent rules, support, and engagement. Other youth explicitly contrasted their grandparents' ability to provide basic essentials such as food and housing with their parents' inability to do so. Oftentimes reflecting on parents' limitations led youth to think about the benefits of living with their grandparents, providing an opportunity for them to express their gratitude for the role the grandparent plays in their lives. One teen described her relationship with her grandmother this way, explicitly contrasting it with that of her mother:

> I have a stronger bond with [grandmother] than my own mother. I don't even call my mother "mommy." *She's* [grandma] my mother, because she's been there for me my whole life. . . . I can't call nobody "mommy" that wasn't there my whole life . . . everything's good. It's the best thing. Better than I would if I lived with my mother.

Another youth took a more cynical approach, but ended with the same conclusion that his life was better with this grandmother than it would have been with his parents:

> My parents were horrible, so why care if they're not here? . . . That's the only difference between you [grandma] and them. You have your faults and all your problems and everything, but at least you know what you're doing. For the most part."

Interestingly, this somewhat negative but clear-eyed view of parents may be adaptive. The average grandparent-grandchild relationship quality in this group was higher, and youth had lower levels of anger compared to the larger group. Perhaps recognizing that the parent is unlikely to ever play a real parental role in their lives allows youth to bond more closely with their grandparent and accept the grandparent taking on a parental role.

Longing for Parent

Other families (6 out of 44) expressed that the youth longed for a parent-child relationship better than the one they currently had. As wistfully expressed by one teenaged girl, "What's the hardest thing? Just being without my mom. I love my mom. I miss my mom. Just thinking about her makes me want to cry!"

These youth often expressed the opinion that their grandparent was not their "real parent" and could not fill the void of their parents, as noted by one teen: "The hardest thing is knowing that you're not with your real parents. That hurts sometimes to think that I have to count on you for everything instead of my mom and my dad. It's hard." Another teen expresses a similar feeling in greater detail:

> You know I thank God for you [grandma] trying to help us and . . . making us comfortable, but our state of mind is still going to be always "This isn't my mom." Reality. Face it. This isn't my mom . . . nobody can really take the place, so . . . that's . . . always going to be there. . . . I remember when I was younger I used to call you my parent. And then when I got older, I'm thinking "This is not my mom." You know?

Indeed, the issue of the use of the word "mother" came up repeatedly in the interviews. Some youth, as indicated in the previous section, felt that a "mother" transcended a literal biological status and instead reflected someone who was reliable and caring. Others, such as the youth quoted above, were unable to let go of the idea that their grandparent, despite raising them, was not their "real mother," and longed for her. It may be the case that unresolved feelings regarding the parent and their role in the youths' lives leads to tension regarding the use of the term "mother."

Strong feelings of loss and missing the absent parent are also found in the divorce literature (Kelly and Emery, 2003). This longing may be related to the fact that youth in this group had been living with their grandparent for a shorter period of time compared to the larger sample (average of 7 years compared to 10 years for the larger group) and were slightly over 7 years old when they came to live with their grandparent. Despite the pain that youth in this group felt regarding the parental absence, these youth had lower levels of anger on average and a higher grandparent-grandchild relationship quality than the sample as a whole; however, such youth did report relatively high levels of behavior problems. Thus, it appears that the parental longing does not interfere with the grandparent-youth relationship quality, but may be linked to maladaptive behavior on the part of the youth.

"I Bonded Them Together": Grandparent Encouraging Parent-Child Relationship

For some families (13 out of 44), the grandparent played a key role in trying to encourage a positive parent-child relationship, described by one grandmother in this way: "She [youth] wasn't talking to her mother and the mother wasn't talking. . . . But I bond them back. It took twice, but I did it, I bonded them together." Sometimes this meant that the grandparent attempted to get a reluctant adolescent to reach out to the parent. As noted by one grandparent, this was oftentimes an uphill battle: "I can't make her . . . call him to wish him happy Easter. She says I'm tired of being a bigger person. He's the adult, he should call me, and she's right, she's right." In other instances, this involved grandparents moving beyond their own feelings about parents' bad behavior in order to attempt to maintain a healthy parent-child interaction. As noted by one grandparent, "I tell [the grandkids] that the mother loves them but she doesn't know how to be a mom. I don't know whether she knows how to be a mother or if she doesn't know how to be a mother."

Other grandparents went out of their way to involve parents in meaningful aspects of their children's lives, including sharing report cards and taking their grandchildren on trips to visit parents who live out of state. Finally, some grandparents reached out directly to the adolescent's parents to try to encourage more positive interactions between their own children and their grandchildren, approached in a very loving way by this grandmother:

> She's [mom] talked to me and she says, "I don't know what to say [about visiting], I'm afraid." . . . I says whenever you decide, you know the phone number, it hasn't changed in 20 plus years, and her last words to me was, and

this was like a good 2 years ago, "I'm afraid, I don't know what to tell him. I don't even know how to face him," and so I says, well, pray to God, when the time is right, you'll show up. They love you.

Other grandparents attempt to connect parents to their own children, but express sadness and frustration at the parents' unwillingness to respond to their requests to engage with their own children:

I said [to the dad], what happened to the quality time, why don't you spend any time? I myself get angry at my son and I just, I don't know, I just can't believe he's doing this. I'm shocked. I didn't raise him this way, that's the hard thing.

Mothers of youth in this group were more likely than those in the larger sample to have given their child to the grandparent voluntarily (58% vs. 40%); perhaps the fact that the child came to live with the grandparent without the involvement of social service agencies is what leads the grandparents to keep the door open for interactions between parents and their children. The active engagement of grandparents in "bonding" their grandchild with their nonresident parents is noteworthy and stands in contrast to the divorce literature, which describes frequent situations of high conflict and resentment between divorced and separated parents which can cause children to feel caught in the middle, ultimately leading to anger and behavioral problems (Hetherington, Stanley-Hagan, and Anderson, 1989). Many custodial grandparents in this sample rose above their anger toward the nonresident parent (usually their own child) in an effort to create a positive relationship between that parent and their grandchild.

Pointing Out the Parent's Faults

There were only two families in which the grandparent tried to influence the parent-child relationship by focusing on the parents' negative attributes. In both cases, this occurred when grandparents felt a need to counteract the idea that the grandparent had "taken" the child from the parent and that the parent would provide a better place for the youth to live. One grandparent finally confronted her granddaughter with court papers detailing the abuse the girl received at the hands of her mother. Another grandmother took this approach:

I told her . . . go live with your father then. You know, call him up and see. He's always telling you how he's always there and all this good stuff. He was telling her on the phone and yet he would never come to see her and wouldn't call her; she was always calling him. I feel that, you know, he should answer for himself. Otherwise, she's just going to keep going on thinking he's Mr. Wonderful.

Interestingly, for both families in this group, the state child welfare agency was involved in the child coming to live with the grandparent. Perhaps in these situations grandparents feel the need to protect the youth from their own parents by setting up barriers to the parent-child relationship. Additionally, youth in this group had been living with their grandparent for much shorter periods of time compared to youth in the other groups (average of 6 years compared to 10 years for the sample as a whole); perhaps these youths' relatively recent arrival caused grandparents to have a greater fear that the youth would seek to return home. Indeed, in both of these situations, the grandparent's focus on the negative traits of the parent occurred in response to a perceived threat that the youth would leave the grandparental home and go live with the parent. Given the ambiguous legal status held by most of the custodial grandparents, this threat likely seemed plausible. In each situation, it was also reported that the nonresident parent was playing an active role in encouraging the youth to leave the grand-parent's home and even suggesting that the grandparent was the reason they were no longer living together. In this case, similar to what is seen in the literature on divorced parents, the youth likely felt caught in the middle between the grandparent and the nonresident parent (Hetherington et al., 1989). The turmoil faced by such youth may also be seen in the fact that they have much higher levels of behavior problems than others.

Anger Toward Parent

Out of 44 families, 8 discussed strong feelings of anger on the part of the youth toward the parent. Oftentimes, this anger became stronger in the teenage years, as noted by one grandmother:

> But as he got older and became a teenager, you know, the hormones are flying anyway and then he starts thinking about, gee, these two are really lousy. So when he got to be a teenager, you know, then it started to get bad with him. He was just so angry at both of them, and I said it would be better if you get it out.

The teenagers' anger toward their parents was often directed toward the grand-parent—the person closest at hand. This anger sometimes took the form of physical violence, as described by one teenage girl:

> At first it was kind of like a tornado. It was bad. It gets better. Like, I fought with you, like, every day, and I bit you. I wasn't expecting what I found. I was definitely really scared, because I didn't really realize I actually lost my father. And I wasn't realizing that my mother didn't really care.

Despite this, grandparents expressed a great deal of sympathy toward the teens, interpreting these outbursts of anger as originating from complicated and painful feelings toward the parents. As noted by one grandmother,

> I had books thrown at me, chairs. I broke the blood vessels in my arms, but through it all, he always cried and said, "Nana, I didn't want to hurt you, I was so angry, I was so angry, I've been so hurt. I don't think I'll ever forgive mommy and daddy."

Youth in this group were much more likely to have been given up voluntarily by their mother (63% vs. 40% in the sample as a whole); perhaps the knowledge that the mother chose to give up the youth, and the increasing awareness of this knowledge over the teenage years, led to intense feelings of anger toward the parent. This is consistent with patterns noted by Hethington et al. (1989), who describe the diverse ways in which children experience the aftermath of divorce, noting that strong negative feelings, including anger, often reemerge during adolescence, a time during which children often challenge and question both their own and others' roles within their families. Interestingly, the numbers of youth in this group were not higher than average in the expressions of anger toward the grandparent, suggesting that the anger may be reserved for the parent only.

Ambivalence

A final group of four families described ambivalent feelings between youth and their parents. Oftentimes, these youth had a strong desire to spend time with their parents, but at the same time withdrew from interactions due to the parents' unpredictable behaviors. As noted by one grandmother, "She wants to be with her mother, but when her mother's there she doesn't interact with her. . . . She interacts with me more than she does with her mother, and yet she wants to be with her mother."

Youth in this group had higher levels of anger and depression in the videotaped observational data. Such youth also had lower-quality grandparent-grandchild relationships than the larger sample, but also lower levels of reported behavior problems. As noted above, when family boundaries are unclear, the functioning of the family unit, as well as the individuals in that family, can suffer (Carroll et al., 2007). Perhaps these youth have not been able to sufficiently establish a clear role in their lives for both their grandparent and their nonresidential parent, as indicated by their lower-quality relationship with their grandparent. It may be the case that their inability to identify a clear role for the nonresident parent hinders their relationship with their custodial grandparent.

Discussion

This chapter examined patterns of parent-child relationships among youth in custodial grandparent households, using unique, multimethod data, including videotaped observational data on the nature of the grandparent-grandchild relationship and on dimensions of youth well-being. Lifecourse and family systems theories highlight the potential for complex interactions among grandparents, parents, and children in custodial grandparent households and suggest that relations between some family members (such as the parent and child) may spill over to influence others (such as the grandparent-grandchild relationship). We draw on the extensive literature on nonresident parents, much of which has focused on children of divorced or never-married parents, to develop themes related to the role of nonresident parents in the lives of children in custodial grandparent households. Our analysis reveals seven such themes.

Some themes highlight the role that the parent is perceived to play in the life of the youth. Whereas some youth were reported to have a friend-like relationship with their parent, others had a jaundiced view of their parent's ability to engage with them, considering the parent to be highly unreliable and unable to support or provide for the child. Interestingly, youth well-being was higher among families in which the parent was considered unreliable, and such youth had higher-quality observed relationships with their custodial grandparent. Perhaps having a clear-eyed, if negative, assessment of the parents' role in the child's life is adaptive and allows youth to develop a parent-like relationship with their custodial grandparent and to appreciate the positive role the grandparent plays in their lives. Future research could more carefully test the ways in which the grandparent-grandchild relationship relates to youth views of the role of the parents in their lives.

Other themes described how youth feel about their nonresident parents, encompassing anger, longing, and ambivalence. In this way, youth responses to parental absence correspond to those discussed by scholars of attachment theory. Youth feelings toward the parent appear to be related to child's age at the time he or she left the parental home, as well as the reasons for doing so. Children who were older when leaving their parents were more likely to express longing for the absent parent; this may be due to having a stronger memory of living with the parent or less time to adjust to not doing so. Our analysis of reasons why the child left the parental home revealed that many did so due to a voluntary decision on the part of the parent; children expressing strong anger toward their parent were more likely to have been "given up" by their parent voluntarily. Perhaps the increasing awareness and feelings of rejection that result from such a situation, emerging in the teenage years, leads to feelings of anger on the part of youth. This may be compounded by the fact that many children live near their nonresident parents, and oftentimes those nonresident parents have moved on to other partners and have other children whom they are raising (note that 80% of this sample had siblings living outside of their household). As described by Hetherington et al. (1989), following divorce, children often experience a second period of distress when their parent remarries. For children being raised by their grandparents, this distress may occur when one or both of their parents moves on to live with other partners and have other children, situations that are quite common.

Finally, youth with ambivalent feelings toward their parent (simultaneously pushing them away and wanting to be with them) had relatively high scores on the observed measure of depression. It is possible that their unresolved feelings toward their parent are internalized in this way. A parallel can be found in the research on ambivalent loss (Boss, 2007), which highlights the trauma and distress that can ensue in such situations. Such youth may have difficulty identifying clear roles for both their parent and their grandparent, hindering both relationships.

Finally, our themes relate to the role played by the custodial grandparent in the parent-child relationship. A particularly noteworthy finding is that many grandparents go out of their way to engage in strategies designed to "bond" their grandchild with the absent parent. Insights from the literature on coparenting highlight what a strong, healthy behavior this is on the part of grandparents, with likely benefits for the child (although some research on nonresident fathers indicates that it may not be healthy to bond a child with a nonresident parent who exhibits problematic behaviors such as substance abuse or mental health problems). Perhaps the motivation to effectively coparent with an absent parent is stronger in custodial grandparent households than in traditional households in which parents are living apart—custodial grandparents have a strong bond with and love for their own children (the child's parent), despite that parent's negative behaviors, and seem to draw upon that relationship in attempting, sometimes against all odds, to form a relationship between their custodial grandchild and that child's parent. Such efforts on the part of the grandparent may in turn lead to greater and more positive involvement by the nonresident parent. Carlson, McLanahan, and Brooks-Gunn (2008) found that when resident mothers and nonresident fathers have a better coparenting relationship, the nonresident father is more involved in the life of the child.

It was much rarer for a grandparent to negatively influence their grandchild's relationship with the parent, and such instances only occurred in cases in which the child was removed from the parental home by child welfare officials. The fact that few grandparents attempt to negatively influence the relationship with the parent is reassuring, given evidence from the divorce literature that hearing a trusted adult bad-mouth a parent is highly destructive to children, creating stress and loyalty conflicts (Kelly and Emery, 2003). Perhaps in this situation, grandparents are motivated to keep children away from parents who have been deemed unsafe, particularly if those parents are actively seeking to convince the child to come live with them instead. Given a lack of clear legal arrangements for most of the custodial grandparent families interviewed, this situation is likely perceived as both plausible and threatening.

Results from this study have several implications for policy and practice. While literature on nonresident parents suggests that youth may benefit if such a parent is able to take on an engaged, authoritative parenting role, many youth in our study did not perceive that their parents were willing or able to do so. This highlights a need for programs designed to enhance the mental health and parenting skills among the parents of children in custodial grandparent households. The majority of such children remain in contact with their parent, yet these parents appear to have problems engaging with their children in healthy ways. While several programs offer parenting skills for custodial grandparents themselves, this study identifies a need for programs designed to promote well-being and skills among the nonresident parents as well.

At the same time, it should be noted that for some youth, disengaging from the parent may be the healthiest option. Indeed, youth who had a cynical, but perhaps realistic, view of their parents' limitations had lower levels of anger and higher-quality relationships with their custodial grandparents. Programs reaching custodial grandparent families may also want to consider coaching grandparents on ways to speak about the child's absent parent in a manner that acknowledges the parents' limitations in an appropriate way and considers what role the parent is able to play in the child's life.

These findings also highlight the ways in which youth experience the loss of their parent. Such feelings may change over time and may become particularly strong in the teenage years, as youth develop an increasing awareness of their parents' absence and the reasons for it, and begin to reexamine the role that various adults play in their lives. That youth exhibit such strong feelings toward their absent parents, despite the fact that most had been living with their grandparents for the vast majority of their lives, suggests a need for counseling or other services to support them in dealing with ongoing issues related to the parental separation.

Finally, results highlight a key role that grandparents play in fostering parent-child relationships in custodial grandparent families. Given the complex and nuanced ways in which parents may influence the family system, programs expressly designed to work with grandparents on negotiating the parent-child relationships may be beneficial.

This study has several limitations that should be noted. The data were gathered through convenience sampling of families with some involvement in social service agencies in their community and are not representative of custodial grandparent families in New York or elsewhere. Additionally, our sample was relatively small, and our data was cross-sectional, making our results descriptive rather than causal. However, taken together, results from this study paint a fuller picture of the complex relationships in custodial grandparent households than previously known. Our results emphasize that children, grandparents, and parents in such households do indeed have "linked lives," and highlight the need for not only more research in this area but for policies and programs designed to meet the unique needs of such families.

References

Amato, P. and Gilbreth, J. 1999. Nonresident fathers and children's well-being: A meta-analysis. *Journal of Marriage and Family*, 61(3): 557-573.

Berger, L. and Langton, C. 2011. Young disadvantaged men as fathers. *Annals of the American Academy of Political and Social Science*, 635: 56-75.

Boss, P. 2007. Ambiguous loss theory: Challenges for scholars and practitioners. *Family Relations*, 56: 105-111.

Bowlby, J. 1982. Attachment and loss: Retrospect and prospect. *American Journal of Orthopsychiatry,* 52(4): 664-687.

Braman, D. 2004. Doing time on the outside: Incarceration and family life in urban America. Ann Arbor, MI: University of Michigan Press.

Carlson, M. and Magnuson, K. 2011. Low-income fathers' influence on children. *Annals of the American Academy of Political and Social Science,* 635: 95-116.

Carlson, M. J., McLanahan, S., and Brooks-Gunn, J. 2008. Coparenting and nonresident fathers' involvement with young children after a nonmarital birth. *Demography,* 45(2): 461-488.

Carroll, J. S., Olson, C., and Buckmiller, N. 2007. Family boundary ambiguity: A 30-year review of theory, research and measurement. *Family Relations,* 56: 210-230.

Cecil, D., McHale, J., Strozier, A., and Pietsch, J. 2008. Female inmates, family caregivers, and young children's adjustment: A research agenda and implications for corrections programming. *Journal of Criminal Justice,* 36: 513-521.

Chase-Lansdale, P. L., Gordon, R., Coley, R., Wakschlag, L., and Brooks-Gunn, J. 1999. Young African-American multigenerational families in poverty. In E. M. Hetherington (Ed.), *Coping with divorce, single parenting, and remarriage* (pp. 165-192). Mahwah, NJ: Lawrence Erlbaum Associates.

Cox, M. and Paley, B. 2003. Understanding families as systems. *Current Directions in Psychological Science,* 12: 193-196.

Crosnoe, R. and Elder, G. H. 2002. Life course transitions, the generational stake, and grandparent-grandchild relationships. *Journal of Marriage and the Family,* 64(4): 1089-1096

Davies, P. and Cummings, E. M. 1994. Marital conflict and child adjustment: An emotional security hypothesis. *Psychological Bulletin,* 116(3): 387-411.

Dolbin-MacNab, M. and Keiley, M. 2009. Navigating interdependence: How adolescents raised solely by their grandparents experience their family relationships. *Family Relations,* 58: 162-175.

Dunifon, R., Ziol-Guest, K., and Kopko, K. 2014. Grandparental co-residence and family well-being: Implications for research and policy. *The Annals of the American Academy of Political and Social Science,* 654(1): 110-126.

Gleeson, J. P., Wesley, J. M., Ellis, R., Seryak, C., Talley, G. W., and Robinson, J. 2009. Becoming involved in raising a relative's child: Reasons, caregiver motivations and pathways to informal kinship care. *Child & Family Social Work,* 14(3): 300-310.

Goodman, C. 2003. Intergenerational triads in grandparent-headed families. *Journal of Gerontology: SOCIAL SCIENCES,* 58B(5): S281-289.

Goodman, C. and Silverstein, M. 2001. Grandmothers who parent their grandchildren: An exploratory study of close relations across three generations. *Journal of Family Issues,* 22(5): 557-578.

Graber, J. and Brooks-Gunn, J. 1996. Transitions and turning points: Navigating the passage from childhood through adolescence. *Developmental Psychology,* 32(4): 768-776.

Hetherington, E. M., Bridges, M., and Insabella, G. 1998. What matters? What does not? Five perspectives on the association between martial transitions and children's development. *American Psychologist,* 53(2): 167-184.

Hetherington, E. M., Stanley-Hagan, M., and Anderson, E. 1989. Marital transitions: A child's perspective. *American Psychologist,* 44(2): 303-312.

Jaffee, S., Caspi, A., Moffitt, E., Taylor, A., and Dickson, N. 2001. Predicting early fatherhood and whether young fathers live with their children: Prospective findings and policy reconsiderations. *Journal of Child Psychology and Psychiatry*, 42(6): 803-815.

Jaffee, S., Moffitt, T., Caspi, A., and Taylor, A. 2003. Life with (or without) father: The benefits of living with two biological parents depend on the father's antisocial behavior. *Child Development*, 74(1): 109-126.

Kelly, J. B. and Emery, R. 2003. Children's adjustment following divorce: Risk and resilience perspectives. *Family Relations*, 52(4): 352-362.

Maccoby, E. E. and Mnookin, R. H. 1992. *Dividing the child: Social and legal dilemmas of custody*. Cambridge, MA: Harvard University Press.

Macomber, J., Geen, R., and Clark, R. 2001. *Children cared for by relatives: Who are they and how are they faring?* Urban Institute Report available online at: http://www.urban.org/publications/310270.html

McKlindon, A., Dunifon, R., Variano, D., Reynolds, B., Byster, L., and Healy, P. 2007. The Hudson Valley Regional Relatives as Parents Program. Research Brief available online at: http://www.human.cornell.edu/pam/outreach/parenting/research/upload/The-20Hudson-20Valley-20Regional-20Relatives-20as-20Parents-20Pr.pdf

Melby, J., Conger, R., Book, R., Rueter, M., Lucy, L., Repinski, D., Rogers, S., Rogers, B., and Scaramella, L. 1998. *The Iowa Family Interaction Rating Scales* (5th ed.). Institute for Social and Behavioral Research, Iowa State University, Ames, Iowa.

Messing, J. T. 2006. From the child's perspective: A qualitative analysis of kinship care placements. *Children and Youth Services Review*, 28(12): 1415-1434.

McHale, J., Salman, S., Strozier, A., and Cecil, D. 2013. Triadic interactions in mother-grandmother coparenting systems following maternal release from jail. *Monographs of the Society for Research in Child Development*, 78(3): 57-74.

McHale, J., Khazan, I., Erera, P., Rotman, T., DeCourcey, W., and McConnell, M. 2008. Coparenting in diverse family systems. In M. Bornstein (Ed.), *Handbook of parenting* (2nd ed., Vol. 3, pp. 75-108). Mahwah, NJ: Lawrence Erlbaum Associates.

McLanahan, S. 2004. Diverging destinies: How children are faring under the second demographic transition. *Demography*, 41(4): 607-627.

Musil, C., Warner, C., McNamara, M., Rokoff, S., and Turek, D. 2008. Parenting concerns of grandparents raising grandchildren: An insider's picture. In B. Hayslip and P. Kaminski (Eds.), *Parenting the custodial grandchild* (pp. 101-114). New York, NY: Springer.

Scarcella, C. A., Ehrle, J., and Geen, R. 2003. *Identifying and addressing the needs of children in grandparent care*. Urban Institute report available online at: http://www.urban.org/uploadedpdf/310842_b-55.pdf

Smith, G., Palmieri, P., Hancock., G., and Richardson, R. 2008. Custodial grandmothers' psychological distress, dysfunctional parenting and grandchildren's adjustment. *International Aging and Human Development*, 67(4): 327-357.

Sroufe, L. A. 2002. From infant attachment to promotion of adolescent autonomy: Prospective, longitudinal data on the role of parents in development. In J. G. Borkowksi, S. L. Ramey, and M. Bristol-Power (Eds.), *Parenting and the child's world* (pp. 187-202). Mahwah, NJ: Lawrence Erlbaum Associates.

Stack, C. and Burton, L. 1993. Kinscripts. *Journal of Comparative Family Studies*, 24(2): 157-170.

Steinberg, L. and Silk, J. 2008. Parenting adolescents. In M. Bornstein (Ed.), *Handbook of parenting* (2nd ed., Vol. 1, pp. 103-134). Mahwah, NJ: Lawrence Erlbaum Associates.

Strozier, A., Armstrong, M., Skuza, S., Cecil, D., and McHale, J. 2011. Coparenting in kinship families with incarcerated mothers: A qualitative study. *Families in Society: The Journal of Contemporary Social Services*, 92(1): 55-61.

Tach, L. and Edin, K. 2011. The relationship contexts of young disadvantaged men. *Annals of the American Academy of Political and Social Science*, 635: 76-94.

U.S. Census Bureau. 2011. America's families and living arrangements: 2011. Available online at: http://www.census.gov/population/www/socdemo/hh-fam/cps2011.html

Wakschlag, L., Chase-Lansdale, P. L., and Brooks-Gunn, J. 1996. Not just "ghosts in the nursery": Contemporaneous intergenerational relationships and parenting in youth African-American families. *Child Development*, 67(5): 2131-2147.

http://dx.doi.org/10.2190/GITC8

CHAPTER 8

An Exploration of the Health of Adolescents Raised by Grandparents

Megan L. Dolbin-MacNab

In the United States, a growing number of grandparents are primarily responsible for the care of their grandchildren. In fact, recent census data indicate that there are approximately 2.7 million grandparents raising grandchildren, which reflects an increase of 16% since 2000 (Murphey, Cooper, and Moore, 2012; Pew Research Center, 2010). These grandparents are providing care for 2.9 million children and adolescents, a number that represents 40% of the approximately one in ten or 7.8 million American children who coreside with a grandparent (Kreider and Ellis, 2011). Numerous explanations have been given for the growth in grandfamilies, a term used to refer to families in which a grandparent is providing the majority of the care and parenting for one or more grandchildren. Most common are difficulties associated with the grandchild's parents and include parental incarceration, death or illness, substance abuse, and/or child abuse and neglect (Hayslip and Kaminski, 2005). However, cultural values of grandmother involvement in the care of children (Goodman and Silverstein, 2006) and federal and state policies that advocate for the placement of foster children with relatives (Pew Charitable Trusts, 2007) have also influenced the growth of grandfamilies.

Although there is growing evidence of resilience among grandfamilies (Hayslip and Smith, 2013), custodial grandparents still experience a variety of challenges, including financial difficulties, legal concerns, disrupted social networks, family conflicts, parenting stress, and physical and psychological stress (Hayslip and Kaminski, 2005). Collectively, these challenges place grandparents at risk for depression and anxiety (Hayslip, Shore, Henderson, and Lambert, 1998; Minkler, Fuller-Thomson, Miller, and Driver, 1997), as well as compromised physical health (Hughes, Waite, LaPierre, and Luo, 2007; Minkler and Fuller-Thomson, 1999). Grandparents are not alone in experiencing negative outcomes; similarly, grandchildren have been found to be at risk for health problems, difficulties in school, and a variety of psychological and behavioral problems (Billing, Ehrle, and Kortenkamp, 2002; Bramlett and Blumberg, 2007; Smith and Palmieri, 2007). Many of these problems stem from grandchildren's histories, which may include abuse/neglect and exposure to drugs and alcohol, but may also relate to grandparents' psychological distress and parenting stress (Smith and Dolbin-MacNab, 2013; Smith et al., 2008) as well as to accumulating and intersecting sources of oppression and marginalization (Keene and Batson, 2010).

Health and Grandfamilies

Of the many challenges and issues facing grandfamilies, researchers have become increasingly interested in the physical health of custodial grandparents. Grandparents raising grandchildren may experience compromised health, chronic health conditions such as heart disease and diabetes, dissatisfaction with their health, and physical limitations (Minkler and Fuller-Thomson, 1999). Additionally, research suggests that grandparents often engage in risky health behaviors, including smoking, alcohol consumption, and lack of exercise (Hughes et al., 2007; Roberto, Dolbin-MacNab, and Finney, 2008). The impact of these risky behaviors on grandparents' overall physical health may also be compounded by their less frequent use of preventive healthcare services such as screenings and vaccinations (Baker and Silverstein, 2008; Roberto et al., 2008). Nonetheless, Hughes and colleagues (2007) note that the act of raising grandchildren itself does not seem to have a dramatic negative impact on grandparents' health; rather, other risk factors such as financial distress are what actually contribute to grandparents' poor health outcomes. Still, these and other researchers conclude that custodial grandparents often have compromised physical health, and their health may worsen during transitions related to caregiving, such as assuming greater responsibility for the care of a grandchild or taking on an additional grandchild (Baker and Silverstein, 2008; Musil, Gordon, Warner, Zausniewski, Standing, and Wykle, 2010).

Despite clear concerns related to the physical health of custodial grandparents and the fact that contextual factors, namely, poverty, may be significant in influencing grandparents' health (Hughes et al., 2007), much less attention has been given to the physical health of the grandchildren. This is unfortunate, as grandchildren's difficult histories of trauma, neglect, exposure to substances, and parental abandonment (Hayslip and Kaminski, 2005) may place them at increased risk for negative health outcomes and chronic health conditions. Having acute or chronic health conditions can significantly compromise grandchildren's future development and well-being (Child and Adolescent Health Measurement Initiative, 2014). Additionally, from an ecological perspective (Bronfenbrenner, 1979), grandchildren live in shared environments with their grandparents and are exposed to similar environmental limitations or advantages that may also influence their health. For instance, just as some grandparents are unable to afford needed medications or medical care for themselves due to poverty or lack of health insurance, it may also be difficult for these grandparents to afford the out-of-pocket expenses associated with the care of their grandchildren's chronic conditions or disabilities. Similarly, grandparents living in isolated rural areas may find it difficult to locate specialists with the expertise necessary to address a grandchild's specific medical needs. Thus, barriers within the larger environments in which grandchildren are embedded may have significant consequences for their health, access to medical care, and future well-being (Centers for Disease Control and Prevention, 2008).

Given the relative lack of empirical attention given to the health of children being raised by grandparents, the purpose of this exploratory study was to examine the physical health and healthcare utilization of a sample of adolescents being raised by custodial grandmothers. The research questions guiding the study included (a) How healthy are adolescents being raised by grandparents? (b) What is the nature of grandchildren's healthcare utilization? (c) What individual and contextual factors predict grandchildren's health and healthcare utilization? Findings from this study can provide important insights into the health needs of grandchildren being raised by grandparents and can also be used to inform practice and policy.

Health of Children Raised by Grandparents

As noted previously, due to their often difficult histories and resulting physical, psychological, and developmental challenges (Billing et al., 2002; Hayslip and Kaminski, 2005; Smith and Palmieri, 2007), children and adolescents being raised by grandparents may be at increased risk for health problems, chronic diseases, or other limiting conditions. These health problems may be further exacerbated by a lack of regular access to healthcare services, stemming from barriers such as financial difficulties or lack of health insurance (Centers for Disease Control and Prevention, 2008). Lack of access to adequate healthcare services may be especially problematic for children and adolescents with special needs (Strickland, Jones, Ghandour, Kogan, and Newacheck, 2011). To date, however, only a few studies have examined grandchildren's health, and none have focused specifically on healthcare utilization or adolescence. Physical health during adolescence is particularly important to examine, as adolescence is a time of significant growth and development (Spear, 2002). It is also a time when adolescents begin assuming responsibility for managing their chronic health conditions and establishing habits related to smoking, diet, and exercise that will impact their future health and well-being (Office of Adolescent Health, 2014).

In one of the first studies to examine the health of children raised by grandparents, Solomon and Marx (1995) used data from the National Children's Health Supplement and found that children being raised by grandparents did not differ significantly from children raised in one- or two-parent families. In this study, health was defined as susceptibility to illness and frequency of health problems such as asthma, headaches, accidents, injuries, and enuresis. Grandchildren's health was also not related to the grandparent's age, the grandchild's race, or the length of time the grandchild had been living with the grandparent. The authors did, however, report some evidence that grandchildren being raised by single grandparents were more susceptible to illness than grandchildren being raised in two-grandparent-headed families (Solomon and Marx, 1995). Male grandchildren were found to be more susceptible to illness as compared to female grandchildren. Despite these demographic variations, Solomon and Marx (1995) still argued that children being raised by grandparents compared favorably to children from other family constellations in terms of physical health, and that this likely reflects the fact that custodial grandparents serve as protective forces in the lives of their grandchildren.

In a more recent study, using data from the National Survey of America's Families, Billing and colleagues (2002) found that 14% of children living with relatives, including grandparents, had some type of limiting condition, and 7% were rated by their caregivers as being in fair or poor physical health. As the authors note, these percentages are approximately double those of children living in two-parent families (Billing et al., 2002). When income was taken into consideration, Billing and colleagues reported, "Children in low-income relative care are as likely to be in fair or poor health as children in low-income parent care, but more likely to have a limiting condition" (p. 4). The authors concluded that, while children living with grandparents experience worse physical health than children in other family constellations, these outcomes may be more likely due to the grandchildren living in poverty or to the grandchildren's histories of parental abuse, neglect, or abandonment (Billing et al., 2002).

Most recently, Bramlett and Blumberg (2007) used data from the National Survey of Children's Health to examine the physical and mental health of children in grandparent-only families, in comparison to children in two-parent, blended, and single-parent families. Their findings revealed that children being raised by grandparents had the worst physical and mental health. Even after controlling for various demographic characteristics, such as household poverty level and race/ethnicity, children living in grandfamilies were still significantly more likely than children in two-parent families to have special health needs, attention deficit hyperactivity disorder (ADHD), or serious emotional and social problems.

In sum, these studies suggest that, while some grandchildren experience health problems at levels similar to those of the general population, a significant portion of children and adolescents being raised by grandparents may experience limiting conditions or other health difficulties (Billing et al., 2002; Bramlett and Blumberg, 2007; Solomon and Marx, 1995). This may be especially likely for grandchildren living in families experiencing other stressors such as a lack of adequate financial resources. Despite the value of this information in providing a snapshot of grandchildren's health, some limitations of these studies are that they did not examine grandchildren's healthcare utilization nor did they examine individual and environmental factors associated with grandchildren's health. By addressing both of these issues, the present study can provide a more comprehensive understanding of grandchildren's health.

Adolescent Healthcare Utilization

Though there have been no studies examining the healthcare utilization of adolescents being raised by grandparents, regular health care is important to adolescents' overall health and development (Office of Adolescent Health, 2014). According to national statistics, approximately 82% of adolescents between the ages of 12 and 17 had a preventive medical visit within the past year, and almost 87% had received some type of medical care, including check-ups, sick care, or hospitalizations (Child and Adolescent Health Measurement Initiative, 2014). Almost 86% of adolescents had also received some type of dental care, and approximately 64% of adolescents who needed mental health services had received them (Child and Adolescent Health Measurement Initiative, 2014). Further, approximately 90% of U.S. adolescents have a medical home and 94% have some type of health insurance (Child and Adolescent Health Measurement Initiative, 2014). While these statistics highlight how most adolescents are able to obtain needed health care, significant disparities in access to health care exist for vulnerable adolescents (Agency for Healthcare Research and Quality, 2011). That is, disparities in access to health care have been associated with racial/ethnic minorities, adolescents with special needs, and low-income families (Agency for Healthcare Research and Quality, 2011). Many of these characteristics are particularly prevalent in grandfamilies (Hayslip and Kaminksi, 2005), which may further elevate grandchildren's risk for negative health outcomes.

An Ecological Perspective on Grandchild Health and Healthcare Utilization

In conceptualizing factors that may influence or be associated with grandchildren's health and healthcare utilization, ecological systems theory (Bronfenbrenner, 1979) emerges as a useful guiding theoretical model. According to ecological systems theory (Bronfenbrenner, 1979), grandchildren are interdependent with their larger environments such that the quality of their proximal and distal environments influences their health and overall well-being. Proximal environments include family, friends, schools, and other environments with a direct impact on the grandchild, while distal environments such as neighborhoods, healthcare agencies, and cultural norms are still influential but have a more indirect impact. Thus, grandchildren embedded in higher-quality proximal and distal environments would be more likely to experience better health outcomes than grandchildren embedded in lower-quality environments.

Based on the existing literature, a number of specific aspects of grandchildren's proximal and distal environments might be relevant to their health and health-care utilization. First, demographic characteristics such as family income, race/ethnicity, and family structure have all been linked to grandchildren's health (Billing et al., 2002; Bramlett and Blumberg, 2007; Solomon and Marx, 1995) and adolescent health and healthcare utilization more generally (Agency for Healthcare Research and Quality, 2011; Case and Paxson, 2002). As implied by ecological systems theory (Bronfenbrenner, 1979), children coming from more vulnerable grandfamilies, which could include racial/ethnic minorities, single-grandparent-headed families, and poor families, may lack the resources and information necessary to make healthy choices and to access needed health care, which may result in more negative health outcomes.

In addition to family demographic characteristics, ecological systems theory (Bronfenbrenner, 1979) would also suggest that characteristics of the grand-parent could influence the grandchild's health. Caregivers are significant to the health of children and adolescents—they model specific health behaviors, make decisions about diet and exercise for their children, and shape the quality of the larger environment (Case and Paxson, 2002). Within grandfamilies, grandparents' mental health has been linked to their grandchildren's well-being, with depressed and anxious grandparents having grandchildren with more serious levels of emotional and behavioral problems (Smith and Dolbin-MacNab, 2013; Smith et al., 2008). In terms of physical health, in the larger literature beyond grandfamilies, mothers' ratings of their own health have been strongly related to their ratings of their children's health (Waters, Doyle, Wolfe, Wright, Wake, and Salmon, 2000). Thus, in examining predictors of grandchildren's health and healthcare utilization, it is important to consider the influence of grandparents' physical and mental health.

Finally, from an ecological perspective (Bronfenbrenner, 1979), personal characteristics of the grandchildren would clearly have the potential to influence their health and healthcare utilization. Of the many characteristics that could be influential, behavior problems emerge as being especially relevant to adolescents being raised by grandparents. As noted previously, children and adolescents living in grandfamilies are often at increased risk for emotional and behavioral problems (Billing et al., 2002; Smith and Palmieri, 2007). Psychological problems in adolescence, such as depression and conduct disorder, have been linked to current and future chronic health conditions and other health problems (Bardone, Moffitt, Caspi, Dickson, Stanton, and Silva, 1998; Naicker, Galambos, Zeng, Senthilselvan, and Colman, 2013). This linkage is typically explained by the fact that mental health difficulties can make it difficult for adolescents to engage in health-promoting behaviors. Additionally, some mental health difficulties manifest themselves physically, and long-standing emotional or behavioral problems may make it difficult for adolescents to adapt to stressors and transitions, which may ultimately negatively impact their physical health (Repetti, Taylor, and Seeman, 2002).

Related to adapting to stressors and transitions, the ability to regulate or manage distressing emotions, also known as emotion regulation, is thought to moderate or mediate the relationship between environmental risk factors and negative physical and mental health outcomes in children and adolescents (Repetti et al., 2002). In terms of its role in physical health, the inability to regulate emotion is thought to result in physiological distress that, over time, can negatively impact health (Repetti et al., 2002). Additionally, the inability to effectively regulate emotion has been related to various mental health issues, such as depression, which are also thought to contribute to poor physical health (Repetti et al., 2002). As emotion regulation has its roots in secure attachment relationships (Repetti et al., 2002), due to their histories of parental abuse, neglect, and abandonment (Hayslip and Kaminski, 2005), grandchildren may be especially at risk for having problems with emotion regulation. Thus, examining emotion regulation in the context of grandchildren's health and healthcare utilization is relevant to an ecological (Bronfenbrenner, 1979) understanding of mechanisms that may explain their health outcomes.

Overview of the Study

Sample

Participants for this study consisted of 81 pairs of adolescents and their custodial grandmothers. Using purposive, convenience methods, families were recruited from 17 states in the southern United States (U.S. Census Bureau, 2007). Specifically, the sample was recruited by sending information about the study to leaders of programs serving grandparents raising grandchildren. Program leaders were asked to distribute information about the study to grandparents raising adolescent grandchildren with whom they were in contact. With regard to inclusion criteria, grandparents were required to be the person primarily responsible for the financial and emotional care of a grandchild between the ages of 12 and 18. Target grandchildren were required to reside with the custodial grandparent full time and the grandchild's parent(s) could not be in coresidence. If more than one grandchild was eligible to participate, the oldest willing grandchild was selected. Sample demographics are presented in Table 1.

Procedures

After learning about the study, interested grandparents contacted the researcher via email or telephone. Families were screened over the telephone for eligibility. If all inclusion criteria were met, a data-collection session was scheduled. Due to the regional approach to sampling, 14 (17%) grandchildren and grandmothers participated in face-to-face data-collection sessions, while 67 (83%) families participated in a data-collection session over the telephone. Prior to data collection, written consent/assent was obtained from all participants. Trained

Table 1. Grandchild and Grandmother Demographic Information (N = 81)

	Grandchildren (GC)			Grandmothers (GM)		
	n (%)	M (SD)	Range	n (%)	M (SD)	Range
Age (years)		14.62 (1.88)	12–18		60.74 (6.46)	47–75
Race						
African American	26 (32)			27 (33)		
Caucasian	46 (57)			51 (63)		
Latino	3 (4)			1 (1)		
Multiracial	4 (5)			0 (0)		
Native American	2 (3)			2 (3)		
Gender						
Female	41 (51)					
Male	40 (49)					
GM education						
Less than HS				15 (19)		
High school				18 (22)		
Some college				22 (27)		
College degree				26 (32)		
Year with GM		9.96 (5.03)	0–18			
Number of GC					2.01 (1.43)	1–10
Annual income						
< $15K				27 (33)		
$15K–$25K				25 (31)		
$25K–$50K				16 (20)		
> $50K				12 (15)		
Refused				1 (1)		
Reason for living with GM[a]						
Substance abuse	44 (54)					
Abuse/neglect	36 (44)					
Incarceration	23 (28)					
Domestic violence	17 (21)					
Illness/disability	16 (20)					
Death	14 (17)					
Abandonment	11 (14)					
Other	16 (20)					
Maternal GM				56 (69)		
Married (Yes)				27 (33)		

[a]These numbers exceed the total sample size because grandmothers could provide multiple reasons for the caregiving arrangement.

interviewers administered questionnaires to grandmothers and grandchildren individually, with data-collection sessions lasting approximately 1 hour for each participant. Each grandmother and each grandchild received a $20 Wal-Mart gift card as compensation for their involvement in the study.

Measures

While a detailed presentation of the self-report measures used in this study is beyond the scope of this chapter, a brief overview of each measure will be given. In addition to a categorical rating of the grandchild's health, an adaptation of the Current Health Scale (Ware, 1976) provided a continuous measure of grandchild health. Grandmothers and grandchildren both completed this scale in reference to the grandchild's physical health. The scale includes 9 items, which assess how the grandchild has been feeling currently, as well as in the past, what doctors have said about the quality of the grandchild's health, and how the grandchild's health compares with their peers. Higher scores reflect better health. In terms of reliability, in the present study, $\alpha = .78$ and $\alpha = .91$ for the grandchild and grandmother reports of grandchild health, respectively. Grandchild healthcare utilization was measured with a series of questions, all of which were completed by the grandmother, about the number of times within the last year the grandchild had accessed dental, mental health, or hospital/emergency room services. Also assessed were the number of times in the last year the grandchild had sick and wellness visits with a physician.

Grandchild behavior problems, including internalizing and externalizing behavior problems, were measured with the Child Behavior Checklist (CBCL) (Achenbach and Rescorla, 2001) and the Youth Self-Report/11–18 (YSR) (Achenbach and Rescorla, 2001). Grandmothers completed the CBCL, while grandchildren completed the YSR. For both measures, respondents reported on the degree to which 120 problem behaviors were true of the grandchild within the previous 6 months. The internalizing scale includes items from the withdrawn/depressed, anxious/depressed, and somatic complaints syndrome scales. The externalizing scale reflects items from the aggressive and rule-breaking behavior syndrome scales. On both the CBCL and the YSR, higher scores reflect more dysfunctional behavior. Both measures are widely used and have substantial evidence for their reliability and validity (Achenbach and Rescorla, 2001).

Grandchild emotion regulation was measured, from the perspective of the grandmother and the grandchild, with the Emotion Regulation Checklist (ERC) (Shields and Cicchetti, 1997). This 24-item scale assesses how frequently the grandchild displays certain affective behaviors related to emotion regulation and emotion lability. In this study, higher scores reflect greater grandchild affect regulation and low emotional dysregulation. The reliability and validity of the ERC have been well established (Shields and Cicchetti, 1997). For this study, $\alpha = .85$ for the grandmother report of the grandchild's emotion regulation and $\alpha = .77$ for the grandchild's self-report.

Grandmothers' physical health and mental health was measured with the two standardized summary scores from the General Health Index of the Medical Outcomes Study Short Form-36 Version 2.0 (SF-36v2) (Ware, Kosinki, and Dewey, 2000; Ware and Sherbourne, 1992). The summary score for physical health includes items related to general perceptions of physical health, physical functioning, limitations on physical roles, and experiences of pain. The mental health scale includes items assessing perceived vitality, social functioning, limitations on emotional roles, and general perceptions of mental health related to depression and anxiety. For both scales, higher scores indicate better overall physical or mental health.

Finally, the degree to which the grandfamily has the resources necessary to meet its needs was measured using the Family Resource Scale (Dunst and Lee, 1987). This 30-item instrument was completed by grandmothers and examines the adequacy of the family's physical and nonphysical resources. Examples of the resources measured by the scale include money, food, transportation, social support, and time. Higher scores indicate that the grandfamily has more adequate resources. The scale has established reliability and validity (Dunst and Lee, 1987). In the current study, Cronbach's alpha was .95.

Data Analysis

Given the lack of information in the literature about grandchildren's health, initial analyses were exploratory and focused on identifying patterns related to grandchildren's health and healthcare utilization. In addition to providing descriptive information about grandchildren's health and healthcare utilization, t-tests were used to compare grandmothers and grandchildren's ratings of the grandchild's health, as well as differences in grandchildren's health and healthcare utilization based on demographic characteristics such as grandchild gender, race/ethnicity, grandmother marital status, family income, number of grandchildren, and length of caregiving. Next, bivariate correlations were used to examine the associations among grandchild, grandmother, and family variables and grandchildren's health and healthcare utilization. Finally, ordinary least squares regression was used to examine ecological (i.e., grandchild, grandmother, and family) predictors of grandchildren's health and healthcare utilization. Given the exploratory nature of the study, p-values for the ordinary least squares regressions were set at .10.

Findings

Grandchild Health and Healthcare Utilization

When asked to rate their overall health categorically, 25% of grandchildren rated it as "excellent," 46% rated it as "very good," 27% gave a rating of "good," and 3% rated their health as "poor." When grandmothers categorically rated their grandchildren's health, 44% rated it as "excellent," 33% rated it as "very good," 15% rated it as "good," 6% rated it as "fair," and 1% rated it as "poor." Overall, 25% of the grandmothers indicated that their grandchildren had a limiting physical, learning, or mental health condition. Via the continuous measure of health (Ware, 1976), grandchildren also appeared to be relatively healthy. However, in comparing the grandmother and grandchild reports, grandmothers' reports of their grandchildren's health were marginally significantly higher than their grandchildren's self-reported health, indicating that grandmothers viewed their grandchildren as being slightly more healthy than grandchildren viewed themselves. Statistical information related to these findings is available in Table 2.

There were some demographic characteristics related to grandchildren's health. Table 2 also provides a summary of these analyses. First, while there were no differences for male and female grandchild health when reported by the

Table 2. Grandchildren's Health ($N = 81$)

	GC report n (%)	GM report n (%)	M (SD)	Range
Categorical Rating of Health				
Excellent	20 (25)	36 (44)		
Very good	37 (46)	27 (33)		
Good	22 (27)	12 (15)		
Fair	—	5 (6)		
Poor	2 (3)	1 (1)		
Continuous Rating of Health (Current Health Scale)				
GC health (GC report)			4.04 (.59)	2.22–5.00
GC health (GM report)			4.23 (.79)	1.67–5.00
Comparison of GC and GM reports			$t(80) = 1.84, p = .07$	
Demographic Variations in GC Health (GC Report)				
GC Gender				
Male			4.29 (.39)	3.44–5.00
Female			3.82 (.66)	2.22–4.89
Comparison of male GC and female GC			$t(79) = 3.92, p = .000$	
GM Marital Status				
Married			3.84 (.58)	2.78–4.78
Not married			4.12 (.57)	2.22–5.00
Comparison of married GM and not married GM			$t(79) = -2.27, p = .03$	

Note: GC = Grandchild; GM = Grandmother; Other demographic variations in GC health, as noted in the text, were nonsignificant.

grandmothers, male grandchildren self-rated themselves as being significantly healthier than female grandchildren. Additionally, grandchildren with married grandmothers reported significantly worse health than grandchildren whose grandmothers were not married. This included grandchildren whose grandmothers were single, never married, divorced, or widowed. There were no other demographic differences, including grandchild racial/ethnic background, household income, grandmother/grandchild age, number of grandchildren in the home, or length of time with the custodial grandmother, related to grandchildren's physical health. No information was available about health insurance coverage for the grandchild or the larger grandfamily.

In terms of healthcare utilization, Table 3 provides a summary of grandchildren's healthcare utilization, as reported by their custodial grandmothers. In the past year, grandchildren had seen a dentist an average of two times and had accessed their general practitioners almost two times for check-ups or wellness visits. Almost 10% of the grandchildren had received no dental care within the last year, while approximately 5% of the grandchildren had not visited a physician for a check-up or wellness visit. With regard to healthcare visits related to illnesses, grandchildren averaged two sick visits in the past year. For mental health care, about half of the grandchildren had been seen by a mental health counselor for an average of six visits. With regard to demographic variations in grandchildren's healthcare utilization, grandchildren of White grandmothers had significantly more sick and mental health visits than grandchildren of non-White grandmothers. Female grandchildren had significantly more sick and emergency room visits than male grandchildren. Finally, grandchildren living in families with annual incomes above $25K utilized hospital and emergency room services less frequently than grandchildren living in families with annual incomes under $25K, though this was only a statistical trend. Statistical information in support of these findings is available in Table 3.

Factors Associated with Grandchild Health and Healthcare Utilization

Grandchildren's self-reported health was correlated with a number of individual and grandmother characteristics. See Table 4 for additional details about these correlations and their significance levels. Specific to characteristics of the grandchildren, grandchildren with better physical health also had significantly fewer internalizing, externalizing, and total self-reported behavior problems. Additionally, grandchildren with better health also self-reported significantly more optimal emotion regulation. Demographically, male grandchildren and grandchildren with single grandmothers self-reported better health. Grandchildren's self-reported health was not associated with their grandmothers' physical health or mental health. Additionally, there was no significant relationship between grandchild self-reported health and the degree of family resources or any other grandmother or grandchild demographic variables.

Table 3. Grandchildren's Healthcare Utilization in the Previous
Year ($N = 81$)

	n (%)	Mean	SD	Minimum	Maximum
Type of health care utilization					
Dental visits	73 (90.1)	2.44	2.03	0	12
Check-up or wellness visits	77 (95.1)	1.80	1.39	0	7
Sick visits	54 (66.7)	1.93	2.71	0	12
Hospital/emergency visits	26 (32.1)	.64	1.40	0	10
Mental health visits	40 (49.4)	6.44	6.44	0	48

Demographic Variations in GC Healthcare Utilization (GP Report)

	M (SD)	Range	Comparison
Sick visits			
GM/GC race/ethnicity			
White	2.47 (3.14)/2.46 (2.93)	0–12	$t(79)_{GM} = 2.92, p = .005$
Non-white	1.00 (1.34)/1.23 (2.34)	0–5	$t(79)_{GC} = 2.14, p = .04$
GC gender			
Female	2.66 (3.34)	0–12	$t(79) = -2.57, p = .01$
Male	1.18 (1.55)	0–5	
Mental health visits			
GM race/ethnicity			$t(79) = -2.51, p = .01$
White	8.33 (12.10)	0–48	
Non-white	3.23 (6.13)	0–24	
Hospital/emergency visits			
GC gender			$t(79) = -2.43, p = .02$
Female	1.00 (1.83)	0–10	
Male	.28 (.55)	0–2	
Annual income			
Over $25K	.32 (.82)	0–3	$t(79) = -1.72, p = .09$
Under $25K	.79 (1.61)	0–10	

Note: Other demographic variations in GC healthcare utilization, including GM/GC age, GM marital status, and number of grandchildren, were nonsignificant.

When grandmothers reported on their grandchildren's health, some similar and different correlations emerged. First, in terms of grandchild characteristics, grandmothers who reported their grandchildren as being in better physical health were significantly less likely to report grandchild internalizing and total behavior problems. In addition, grandmothers' reports of their grandchildren's health were positively and significantly correlated with their ratings of their grandchildren's emotion regulation, such that better grandchild health was associated with more optimal grandchild emotion regulation. With regard to grandmother

Table 4. Correlates of Grandchild Health and Health Care
Utilization (*N* = 81)

Variable	Correlate	*r (p)*
GC Health (GCR)	GC Internalizing Problems (GCR)	−.47 (.000)
	GC Externalizing Problems (GCR)	−.31 (.005)
	GC Total Problems (GCR)	−.41 (.000)
	GC Emotion Regulation	.30 (.006)
	GM Married	−.25 (.03)
	GC Male	.40 (.000)
GC Health (GMR)	GC Internalizing Problems (GMR)	−.38 (.000)
	GC Total Problems (GMR)	−.25 (.03)
	GC Emotion Regulation (GMR)	.31 (.004)
	GM Physical Health	.28 (.01)
	Check-Up/Well Visits	−.39 (.000)
	Sick Visits	−56 (.000)
	Hospital/Emergency Visits	−.53 (.000)
	Mental Health Visits	−.23 (.04)
Check-Up/ Wellness Visit	GM Physical Health	−.23 (.04)
Sick Visits	GC Internalizing Problems (GMR)	.49 (.000)
	GC Internalizing Problem (GCR)	.26 (.02)
	GC Externalizing Problems (GMR)	.23 (.04)
	GC Total Problems (GMR)	.40 (.000)
	GC White	.23 (.01)
	GM White	.26 (.02)
	GC Male	−.28 (.01)
Hospital/Emergency Visits	GC Internalizing Problems (GMR)	.36 (.001)
	GC Total Problems (GMR)	.29 (.008)
	GC Male	−.26 (.02)
Mental Health Visits	GC Internalizing Problems (GMR)	.30 (.007)
	GC Total Problems (GMR)	.35 (.002)
	GM White	.24 (.04)

Note: GCR = Grandchild Report; GMR = Grandmother Report; All other demographic variables, as noted in the text, were not significantly associated with the grandchild health and health care utilization variables.

characteristics, grandmothers who were physically healthy were significantly more likely to report having grandchildren who were also physically healthy. There were no significant associations among grandmothers' reports of their grandchildren's health and grandmother mental health, grandmother and grandchild demographic characteristics, or family resources.

Expectedly, grandchildren's health was associated with their healthcare utilization; grandchildren's physical health, as reported by their grandmothers, was significantly and negatively associated with their number of wellness visits, mental health visits, sick visits, and hospital/emergency room visits. Again, Table 4 details these correlations. In each of these cases, better grandchild health was associated with fewer healthcare visits. None of the healthcare utilization variables were significantly related to the grandchild's self-reported health.

Grandchildren's healthcare utilization was associated with a number of grandchild and grandmother characteristics. Noteworthy relationships were those among grandchildren's number of dental, sick, hospital/emergency room, and mental health visits and their behavior problems, namely, internalizing, externalizing, and total behavior problems, such that a greater number of each type of healthcare visits was significantly associated with higher levels of grandchild behavior problems. Internalizing and total behavior problems were particularly likely to be associated with greater grandchild healthcare utilization. Another association of note was the significant, negative correlation between grandchildren's number of wellness visits and grandmothers' physical health. Grandchildren with physically healthier grandmothers received fewer wellness visits. Demographically, there were significant, negative correlations between grandchild gender and their number of sick and hospital/emergency room visits such that more of these types of visits were associated with female grandchildren. Additionally, being a White grandchild and/or grandmother was significantly correlated with a greater number of grandchild sick visits and the number of mental health visits. No other demographic characteristics were significantly correlated with grandchildren's healthcare utilization. Detailed information about these correlations is presented in Table 4.

Ecological Predictors of Grandchild Health and Healthcare Utilization

As presented in Table 5, a series of multiple regression analyses were conducted in order to gain further insight into proximal and distal ecological predictors of grandchildren's health and healthcare utilization. The predictors included grandmother, grandchild, and family characteristics and were identified based on the literature and the correlational analyses presented previously. The overall goal of these analyses was to extend the previous research by examining grandchild, grandmother, and family factors that might be predictive of or help explain variations in grandchildren's health and healthcare utilization.

Table 5. Multiple Regression Analyses for Grandchild Health (N = 81)

Variable	GC Health (GC Report)			GC Health (GM Report)			GC Sick Visits (GM Report)			GC Hospital/ Emergency Visits (GM Report)		
	B	SE B	β	B	SE B	β	B	SE B	β	B	SE B	β
GM Marital Status – Married	-.32	.13	-.26*	.06	.17	.03	.03	.52	.006	-.23	.30	-.08
GC Gender – Male	.29	.14	.25*	.09	.18	.06	-.95	.53	-.18†	-.41	.30	-.15
GC/GM Race – White	.11	.13	.09	-.13	.17	-.08	.95	.52	.17†	.12	.30	.04
GM Physical Health	.002	.005	.04	.01	.007	.18†	-.008	.02	-.04	.005	.01	.04
GM Mental Health	.003	.006	.05	-.002	.009	-.03	-.03	.03	-.10	-.02	.02	-.11
Family Resources	-.13	.10	-.15	.02	.14	.01	.49	.43	.13	.10	.25	.05
GC Internalizing Problems	-.02	.01	-.30†	-.04	.01	-.39**	.08	.05	.22†	.03	.03	.14
GC Externalizing Problems	-.001	.01	-.01	.04	.01	.49**	.07	.04	.25†	.03	.03	.20
GC Emotion Regulation	.27	.23	.15	.88	.28	.44**	1.38	.90	.20	.91	.51	.26†
GC Health (GM Report)							-1.65	.36	-.48***	-.92	.21	-.52***
	$F(9,71) = 4.30$, $p = .000$, $R^2 = .35$			$F(9,71) = 4.03$, $p = .000$, $R^2 = .34$			$F(10,70) = 6.90$, $p = .000$, $R^2 = .50$			$F(10,70) = 4.13$, $p = .000$, $R^2 = .37$		

Note: GM = Grandmother; GC = Grandchild; The demographic variables included in these analyses were informed by the results presented in Table 4.
†$p \leq .10$; *$p \leq .05$; **$p \leq .01$; ***$p \leq .001$.

With regard to predictors of grandchildren's self-reported physical health, as shown in Table 5, being raised by a married grandmother, being a female grandchild, and having more internalizing problems were predictive of poorer grandchild health. In the regression model predicting the grandmother's report of the grandchild's health, significant predictors included grandmother physical health and grandmother reports of their grandchildren's emotion regulation, internalizing behavior problems, and externalizing behavior problems. That is, better grandmother-reported grandchild physical health was predicted by better grandmother physical health, more optimal grandchild emotion regulation, fewer grandchild internalizing behavior problems, but greater externalizing behavior problems.

With regard to grandchildren's healthcare utilization, the significant regression models were those predicting grandchildren's number of hospital/emergency visits and grandchildren's number of sick visits. Results of these analyses are also presented in Table 5. Across both regression models, grandmothers' reports of their grandchildren's health were significant predictors, such that poorer grandchild physical health predicted a greater number of grandchild sick visits and more utilization of hospital/emergency services. Beyond grandchild health, in the model predicting utilization of sick visits, grandmothers' reports of their grandchildren's internalizing and externalizing behavior problems were trends, with greater grandchild behavior problems being predictive of a greater number of grandchild sick visits. Grandchild gender and grandmother race were also trends, such that being a female grandchild and a White grandmother were predictive of more grandchild sick visits. For the hospital/emergency visits, grandmothers' reports of their grandchildren's emotion regulation approached significance, with more optimal grandchild emotion regulation predicting a greater number of hospital or emergency room visits.

Discussion and Implications

Despite the attention that has been given to the health of custodial grandparents, much less is known about the physical health and healthcare utilization of children being raised by their grandparents. As such, the purpose of the present study was to examine the health and healthcare utilization of adolescents being raised by grandmothers. A related purpose was to explore grandchild, grandmother, and family ecological factors (Bronfenbrenner, 1979) that might be related to and predictive of grandchildren's health and healthcare utilization.

Compared to adolescents in the southern United States (Child and Adolescent Health Measurement Initiative, 2014), the grandchildren in the present study reported worse health. Specifically, approximately 85% of adolescents in the southern United States rated their health as "excellent/very good" versus 71% of grandchildren and 77% of grandmothers in the present study. Grandchild health was, however, comparable to national studies of children in relative care (i.e.,

Billing et al., 2002). In terms of preventive healthcare utilization, the grand-children in this study performed better than children/adolescents from the southern United States. Approximately 95% of the grandchildren versus almost 83% of southern U.S. children and adolescents had received a preventative healthcare visit in the last year, while 90% of the grandchildren had received preventive dental care, as compared to 74% for the region (Child and Adolescent Health Measurement Initiative, 2014). With regard to mental health care, just about half of the grandchildren in the present study had received services, unlike the almost 57% of southern respondents. Additionally, grandmothers in the current study were almost two times more likely to report that their grandchildren had a limiting condition, as compared to a national sample of children in relative care (Billing et al., 2002). Based on these findings, while grandchildren may not be uniformly compromised in terms of their physical health (Solomon and Marx, 1995), it does appear that a portion of grandchildren may be experiencing less-than-optimal health and may be in need of physical and mental health services (Billing et al., 2002; Bramlett and Blumberg, 2007). Practitioners can assist grandfamilies in this regard by providing custodial grandparents with needed medical and mental health referrals and encouraging grandparents to seek pre-ventative health care for their grandchildren.

The findings from this study also demonstrate the value of an ecological (Bronfenbrenner, 1979) perspective in understanding individual, family, and contextual factors influencing grandchildren's health. Specifically, as suggested by previous research with general populations of adolescents (Bardone et al., 1998; Naicker et al., 2013), the findings from this study support the linkages between grandchildren's behavior problems and their health and healthcare utilization. With grandchildren being at increased risk for psychological and behavioral problems (Billing et al., 2002; Smith and Palmieri, 2007), these youth may also be at risk for health problems, especially as they transition into young adulthood. This appears to be especially true for adolescents experiencing internalizing behavior problems, as depression has been consistently linked to difficulties with emotion regulation and compromised physical health (Repetti et al., 2002). Relatedly, in the present study, the positive association between grandchildren's emotion regulation and physical health provides further support for the notion that emotion regulation may be an important mechanism in explaining the influence of personal, familial, and environmental stressors on grandchildren's health and well-being (Repetti et al., 2002).

Regarding the implications of these findings, practitioners should provide interventions that teach grandchildren effective strategies for regulating difficult emotions. Additionally, practitioners should be attentive to internalizing behavior problems among grandchildren and work to address these problems via individual and family therapy. Grandparents could also be taught the linkages among physical and mental health, the importance of effective emotion regulation, and how to identify when their grandchildren might need professional help. Future research with children being raised by grandparents should continue to explore the role of emotion regulation as a potential mediator and moderator of the relationship between stressors or risk factors and grandchildren's physical and mental health. Further examination of the link between behavior problems and physical health would also be valuable.

In the present study, better grandmother physical health was associated with more optimal grandchild health. Custodial grandparents are often at risk for compromised physical health (Baker and Silverstein, 2008; Hughes et al., 2007; Minkler and Fuller-Thomson, 1999; Musil et al., 2010; Roberto et al., 2008). Given the relationship between the health of caregivers and their children (Case and Paxson, 2002; Waters et al., 2000), grandchildren's health appears to be influenced by the quality of their larger environments (Bronfenbrenner, 1979); thus, attending to the health of custodial grandparents is important when trying to support the optimal health and development of adolescents being raised by grandparents. In this regard, practitioners can remind custodial grandparents of the importance of monitoring and maintaining their own health, setting healthy examples for their grandchildren, and obtaining needed preventive healthcare services. Grandparents can also be connected to options for low-cost health insurance and medical services, if affording health care is a source of difficulty. Future research can also continue to explore the intersection between grandparent and grandchild health.

With regard to family and demographic characteristics, in contrast to a number of other studies (Billing et al., 2002; Bramlett and Blumberg, 2007), in the present study, household income and family resources were not consistently related to grandchildren's health or healthcare utilization. This is surprising, since poverty often explains much of the variation in grandparent and grandchild outcomes (Billing et al., 2002; Hughes et al., 2007), and grandfamilies often struggle financially (Hayslip and Kaminski, 2005). The lack of association in the present study could be because the sample was constrained to grandfamilies and, therefore, lacked the economic variation of a more general population. Also in contrast to previous research (e.g., Solomon and Marx, 1995), female grandchildren in the present study self-reported worse physical health. This finding may reflect the fact that the granddaughters in this particular sample appear to be particularly "at risk," as reflected by their clinical levels of internalizing and externalizing behavior problems, which have been linked to compromised physical health (Bardone et al., 1998; Naicker et al., 2013). With regard to grandmother marital status, having a married grandmother was predictive of poorer self-reported grandchild health. In other literature, single grandparenting has been associated with negative health outcomes for grand-children (Solomon and Marx, 1995), perhaps as a reflection of financial or parenting stress. While the explanation for this finding is not readily apparent, it does highlight the complex nature of grandchildren's physical health and how it is ultimately influenced by numerous elements within the grandchild's larger environment. Finally, results confirm previous research suggesting that racial/ethnic minority grandchildren may be at a disadvantage in terms of healthcare utilization (Agency for Healthcare Research and Quality, 2011). Future research should continue to examine and tease apart those elements of the larger environment, including family structure and family resources, which are most influential in terms of grandchildren's health and healthcare utilization.

Conclusion

Although this study is not without limitations, including the relatively small sample size and the fact that the overall study was not designed to focus specifically on grandchildren's health, the findings provide valuable insights about the health and healthcare utilization of adolescents being raised by grandparents. While a proportion of grandchildren appear to be healthy, there are grandchildren who are already experiencing negative health outcomes or may be at risk for future health problems related to personal and ecological factors such as emotional dysregulation, internalizing and externalizing behavior problems, or their grandparents' own health problems. Implications of the findings include the need to identify grandchildren most at risk for negative health outcomes and to provide grandfamilies with strategies and services to minimize the impact of risk factors and optimize grandchild health.

Acknowledgment

This research was supported by "A Support Program for Innovative Research Strategies" (ASPIRES) grant from Virginia Tech, Blacksburg, VA.

References

Achenbach, T. M. and Rescorla, L. A. 2001. *Manual for the ASEBA School-Age Forms & Profiles.* Burlington, VT: University of Vermont.

Agency for Healthcare Research and Quality. 2011. *Child and adolescent health care: Selected findings from the 2010 National Healthcare Quality and Disparities Report.* Rockville, MD: Agency for Healthcare Research and Quality. Available at: http://www.ahrq.gov/research/findings/nhqrdr/nhqrdr10/children.pdf

Baker, L. A. and Silverstein, M. 2008. Preventive health behaviors among grandmothers raising grandchildren. *The Journals of Gerontology: Social Sciences,* 63B(5): S304-S311.

Bardone, A. M., Moffitt, T. E., Caspi, A., Dickson, N., Stanton, W. R., and Silva, P. A. 1998. Adult physical health outcomes of adolescent girls with conduct disorder, depression, and anxiety. *Journal of the American Academy of Child and Adolescent Psychiatry,* 37(6): 594-601.

Billing, A., Ehrle, J., and Kortenkamp, K. 2002. *Children Cared for by Relatives: What Do We Know about Their Well-Being? New Federalism* (Policy Brief B-46). Washington, DC: The Urban Institute.

Bramlett, M. D. and Blumberg, S. J. 2007. Family structure and children's physical and mental health. *Health Affairs,* 26(2): 549-558.

Bronfenbrenner, U. 1979. *The ecology of human development: Experiments by nature and design.* Cambridge, MA: Harvard University Press.

Case, A. and Paxson, C. 2002. Parental behavior and child health. *Health Affairs,* 21(2): 164-178.

Centers for Disease Control and Prevention. 2008. National Health Interview Survey. Washington, DC: Centers for Disease Control and Prevention. Available at: http://www.cdc.gov/nchs/hdi.htm

Child and Adolescent Health Measurement Initiative. 2014. *National Survey of Children's Health.* Portland, OR: The Data Resource Center for Child and Adolescent Health. Available at: http://childhealthdata.org/browse/survey

Dunst, C. J. and Lee, H. E. 1987. Measuring the adequacy of resources in households with young children. *Child: Care, Health, and Development,* 13(2): 111-125.

Goodman, C. C. and Silverstein, M. 2006. Grandmothers raising grandchildren: Ethnic and racial differences in well-being among custodial and coparenting families. *Journal of Family Issues,* 27(11): 1605-1626.

Hayslip, B. and Kaminski, P. 2005. Custodial grandchildren. In G. G. Bear and K. M. Minke (Eds.), *Children's Needs III: Understanding and Addressing the Needs of Children* (pp. 771-782). Washington, DC: National Association of School Psychologists.

Hayslip, B. and Smith, G. C. 2013. *Resilient grandparent caregivers: A strengths-based perspective.* New York, NY: Routledge.

Hayslip, B., Shore, R. J., Henderson, C. E., and Lambert, P. L. 1998. Custodial grandparenting and the impact of grandchildren with problems on role satisfaction and role meaning. *Journal of Gerontology: Social Sciences,* 53B(3): S164-S173.

Hughes, M. E., Waite, L. J., LaPierre, T. A., and Luo, Y. 2007. All in the family: The impact of caring for grandchildren on grandparents' health. *Journal of Gerontology: Social Sciences,* 62B(2): S108-S119.

Keene, J. R. and Batson, C. D. 2010. Under one roof: A review of research on intergenerational coresidence and multigenerational households in the United States. *Sociology Compass,* 4(8): 642-657.

Kreider, R. M. and Ellis, R. 2011. *Living arrangements of children: 2009* (Current Population Reports, P70-P126). Washington, DC: United States Census Bureau. Available at: http://www.census.gov/prod/2011pubs/p70-126.pdf

Minkler, M. and Fuller-Thomson, E. 1999. The health of grandparents raising grandchildren: Results of a national study. *American Journal of Public Health,* 89(9): 1384-1389.

Minkler, M., Fuller-Thomson, E., Miller, D., and Driver, D. 1997. Depression in grandparents raising grandchildren: Results of a national longitudinal study. *Archives of Family Medicine,* 6(5): 445-452.

Murphey, D., Cooper, M., and Moore, K. A. 2012. *Grandparents living with children: State-level data from the American Community Survey.* Bethesda, MD: Child Trends. Available at: http://www.childtrends.org/wp-content/uploads/2012/10/Child_Trends-2012_10_01_RB_Grandchildren.pdf

Musil, C. M., Gordon, N. L., Warner, C. B., Zauszniewski, J. A., Standing, T., and Wykle, M. 2010. Grandmothers and caregiving to grandchildren: Continuity, change, and outcomes over 24 months. *The Gerontologist,* 51(1): 86-100.

Naicker, K., Galambos, N. L., Zeng, Y., Senthilselvan, A., and Colman, I. 2013. Social, demographic, and health outcomes in the 10 years following adolescent depression. *Journal of Adolescent Health,* 52(5): 533-538.

Office of Adolescent Health. 2014. *Physical health and nutrition.* Rockville, MD: Office of Adolescent Health. Available at: http://www.hhs.gov/ash/oah/adolescent-health-topics/physical-health-and-nutrition/

Pew Charitable Trusts. 2007. *Time for reform: Support relatives in providing foster care and permanent families for children.* Philadelphia, PA: The Pew Charitable Trusts. Available at: http://www.pewtrusts.org/our_work_report_detail.aspx?id= 48986

Pew Research Center. 2010. *Since the Great Recession, more children raised by grand-parents.* Philadelphia, PA: The Pew Charitable Trusts. Available at: http://pew research.org/pubs/1724/sharp-increase-children-with-grandparents

Repetti, R. L., Taylor, S. E., and Seeman, T. E. 2002. Risky families: Family social environments and the mental and physical health of offspring. *Psychological Bulletin,* 128(2): 330-366.

Roberto, K. A., Dolbin-MacNab, M. L., and Finney, J. W. 2008. Promoting the health of grandmothers parenting young grandchildren. In B. Hayslip and P. Kaminski (Eds.), *Parenting the custodial grandchild* (pp. 75-89). New York, NY: Springer.

Shields, A. and Cicchetti, D. 1997. Emotion regulation among school-age children: The development and validation of a new criterion Q-Sort Scale. *Developmental Psychology,* 33(6): 906-916.

Smith, G. C. and Dolbin-MacNab, M. L. 2013. The role of negative and positive care-giving appraisals in key outcomes for custodial grandmothers and grandchildren. In B. Hayslip and G. C. Smiths (Eds.), *Resilient grandparent caregivers: A strengths-based perspective*) pp. 3-24). New York, NY: Routledge.

Smith, G. C. and Palmieri, P. A. 2007. Risk of psychological difficulties among children raised by custodial grandparents. *Psychiatric Services,* 58(10): 303-310.

Smith, G. C., Palmieri, P. A., Hancock, G. R., and Richardson, R. A. 2008. Custodial grandmothers' psychological distress, dysfunctional parenting, and grand-children's adjustment. *International Journal of Aging and Human Development,* 67(4): 327-357.

Solomon, J. C. and Marx, J. 1995. To grandmother's house we go: Health and school adjustment of children raised solely by grandparents. *The Gerontologist,* 35(3): 386-394.

Spear, B. A. 2002. Adolescent growth and development. *Journal of the American Dietetic Association,* 102(3 Suppl): S23-S29.

Strickland, B. B., Jones, J. R., Ghandour, R. M., Kogan, M. D., and Newacheck, P. W. 2011. The medical home: Health care access and impact for children and youth in the United States. *Pediatrics,* 127(4): 604-611.

U.S. Census Bureau. 2007. *Census regions and divisions of the United States.* Washington, DC: U.S. Census Bureau. Available at: http://www.census.gov/geo/www/us_ regdiv.pdf

Ware, J. E., Kosinski, M., and Dewey, J. E. 2000. *How to Score Version Two of the SF-36 Health Survey.* Lincoln, RI: Quality Metric.

Ware, J. E. 1976. Scale for measuring general health perceptions. *Health Services Research,* Winter: 396-415.

Ware, J. E. and Sherbourne, C. D. 1992. The MOS 36-Item Short-Form Health Survey (SF-36): I. Conceptual framework and item selection. *Medical Care,* 30(6): 473-483.

Waters, E., Doyle, J., Wolfe, R., Wright, M., Wake, M., and Salmon, L. 2000. Influence of parental gender and self-reported health and illness on parent-reported child health. *Pediatrics,* 106(6): 1422-1428.

http://dx.doi.org/10.2190/GITC9

CHAPTER 9

Young Adults' Perceptions of Living With Their Grandparents During Childhood

Laura D. Pittman, Micah Ioffe,
and Christine R. Keeports

Grandparents are often overlooked as key members of the family system (Bengston, 2001), but a growing literature indicates they can be influential in their grandchildren's development (e.g., Dunifon, 2013; Silverstein, Giarrusso, and Bengtson, 1998). Much of this research has focused on whether grandchildren live in the same household as a grandparent in either multigenerational households (e.g., Gleeson, Strozier, and Littlewood, 2011) or in custodial grandparent households (e.g., Pinazo-Hernandis and Tompkins, 2009). However, typically in these studies it is just the presence or absence of the grandparent in the home that is considered and not other characteristics of the grandparents' involvement. Research has considered specific aspects of grandparent involvement when the grandparents are not living in the home. For example, how close grandchildren feel to their grandparents or the level of emotional support they receive has been found to be important (e.g., Sheehan and Petrovic, 2008; Van Ranst, Verschueren, and Marcoen, 1995). The level of grandparents' investment through time and money also has sometimes been considered (e.g., Coall and Hertwig, 2013; Haxton and Harknett, 2009). Mentioned, but rarely examined, are how grandparents may serve as teachers of family traditions, morals, and values (Mahne and Huxhold, 2012; Silverstein et al., 1998). Thus, considering whether these and other specific factors are viewed as important in both multigenerational and custodial grandparent households will help increase our understanding of how living in these households influences children and adolescents as they grow up.

Census data suggests it is becoming increasingly common for children to live with their grandparents. Between 2008 and 2010, about 5.2 million children in the United States (7%) lived with their grandparents, which is an increase from previous years (Murphey, Cooper, and Moore, 2012). About two-thirds of these households are multigenerational households, where both the parent and grand-parent live in the home, while the remaining one third are custodial grandparent households, where the parent generation is not in the home (Vespa, Lewis, and Kreider, 2013). Fuller-Thomson, Minkler, and Driver (1997), however, suggest these statistics are only snapshots of current living situations and do not reflect the number of children who have ever lived with a grandparent. Specifically, they found that 11% of grandparents indicated in the National Survey of Families and Households (NSFH) that they have had primary responsibility for raising a grandchild for a period of at least 6 months. Given these trends, there is a growing literature considering how living with grandparents may influence the grandchildren's well-being.

Multigenerational Households

Studies using nationally representative samples have found both children and adolescents living in multigenerational households fare better academically and psychologically than those who are living with a single parent (Barbarin and Soler, 1993; DeLeire and Kalil, 2002). However, samples focusing on specific populations have more mixed findings. For example, a longitudinal study of low-income families found adolescents reporting lower internalizing symptoms after consistently living in a multigenerational household compared to those not living in multigenerational households (Pittman, 2007); yet, preschool-aged children in multigenerational households were reported to have worse socio-emotional outcomes over time than those not living in multigenerational households (Pittman and Boswell, 2007). Studies looking at young children with adolescent mothers also had mixed results. Some studies have found that children of young mothers coresiding with their grandmothers have better cognitive and socioemotional outcomes compared to children of young mothers who live alone (e.g., Furstenberg, Brooks-Gunn, and Morgan, 1987; Leadbeater and Bishop, 1994); however, other studies have found the reverse with poorer cognitive and physical development in toddlers of adolescent mothers in multigenerational households (e.g., Black and Nitz, 1996). Some have suggested that other factors need to be considered to understand the influence of living in multigenerational households, including the reasons these households form (Pittman, 2007) and the quality of the relationships between parents and grandparents (Coley and Chase-Lansdale, 1998; Kalil, Spencer, Spieker, and Gilchrist, 1998).

Custodial Grandparents

The interest in children being raised by custodial grandparents has increased dramatically in the last few decades. Solomon and Marx (1995), using the 1988 National Child Health Supplement of the National Health Interview Survey, found no differences in health or behavior problems between children raised solely by grandparents and those living with two biological parents. However, children who are living with custodial grandparents because they have a kinship care arrangement through foster care, not surprisingly, appear to have higher rates of behavioral and socioemotional problems than children not in the child welfare system (e.g., Dubowitz, Feigelman, Harrington, Starr, Zuravin, and Sawyer, 1994), but fewer behavioral and socioemotional problems than those placed in the regular foster care system (Brooks and Barth, 1998). Among low-income families, young children living with custodial grandmothers fared worse academically compared to other low-income children, but were similar with regard to their socioemotional outcomes (Pittman and Boswell, 2007). However, among adolescents, living with custodial grandmothers was linked to more externalizing problems over time (Pittman, 2007). Like with multigenerational households, the reasoning as to why children live with the grandparents without a parent present and the dynamics within the family may be influential in these outcomes.

This Study

While much of the previous research has focused on the outcomes of children and adolescents who live in these specific household types, less has been done to consider the family dynamics and characteristics of these households. Also, much of the previous research has focused on specific at-risk groups like low-income families and families with drug-addicted or young mothers (e.g., Eshbaugh and Luze, 2007; Gordon, Chase-Lansdale, and Brooks-Gunn, 2004; Minkler, Roe, and Robertson-Beckley, 1994), which may limit our understanding of what children experience when living with grandparents. Therefore, to better understand the impact of living with grandparents, qualitative interviews with young adults were conducted to identify and better understand the factors that influence the grandchildren in these types of households. In this study, young adults were recruited to participate if they had ever lived with a grandparent, without limiting the reason for household formation. Thus, a broader sample of children who had lived in either multigenerational or custodial grandparent households was collected. Specifically, we were interested in getting a better understanding of why these households formed and gathering young adults' perceptions of the positive and negative aspects of these experiences. Our hope is with this more nuanced information future research can consider how specific aspects of these experiences may influence children and adolescents' psychological and behavioral outcomes.

Method

Sample

A total of 82 young adults were recruited through an undergraduate research participant pool at a large midwestern university and received course credit for participating. Only students who had ever lived with a grandparent for 1 month or longer were eligible for the study. All participants were between the ages of 18 and 27 years ($M = 19.49$, $SD = 1.59$). See Table 1 for additional participant characteristics.

Table 1. Participant Characteristics ($N = 82$)

Characteristic	Percentage
Gender	
Male	40
Female	60
Ethnicity	
Caucasian	32
African American	37
Hispanic American	10
Asian American	9
Biracial	7
Other	5
Year in college	
Freshmen	42
Sophomore	38
Junior	16
Senior	4
Parental marital status	
Married/Cohabiting	49
Divorced or separated	25
Never married and not currently living together	26
Parental education	
Mother	
Less than high school	6
High school diploma	64
College degree	30
Father	
Less than high school	10
High school diploma	59
College degree	31
Family's standard of living	
Meager conditions or poverty	15
Enough money for basic essentials	33
Comfortable	49
More than enough money	3

Procedures

Experimenters conducted a qualitative interview with each participant. Each interview was audio-recorded and later transcribed for analyses. Consent for participation and audio recording of the interviews was obtained. Interviews started with gaining information about the living arrangement with the grandparent. For example, questions probed about the type of grandparent with whom they lived, the duration of time, and participants' ages while living with grandparents. Additionally, participants were asked about why these households formed (i.e., "What led to this living arrangement with your grandparent?"). Other questions explored participants' perceptions of their relationship with their grandparent during different time points of living together (i.e., before, during, and after) and currently, as was applicable. Participants were also asked about aspects of the living arrangement that they enjoyed or liked as well as things they disliked about living with their grandparent. Additionally, participants were asked about their parents' relationships with their grandparent and whether or not they thought the living arrangement had helped their parents. Finally, participants were asked about any financial and/or emotional support that grandparents had provided while living together. The same set of questions was asked again for each distinct period when they had lived with a grandparent. After all interviews were completed and transcribed, a coding scheme was developed based on themes presented in participant responses. Two trained research assistants independently coded when the identified themes were present in each interview. Discrepancies in coding were resolved in weekly meetings with the lead coder.

Grandparent Information

Most participants ($n = 54$) reported only one distinct period when they lived with a grandparent, but some reported two ($n = 20$) or three ($n = 8$) periods. Thus, 118 periods of living with a grandparent were identified. Table 2 presents details about these periods of living with grandparents. In approximately two-thirds of these periods a parent also lived in the household (i.e., multigenerational household), with no parent being present in the remaining one-third of periods (i.e., custodial grandparent household). As would be expected (e.g., Mahne and Huxhold, 2012), participants more often reported having lived during these time periods with their maternal grandparents, including sometimes with their great-grandmother. In contrast, many fewer participants indicated having periods where they lived with their paternal grandparents, and none reported living with only their paternal grandfather. On rare occasions, participants lived with a combination of maternal and paternal grandparents at the same time.

Participants reported living with their grandparents at various points during their development, although few lived with their grandparents consistently across their childhood. It was more common to live with their grandparents when they were young.

Table 2. Grandparent Household Information and Participants'
Developmental Period When Living with Grandparents

	Percentage
Type of household[a]	
Multigenerational	68
Custodial grandparent	32
Type of grandparents in household[a]	
Maternal grandparents only	
Maternal grandmother and grandfather	29
Maternal grandmother only	36
Maternal grandfather only	2
Maternal great-grandmother only	5
Maternal grandmother and step-grandfather	2
Maternal grandmother and great-grandmother	2
Paternal grandparents only	
Paternal grandmother and grandfather	9
Paternal grandmother only	10
Paternal grandfather only	0
Paternal great-grandmother only	1
Both maternal and paternal grandparents	
Maternal and paternal grandparents (all four grandparents)	1
Maternal grandparents and paternal grandmother	2
Paternal grandparents and maternal grandmother	1
Developmental Periods When Ever Lived with Grandparent[b]	
Infancy and preschool	67
Elementary school	73
Middle school	38
High school	57
College	24
Majority of life	16

[a]The sample size for this household characteristic is the number of time periods participants had lived with a grandparent ($n = 118$).

[b]The sample size for this participant's characteristic is 82. Each percentage point represents the number of participants out of 82 who lived with a grandparent during each developmental period.

Reasons for Household Formation

Much of the existing research has focused on multigenerational households and custodial grandparent households that have formed because of a specific reason like teen parenthood (e.g., Furstenberg et al., 1987). In addition, several large-scale studies document that grandchildren have lived with their grandparents, but have not asked about the reason for the household formation because the grandparent coresidence was not a focus of the original study (e.g., Fuller-Thomson et al., 1997). In this study, participants reported on the reasons households were formed with grandparents, based on their recollections or what they had been told (i.e., they typically were not part of the decision-making process). As shown in Figure 1, in this less specific sample, multiple reasons were given by participants and ranged from the needs of the younger generation for the help of the grandparents to the needs of the grandparent for help from the younger generation.

Grandparent Help

Broadly, the most common reason grandchildren had lived with grandparents during their childhood was so that grandparents could help the parent and child generations. For example, a 19-year-old African American female who lived with her maternal grandmother stated, "It was easier that way so my mom can work because she worked three jobs." Included within this broad category are multiple specific reasons, which often were mentioned simultaneously. The most common specific way grandparents helped was through the provision of childcare. As stated by a 19-year-old Asian American female who lived with her maternal grandmother, "Because both of my parents worked a lot, it was a way for my mom not to have to get a babysitter." Also, participants mentioned that their parents

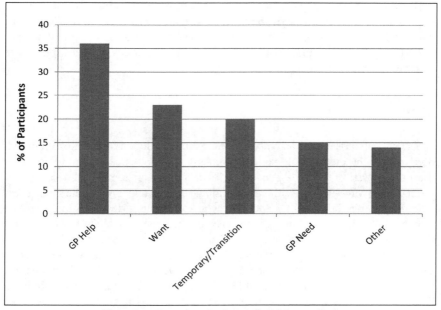

Figure 1. Reasons for household formation.

were young when they were first born or wanted to pursue more education. A 19-year-old Hispanic American female shared, "They were fairly young. So it was just more convenient [to live with my paternal grandparents] 'cause my dad was going to college [and] my mom was working." The need of grandparent help was more often raised by those who had lived in custodial grandparent households (58%) as compared to multigenerational households (26%). This was particularly true when the specific reason given was so that parents could seek an education (i.e., 16% for custodial grandparent households as compared to 0% of multigenerational households).

Financial concerns of the parent generation also were reported as a reason grandparents lived with their grandchildren. For example, an 18-year-old African American female who moved in with her maternal great-grandmother indicated, "We didn't have anywhere else to go." Forming a multigenerational household was sometimes clearly viewed as mutually beneficial. One 20-year-old biracial male who lived with his paternal grandmother stated, "Financially my mother and grandmother couldn't support themselves, so they came together for financial reasons."

Grandparents also stepped in because of concerns about the grandchildren's well-being when parents were addicted to drugs or alcohol, struggling with mental illness, or just irresponsible. For example, a 20-year-old biracial female described it as follows: "My mom was irresponsible. That is why we lived with my great grandma. . . . [My mom] would rather go out than pay her bills." A 19-year-old African American male, who lived with his paternal grandparents, summed it up best by stating that grandparents can sometimes provide children with "the most stable environment." Thus, the most common reason for grandchildren to be living with their grandparents was when grandparents were stepping in to help the family.

Want

The second most common reason participants mentioned for living with grandparents was the desire to do so. Sometimes this was expressed as the desire of the parent, such as the 19-year-old African American female who said, "My mom had always stayed with my grandma, so me and my brother just came in." Other times it was the grandchild who expressed a desire to live with the grandparent, often after having lived part of the time with them before. "I just liked staying there," reported a 20-year-old African American female who had lived with her paternal grandparents. However, living together was not always long term, but was reported to be an extended vacation that they both desired. For example, a 19-year-old biracial female shared that her maternal grandmother "just came to visit over the summer." Thus, living with grandparents was not always because of need.

Transitions

The next most common reason grandchildren lived with grandparents was because of transitions in the family's life. This included times when parents were going through a divorce, as well as other transitions like when families were moving between homes and had a few months without a house. For example, one 19-year-old Caucasian male shared, "My mom and my biological dad broke up . . . my mom moved in with my grandma and it's just always been the same." Another 19-year-old Caucasian female who had lived with her maternal grandparents reported, "My dad passed away that summer and it was just easier for our family if we just stayed with our grandparents at the time." Thus, when families had a short-term need, they often would turn to grandparents for help.

Grandparent Need

Although less commonly reported, sometimes it was the needs of the grandparent that led families to form multigenerational households. In fact, only multigenerational households were formed because of the needs of the grandparents, which is not surprising given the parent generation, not the grandchild generation, was likely providing the help to the grandparent. The reported specific needs of the grandparent included health issues of the grandparent, concerns about the safety of the neighborhood in which the grandparent lived, and grandparent financial instability. As shared by an 18-year-old Caucasian female about her maternal grandmother, "She just came to live with us because she was really sick. She had a bad case of pneumonia, and . . . she was just getting worse and worse and worse up until the time she had to be hospitalized." Sometimes grandparents lived only temporarily with the family as they sought other care, like the 19-year-old Caucasian male described about his paternal great-grandmother:

> Yeah, she got too old. She kept on crashing her car and saying people kept hitting her, when it was her hitting cars. So we decided it was time to move her into a home and it had a real long waiting list to get in; so that's why she moved in.

Thus, while less common, households sometimes were formed because of the needs of the grandparent. It is likely that these three-generation households that were formed because of the needs of the grandparent are quite different than those that form because of the needs of the younger generations.

Other Reasons

Participants also provided other reasons that were too few in number to provide meaningful groups. Four participants noted it was their safety that led to the household being formed. For example, a 19-year-old African American female who lived with her maternal grandmother explained, "Our house . . . was kind of in a bad neighborhood and people were breaking in. So we went back to my grandma's house until my mom found a better house in a better . . . community." Others indicated it was a cultural expectation to live in multigenerational households. For example, one 18-year-old Hispanic male indicated, "It was kind of the custom; it was like the tradition . . . to live with your dad's parents when you get married." Similarly, an 18-year-old female who lived with her maternal grandparents shared, "Since we are Hispanic, we are all really close. . . . [Our] family wanted to all be together and my parents thought it was a very good opportunity to have the whole family together under one household." Considering the multiple reasons given, research that has focused on just specific subgroups and then generalizes to a wider sample of households with grandparents is likely missing much within group variation.

Emerging Themes

As participants shared their experiences of living with their grandparents, several themes emerged. Most commonly, positive aspects of their relationship with the grandparent were shared including enhanced relationships with grandparents, decreased family stress, and improved financial resources. However, intergenerational conflict also was raised where family members from different generations did not always have common views about family issues. The following sections describe these themes in more detail.

Relationships with Grandparents

As shown in Figure 2, many participants mentioned how living with their grandparent improved the quality of their relationship with them. This included reporting that living with their grandparent led to having a closer relationship with them or even viewing their grandparent as one of their primary parents. While sometimes they mentioned their grandparent being either too strict or too lenient, they more often mentioned enjoying their time with their grandparents and learning specific skills as well as family and cultural history from them.

Closer Relationships to Grandparents

The majority of participants indicated that their relationships with their grandparents grew stronger because of living with them, regardless of the reason for household formation. For example, a 19-year-old Caucasian female described her relationship with her maternal grandfather: "I got a lot closer with him. He is actually really funny and has a good sense of humor. It was just nice seeing a different side of him that I couldn't see over the phone." Some participants felt so close to their grandparents that they felt they could talk to them about anything; some even equated them to close friends. For example, a 19-year-old African American female described her relationship with her maternal

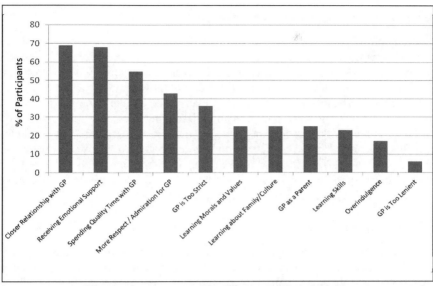

Figure 2. Themes regarding enhanced relationships
with grandparents.

grandmother: "I can say, honestly, I think we got closer. We were able to open up more. . . . I can talk to her about everything . . . me and my grandmother talk, like that's my best friend."

Receiving Emotional Support from Grandparents

Similarly, many participants also expressed that their grandparents provided them with emotional support, either offering advice or consoling them during difficult times. For example, a 19-year-old Caucasian male described his maternal grandmother as always being supportive and helpful: "I can talk to my grandma about anything. . . . When you tell her something, she takes it in a very calm and a professional demeanor and she helps me make decisions." Those who had lived in a custodial grandparent household were more likely to mention grandparents providing emotional support (84%), although the majority of those who had lived in a multigenerational household also mentioned this (60%). Among those who lived in a multigenerational household during a period of transition reported grandparents providing emotional support at particularly high rates (93%). This suggests that certain circumstances likely led to the grandchildren needing or seeking out more emotional support than other circumstances.

Spending Quality Time with Grandparents

Many participants fondly recalled spending quality time or engaging in leisure activities with their grandparents such as gardening or watching television shows. As a 19-year-old Caucasian male described his time with his paternal grandfather, "[We did] different activities I didn't always do . . . with my dad . . . more like old-school type of stuff . . . like building, like shooting bows and arrows . . . making stuff out of wood, fixing benches and stuff like that." Other activities with grandparents included quality time at home. "We [would] watch judge shows, cook, go outside and garden, plant, you know, just watching people walking past," a 20-year-old African American female shared about her maternal grandmother. This quality time likely laid the foundation for the sense of closeness that many participants reported.

More Respect and Admiration for Grandparents

A number of participants indicated that while living with grandparents, they grew to respect and admire them more than they had before living together. A 20-year-old biracial male shared about his paternal grandmother, "She influenced me a lot. She is 74 and she is still a nurse so I feel like she has to be strong. . . . Her strength and dedication to provide for her family, that's where I get my motivation from." Another participant, an 18-year-old biracial female, described her admiration for her maternal great-grandmother as follows: "She wouldn't let her problems consume her. She would . . . find a way to make it better. She had a positive outlook on people. She is not judgmental. She was wise and that is what I like about her." Thus, participants got to know their grandparents in a way that they would not have without living with them.

Grandparents as Teachers

Grandparents actively teaching their grandchildren was another theme that emerged in the interviews. Several participants mentioned explicitly that their grandparents helped teach them good morals and values. For example, a 19-year-old Asian American female discussing her maternal grandparents and paternal grandmother, with whom she had lived, indicated, "All of them [grandparents], including my parents, taught me to be respectful and that family comes first." In addition, sometimes grandparents taught participants about their family or cultural history. A 19-year-old African American female expressed her appreciation for hearing her maternal grandmother's stories from the past: "I loved listening to her stories . . . I learned about history in general, because you know about the civil rights and stuff, but never get to hear about how someone lived through that [time]." Participants also mentioned that their grandparents taught them specific skills like cooking or gardening. For example, an 18-year-old Hispanic male shared how his paternal grandfather taught him important skills:

"With my grandpa, he was always trying to teach me how to do stuff on my own, like . . . this is how you fix this. I would always be trying to learn from him, to impress him." Thus, participants reported valuing what their grandparents had taught them as they lived with them.

Grandparent as a Parent

Throughout the interviews, while not specifically asked, many participants indicated that their grandparent was like a primary parent to them. They either reported them to serve as a parent instead of or in addition to their "real" parent(s), often referring to them as a "second" parent. A 20-year-old Caucasian female shared about her maternal grandmother, "[She was] definitely a parent more than a babysitter because she was just like my mom. She would set the rules. She made us clean all the time, help her out. Yeah, she was definitely a parent." Participants did sometimes indicate that the grandparent did replace the parent. For example, a 20-year-old African American female stated about her maternal grandmother, "I call her Granny, but I consider my grandmother my mother. No disrespect to my actual mother. It's just I feel my grandmother really raised me." This was frequently stated about the grandfather explicitly, especially when the participant had no interactions with their father. "I got really, really attached to them and since my dad wasn't there, he was like my father figure that I had. So there was a point where I would consider him more my dad than my real dad," shared an 18-year-old Hispanic male about his maternal grandfather. Thus, grandparents in these households often became like parents to their grandchildren, both supplementing and sometimes taking over the caregiving role of the parent.

Too Strict or Too Lenient

However, sometimes grandparents were viewed as too strict, setting limits for their grandchildren's freedom. For instance, one 20-year-old male reported about his paternal grandmother, "Sometimes when I come [home] late, I open the door carefully to sneak in, and [my grandmother is] standing in the kitchen watching me. She tells me, 'Look at your watch. What time it is?'" Participants often indicated that their grandparents became stricter when they transitioned to living in one household together, and some participants reported that their grandparents seemed stricter than their parents had ever been. In contrast, fewer participants indicated their grandparents were too lenient. One 19-year-old African American explained about her maternal grandmother, "She didn't really say no to anything . . . she let us do whatever we wanted." Thus, like parents, there was great variation in how grandparents chose to serve in the parental role—sometimes being more strict and other times being more lenient than what the grandchild would have wanted.

Overindulgence

Unrelated to parenting, participants also sometimes indicated that living with their grandparents resulted in being spoiled. One 20-year-old Hispanic female referred to herself as "a spoiled brat" after this treatment from her maternal grandmother. Another 18-year-old Hispanic female participant reported that her maternal grandfather "would buy me little treats against my parents' wishes. He would sneak some chocolate and give me some." While this special attention could be viewed as negative, the participants tended to be quite positive about the extra gifts or attention. Across all these specific themes, most participants reported enhanced relationships with grandparents while living with them.

Influences on the Household

As Figure 3 shows, participants reported living with grandparents influenced the households, both positively and negatively. Many participants found living with grandparents helped the household both financially and through having extra help to care for the needs of the family like cooking meals and providing childcare. Yet, in some households, living with the grandparent increased stress through negative interactions with the grandparent, the need to

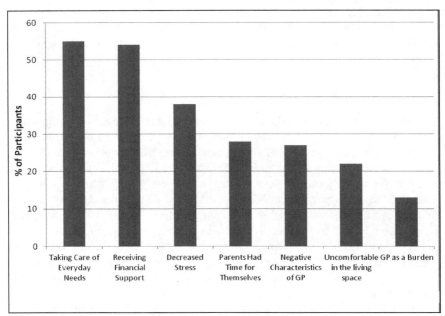

Figure 3. Themes regarding influences on the household.

care for the grandparent, or just the limitations on the physical space available to family members.

Taking Care of Everyday Needs

Many participants mentioned that grandparents eased the burden for parents of running the household by taking care of typical household chores including cooking, cleaning, and laundry. For example, an 18-year-old Asian American female stated that her maternal grandmother would take care of her and her family's needs: "[If] I would forget to do my laundry or something, she would go ahead and do it . . . she would know I didn't have time to do it [cook dinner], so she would have food for the whole family." A 19-year-old Caucasian male also explained, "She [his mother] didn't have to worry about cooking or cleaning."

Financial Support

While living with grandparents, many participants reported receiving financial support. For some participants, this came in the form of monetary gifts for nonessential items like video games and clothing. As one 21-year-old Caucasian female stated, "I get financial support from her [maternal grandmother] all the time, anything I need . . . Like anything, if I like a pair of shoes I could just tell her and she gave me the money for it." Participants also reported that their grandparents helped to pay their bills, including for school. For example, a 19-year-old African American mentioned, "They [maternal grandparents] are helping me through school now actually, [with] tuition." For some participants, grandparents seemed to be the only source of financial support for participants, especially if their parents were absent. One 20-year-old African American explained that she could only rely on her maternal grandmother for financial support: "Because my parents are addicts, you know drug addicts, so living with her I had clothes, I had food, I had everything I was supposed to have. So, yeah, she was the biggest financial support." Many participants also acknowledged that while they may not have received monetary support from grandparents, simply living in their grandparents' house allowed them or their parents to save money. An 18-year-old Hispanic female, explaining how her maternal grandparents helped out, stated, "I know that my mom always said it made things easier because we didn't have to pay for a house yet and we could save money." Thus, for many, grandparents served to ensure their grandchildren had what they physically needed.

Decreased Stress

Many participants explicitly indicated that living with their grandparents helped decrease stress in the family. For example, the stress that would have been caused by needing to find reliable childcare was removed. As shared by a 21-year-old Caucasian male who lived in a multigenerational household with his maternal grandparents: "I think it took a lot of stress off my mom just because she didn't have to worry about finding a babysitter or anything after school. She always had a place I could go and it was reliable." Easing the stress associated with financial burdens was also mentioned. As a 19-year-old African American male who had lived with his paternal grandparents stated, "It helped them [parents] out a lot 'cause until I got older, neither one of them had a lot of financial stability and my grandparents really stepped in . . . [they would] give me food, give me clothes." Related to this theme, many participants mentioned that living with grandparents helped their parents have time for themselves. As one 26-year-old Asian American female stated about living with her maternal grandparents, "It just gave them [her parents] a break probably." An 18-year-old Hispanic female who lived with her custodial maternal grandmother also described her mother: "It's taught her to pay attention to herself and get her life situated. She didn't have to worry about me. . . . If she had to raise me, me or her wouldn't be in the situation that we are in now." Thus, while many recognized grandparents helping the household through taking care of tasks and making financial contributions, many recognized how these actions helped ease the stress in the family.

Negative Characteristics of Grandparents

While the majority of things talked about were positive, some participants noted that their grandparents had negative characteristics that made living together unpleasant for the grandchild. For example, grandparents sometimes had "annoying" habits like smoking, yelling, or nagging behaviors that participants disliked. For instance, one 18-year-old African American female participant reported about her paternal grandfather, "[He] was partially deaf and I had to scream everything. That was quite annoying." Another 19-year-old Caucasian male indicated that his paternal great-grandmother would do "old lady things, like she wanted [to eat] dinner at 4 o'clock." While consistently brought up by a minority of participants, those who had lived in multigenerational households were more likely to bring up negative characteristics of the grandparent (33%) as compared to those who had lived in custodial grandparent household (16%).

Uncomfortable in Living Space

Additionally, many participants reported that they frequently felt uncomfortable in the physical living space when they cohabited with a grandparent. A 20-year-old Asian American male participant summarized this feeling by indicating about his maternal grandmother, "When you wanted to be on your own, she was always there so it was kind of awkward. . . . So we couldn't really have privacy." This feeling of being uncomfortable in the living space ranged from grandparents leaving personal items lying around the house to grandchildren who felt uncomfortable because they did not have a permanent bedroom. As one

18-year-old Caucasian female participant reported, "Living there [with her paternal step-grandmother] was like renting [a room]." Thus, for some, living with a grandparent created challenges that would not otherwise have been present.

Grandparent as Burden

Finally, some of the time participants indicated that living with a grandparent was a burden to the household. One 27-year-old biracial, female reported that her paternal grandmother could not take care of herself and that "It seems like I had to take on a parenting role, especially if my mom was out of the room 'cause [my grandmother] had to be watched. It was intense—you never knew what was going to happen next." Many participants who acknowledged feeling as if their grandparent was a burden typically also indicated that their grandparent was ill or unable to live independently. Specifically, 50% of participants who had reported a multigenerational household being formed because of the grandparents' needs mentioned that they viewed the grandparent as a burden.

Intergenerational Issues

As shown in Figure 4, many participants raised themes related to how living with grandparents influenced their interactions with their own parents as well as their observations of parent-grandparent interactions. In addition, in a small

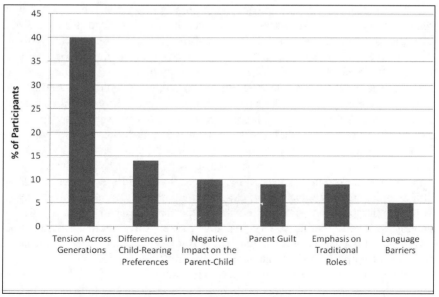

Figure 4. Themes regarding intergenerational issues.

number of households, generational differences in beliefs and language influenced their interactions with their grandparents.

Tension Across Generations

In each interview, participants were asked what kind of relationship their parents had with the grandparent with whom they lived. In response, a large minority of participants mentioned that there was often conflict between the parent and grandparent. For example, a 19-year-old Caucasian male indicated that his maternal grandmother and his mother "clashed a lot. . . . They're both dominant personalities. I guess you would say they both run the house, and you get two people that run the house in the same house [and] they don't know who's running the house anymore." Participants also noted differences in the expectations between their parents and grandparents about how they should behave both in and out of the home. For example, a 22-year-old Caucasian male stated, "It was just weird going from the rules of my parents to my [maternal] grandparents and back to my parents." Thus, for the grandchild, it could be confusing and frustrating. In fact, some of these families had parent-grandparent conflicts about how to raise the grandchild. An 18-year-old Hispanic female shared about her maternal grandmother and mother, "They just never saw eye to eye about how to raise me. . . . My mom thought I could use some more leniency and that my grandma was too strict."

Others noted the negative impact living with their grandparents had on their relationship with their parents. For some it was their preference to spend time with their grandparents that strained the relationship with their parents. A 20-year-old African American female stated, "I always wanted to go over there [to my paternal grandmother's house]. I didn't want to be with my parents, so it made them feel bad." The tension with the parent-child relationship also could be rooted in how the grandparents perceived their parent. For example, a 20-year-old Caucasian female stated, "She [maternal grandmother] never spoke nice about my dad, ever, so I grew up thinking my dad was this horrible person my whole life. I would go over there and I would not want that much to do with him."

In addition, just the living situation, and not what was said by grandparents, was perceived to make parents feel guilty. As an 18-year-old biracial female stated about living with her maternal great-grandmother, "My mother was always a good mother but she probably felt inside that she was bad because I wasn't staying with her." Similarly, a 19-year-old African American male shared about living with his paternal grandparents, "As I've gotten older, I can tell it had a toll on her [mother] . . . She kinda thinks that I think that she gave me up . . . That's something that haunts her 'cause she knows she did it for my benefit." Not surprisingly, more participants who lived with custodial grandparents, where the parents were not in the home, reported perceiving their parents feeling guilty as compared to those living in multigenerational households where the parents were present (21% vs. 3%, respectively).

Generational Differences

Less frequently participants pointed out challenges created by generational differences between grandparents, parents, and themselves. This included grandparents who emphasized traditional gender roles, which parents or grandchildren sometimes did not agree with. For example, an 18-year-old Hispanic female stated about her maternal grandfather, "My grandfather is very old fashion, like he . . . thinks that a girl should stay in the kitchen and a girl shouldn't go to school and my father doesn't agree with . . . that stuff." In addition, a few participants noted that there were language barriers limiting their interactions with their grandparents. For example, an 18-year-old African female indicated she did "not really [have] a relationship with her [paternal grandmother] because she didn't speak English."

Discussion

Young adult grandchildren reflecting on living with grandparents in their childhood were generally positive about these experiences, perceiving more emotional support and feeling closer to their grandparents compared to what they thought their peers who had not lived with a grandparent had experienced growing up. While other studies have suggested grandchildren often report feeling close to their grandparents and benefiting from their emotional support (e.g., Elder and Conger, 2000), the degree to which this is true in this sample suggests the centrality of this relationship for these young adults. Additionally, about one-quarter spontaneously reported that their grandparent was like a parent to them, whether their parents were in the home or not. Given most of these young adults did not live with their grandparent throughout their childhood, asking youth about their grandparents even when they are not living with them may be important, especially when identifying potential mentors or confidants that may help children in times of difficulty.

In addition to the emotional bonds formed while living with grandparents, the majority of participants reported the importance of the grandparent providing instrumental help both through financial support as well as through help with everyday chores. Based on these interviews, it is clear that in many families, the grandparents have stepped in at times of need. However, often the grandparent help is temporary, with much fluidity in the living arrangements. In addition to the benefits from living in a household that likely had more financial resources than it would have had without the presence of the grandparent, young adults mentioned how the provision of this kind of help decreased the stress in the household, helping their parents focus on other important goals like employment or furthering their education rather than needing to worry about things like childcare. While some have taken an intergenerational approach to understanding the influence of grandparents on their grandchildren (e.g., Tomlin, 1998), more research is needed to consider how grandparents may indirectly influence grandchildren through their influence on the parent generation.

While the majority of comments were positive in nature, young adults also acknowledged that they sometimes observed tension between grandparent and parent, especially related to approaches to parenting or the handling of daily chores. In addition, when households were formed because of the needs of the grandparent, grandchildren often mentioned they viewed the grandparent as a burden. Finally, some mentioned how their close relationships with grandparents negatively impacted their relationships with their parents. Thus, while young adults usually reported many more benefits than costs, recognizing these negative aspects and considering how they may be impacting grandchildren may be important. Further research is needed to consider both their impact and possible ways that could support these families to minimize the possible tensions in the intergenerational relationships.

Future research will want to continue to consider the type of grandparent household grandchildren live in (i.e., multigenerational households vs. custodial grandparent household) as some notable differences did emerge. For example, young adults who had lived in a custodial grandparent household were more likely to report both emotional support received from their grandparent as well as the perception that their parents felt guilty about this arrangement. However, few differences in themes emerged based on the reason households were formed among multigenerational households (i.e., wanting to live together, the need for the grandparent to help, or the family being in the midst of a transition). Yet households formed because of the needs of the grandparent did have more frequent negative themes such as the perception that the grandparent was a burden. However, the reason for household formation was gathered through the young adult, who may not be fully aware of the reason. Thus, further research gaining the parents or grandparents' perception of why grandparents lived in the household may provide additional insights.

While this sample was not representative of all young adults who have lived with their grandparents, and likely are faring better than the general population based on their enrollment at a university, getting a broader understanding of these experiences outside of specific at-risk samples is important. However, compared to census data that suggests living with grandparents is more common under the age of 6 years than at older ages (Murphey et al., 2012), our sample reported living with a grandparent just as frequently during elementary school as when younger and almost as often during high school. Investigating how children's experiences of living with grandparents is similar or different across development may be helpful for gaining further understanding of these processes. In addition, given the retrospective reporting, participants' reports may have been biased by their current circumstances. Thus, more real-time documentation of experiences living with grandparents would add to the literature. This study highlights young adults' perceptions of the benefits and costs of living with grandparents. Further research considering the link between each of these aspects and how grandparents may influence grandchildren, rather than the type of grandparent household (i.e., custodial grandparent household, multigenerational household), would further research in this area. Overall, while there appear to be a few negative aspects identified about living with grandparents, most young adults reported multiple positive aspects of living with their grandparents that likely have influenced their development positively.

References

Barbarin, O. A. and Soler, R. E. 1993. Behavioral, emotional, and academic adjustment in a national probability sample of African American children: Effects of age, gender, and family structure. *Journal of Black Psychology*, 19: 423-446.

Bengtson, V. L. 2001. Beyond the nuclear family: The increasing importance of multigenerational bonds (The Burgess Award lecture). *Journal of Marriage and the Family*, 63: 1-16.

Black, M. M. and Nitz, K. 1996. Grandmother co-residence, parenting, and child development among low income, urban teen mothers. *Journal of Adolescent Health*, 18: 218-226.

Brooks, D. and Barth, R. P. 1998. Characteristics and outcomes of drug-exposed and non drug-exposed children in kinship and non-relative foster care. *Children and Youth Services Review*, 20: 475-501.

Coall, D. A. and Hertwig, R. 2013. Grandparent investment: A relic of the past or a resource for the future? *Current Directions in Psychological Science*, 20: 93-98.

Coley, R. L. and Chase-Lansdale, P. L. 1998. Adolescent pregnancy and parenthood: Recent evidence and future directions. *American Psychologist*, 53: 152-166.

DeLeire, T. and Kalil, A. 2002. Good things come in threes: Single-parent multigenerational family structure and adolescent adjustment. *Demography*, 39: 393-413.

Dubowitz, H., Feigelman, S., Harrington, D., Starr, R. H., Zuravin, S., and Sawyer, R. 1994. Children in kinship care: How do they fare? *Children and Youth Services Review*, 16: 85-106.

Dunifon, R. 2013. The influence of grandparents on the lives of children and adolescents. *Child Development Perspectives*, 7: 55-60.

Elder, G. H. and Conger, R. 2000. *Children of the land: Adversity and success in rural America*. Chicago, IL: University of Chicago Press.

Eshbaugh, E. M. and Luze, G. J. 2007. Adolescent and adult low-income mothers: How do needs and resources differ? *Journal of Community Psychology*, 35: 1037-1052.

Fuller-Thomson, E., Minkler, M., and Driver, D. 1997. A profile of grandparents raising grandchildren in the United States. *Gerontologist*, 37: 406-411.

Furstenberg, F. F., Jr., Brooks-Gunn, J., and Morgan, S. P. 1987. *Adolescent mothers in later life*. Cambridge, MA: Cambridge University Press.

Gleeson, J. P., Strozier, A. L. and Littlewood, K. A. 2011. Coparenting in multigenerational family systems: Clinical and policy implications. In J. P. McHale and K. M. Lindahl (Eds.), *Coparenting: A conceptual and clinical examination of family systems* (pp. 269-288). Washington, DC: APA Press.

Gordon, R. A., Chase-Lansdale, P. L., and Brooks-Gunn, J. 2004. Extended households and the life course of young mothers: Understanding the associations using a sample of mothers with premature, low birth weight babies. *Child Development,* 75: 1013-1038.

Haxton, C. L. and Harknett, K. 2009. Racial and gender differences in kin support: A mixed-methods study of African American and Hispanic couples. *Journal of Family Issues,* 30: 1019-1040.

Kalil, A., Spencer, M. S., Spieker, S. J., and Gilchrist, L. D. 1998. Effects of grandmother coresidence and quality of family relationships on depressive symptoms in adolescent mothers. *Family Relations: Interdisciplinary Journal of Applied Family Studies,* 47: 433-441.

Leadbeater, B. J. and Bishop, S. J. 1994. Predictors of behavior problems in preschool children of inner-city Afro-American and Puerto Rican adolescent mothers. *Child Development,* 65: 638-648.

Mahne, K. and Huxhold, O. 2012. Social contact between grandparents and older grand-children: A three-generational perspective. In S. Arber and V. Timonen (Eds.), *Contemporary grandparenting: Changing family relationships in global contexts* (pp. 225-246). Bristol, UK: The Policy Press.

Minkler, M., Roe, K. M., and Robertson-Beckley, R. J. 1994. Raising grandchildren from crack-cocaine households: Effects on family and friendship ties of African-American women. *American Journal of Orthopsychiatry,* 64: 20-29.

Murphey, D., Cooper, M., and Moore, K. A. 2012. *Children living with and cared for by grandparents: State-level data from the American community survey.* Washington, DC: Child Trends. Available at: http://www.childtrends.org/wp-content/uploads/2012/10/2012-30Grandparents.pdf

Pinazo-Hernandis, S. and Tompkins, C. J. 2009. Custodial grandparents: The state of the art and the many faces of this contribution. *Journal of Intergenerational Relationships,* 7: 137-143.

Pittman, L. D. 2007. Grandmothers' involvement among young adolescents growing up in poverty. *Journal of Research on Adolescence,* 17: 89-116.

Pittman, L. D. and Boswell, M. K. 2007. The role of grandmothers in the lives of preschoolers growing up in urban poverty. *Applied Developmental Science,* 11: 20-42.

Sheehan, N. W. and Petrovic, K. 2008. Grandparents and their Adult Grandchildren: Recurring themes from the literature. *Marriage and Family Review,* 44: 99-124.

Silverstein, M., Giarrusso, R., and Bengston, V. L. 1998. Intergenerational solidarity and the grandparent role. In M. E. Szinovacz (Ed.), *Handbook of grandparenthood* (pp. 144-158). Westport, CT: Greenwood Press.

Solomon, J. C. and Marx, J. 1995. "To grandmother's house we go": Health and school adjustment of children raised solely by grandparents. *Gerontologist,* 35: 386-394.

Tomlin, A. M. 1998. Grandparents' influences on grandchildren. In M. E. Szinovacz (Ed.), *Handbook of grandparenthood* (pp. 159-170). Westport, CT: Greenwood Press.

Van Ranst, N., Verschueren, K., and Marcoen, A. 1995. The meaning of grandparents as viewed by adolescent grandchildren: An empirical study in Belgium. *International Journal of Aging and Human Development,* 41: 311-324.

Vespa, J., Lewis, J. M., and Kreider, R. M. 2013. *America's families and living arrangements: 2012.* Washington, DC: U.S. Census Bureau. Available at: http://www.census.gov/prod/2013pubs/p20-570.pdf

http://dx.doi.org/10.2190/GITC10

Noncaregiving Grandparent Peers' Perceptions of Custodial Grandparents: Extent of Life Disruption, Needs for Social Support, and Needs for Social and Mental Health Services

Bert Hayslip, Jr., Rebecca J. Glover, and
Sara E. Pollard

Introduction

The role of grandparent for many has shifted from a traditional, noncaregiving role to a nontraditional caregiver/parental role, with grandmothers typically assuming a custodial role twice as often as grandfathers (Fuller-Thomson and Minkler, 2000). Factors contributing to custodial grandparenting include the death or incarceration of the grandchild's parent as well as the termination or interruption of the parent-child relationship as a result of various forms of abuse, separation or abandonment, substance abuse, job loss, and divorce (Hayslip and Kaminski, 2005; Park and Greenberg, 2007). Qualitative research has found that custodial grandparents report challenges such as the generation gap between themselves and their grandchild, health concerns, discipline difficulties, and strain in their marital relationships (Robinson and Wilks, 2006).

Despite the challenges many grandparents face in raising their grandchildren, such persons more often than not take on this responsibility with the grandchildren's best interests in mind and dedicated to the children's utmost well-being, even above their own, ignoring their own health needs in the process (Baker and Silverstein, 2008). Yet despite its challenges, custodial grandparenting can bring such benefits as feeling closer to the grandchildren and a new sense of meaning to the grandparent's life (Hayslip and Page, 2012).

Perceptions of Custodial Grandparents

Grandparents raising their grandchildren face many challenges with which they must cope: their adequacy as a parent, maintaining their physical and psychological well-being, their need for social services, and their need for social support (see Park and Greenberg, 2007; Hayslip and Kaminiski, 2005; Hayslip and Patrick, 2003). In this light, two distinct groups of custodial grandparents have been identified: those whose difficulties primarily stem from the demands of the newly acquired parenting role, and those whose difficulties also relate to a grandchild with developmental delays, physical illness, or emotional or behavioral problems, most of whom are male (Emick and Hayslip, 1999; Hayslip and Shore, 2000; Hayslip, Shore, Henderson, and Lambert, 1998). In many cases a grandchild's problems, such as attention deficit/hyperactivity disorder, substance abuse, or depression, may exacerbate the challenges custodial grandparents face (Kolomer, McCallion, and Overeynder, 2003), placing many at increased risk for depression and declining physical health. Hayslip and Shore (2000) found custodial grandparents who reported more problem behaviors in their grandchildren experienced more psychosocial distress. In addition, those custodial grandparents who had sought mental health care assistance were the most psychosocially impaired and had the most negative and conflictual relationships with their grandchildren. For some custodial grandparents, then, the effects of the demands of assuming a parental role in midlife or beyond are aggravated by raising a grandchild who is experiencing physical, emotional, or behavioral difficulties and further complicated by isolation from age peers and/or a lack of social support (Emick and Hayslip; 1999; Hayslip et al., 1998).

Many custodial grandparents also report numerous psychological and physical difficulties that stem, in part, from the grandparents' perceptions of their responsibilities as parents. Effective parenting often requires substantial effort and the belief that one has the power to benefit a child, that is, parental efficacy (Gettinger and Guetschow, 1998). In this respect, many custodial grandparents may face barriers such as a lack of energy to actively parent or a lack of recent experience in raising children, leading to experienced parenting stress, depression, and inconsistent parenting practices, and they often may lack the monetary resources of a household led by two employed persons and grieve the loss of a more traditional grandparent role (Hayslip and Kaminiski, 2005). Thus, some custodial grandparents may have more difficulty meeting broader social expectations related to parenting and/or their grandchildren's needs due to the often unforeseen nature of this responsibility and the circumstances surrounding their role acquisition.

Both anecdotal and experimental evidence suggest that there may be a basis for grandparents feeling stigmatized in that they perceive themselves as being viewed by their traditional grandparent peers as having failed as parents in raising children who have become incompetent or irresponsible parents (Baird, 2003;

Hayslip and Glover, 2008; Wohl, Lahner, and Jooste, 2003). At present, while it is unclear whether and how the negative perceptions of others—traditional grandparents, service providers, or social workers—contribute to this picture, many grandparent caregivers report feeling negatively judged or blamed by others about their poor parenting of their own children contributing to their present situation raising a grandchild (Baird, 2003; Hayslip, 2010). This likely contributes to isolation from others borne of shame for having failed as a parent (Baird, 2003; Hayslip, 2010; Hayslip and Page, 2012; Wohl et al., 2003). Consequently, their lower levels of parenting efficacy are not surprising (Gettinger and Guetschow, 1998). However, while grandparents may struggle with becoming a surrogate parent, this second chance at parenting often leads to an effort to perform better in their parenting role with a grandchild compared to their own children (Emick and Hayslip, 1999).

From a broader social perspective, societal perceptions and prejudices are also likely to have an impact on grandparent-headed households. Joslin (2000), for example, pointed out that for grandparent caregivers who are taking care of grandchildren orphaned by HIV/AIDS, social stigma can threaten the grandparent's self-esteem and social support. Along these lines, Miltenberger, Hayslip, Harris, and Kaminski (2003–2004) explored young adults' perceptions of the losses experienced by grandparent caregivers. They found that the depth and intensity of sensitivity to this loss was influenced by feelings regarding both the diverse reasons the grandparent assumed a caregiving role and the level of the grandchild's adjustment problems. Miltenberger et al. (2003–2004) found that a greater sensitivity to loss was present when the grandparent took on the caregiving role due to parental death, abandonment, child abuse, drug abuse, and incarceration rather than parental divorce or job loss. This might suggest that those with whom custodial grandparents interact might underestimate the level of disappointment they experience regarding the loss of intimacy with a partner (Erhle and Day, 1994), disruption in life plans (e.g., traveling, retirement) (Jendrek, 1993), or the loss of the desired relationship with either the adult child or the grandchild. Additionally, many grandparents are forced to cope with the loss of the view that they were good parents, based upon societal assumptions that the grandparent caregiver's own poor parenting or failure to model marital or vocational success may have contributed to the now adult child's lack of success in parenting, marriage, or career. Miltenberger et al. (2003–2004) also found a greater sensitivity to loss when the grandchild exhibited behavioral or emotional problems. This is important in light of the fact that even grandparents who are raising children without serious behavioral or emotional problems experience difficulties due to the demands of their newly acquired parental roles (Emick and Hayslip, 1999; Hayslip et al., 1998) and may desire help. Indeed, many custodial grandparents express feeling overwhelmed, isolated, and in need of emotional support from others in the form of support groups, mentoring by other grandparent caregivers, or counseling services (Hayslip, King, and Jooste, 2008).

Wohl et al. (2003) noted the most prominent themes emerging from a group intervention program with custodial grandparents were difficulties involving relationships with others, relationships with the parents of the grandchildren, and relationships with the grandchildren themselves. Given that the grandparents' age peers typically do not have ongoing caregiving responsibilities for children, it is not surprising to observe that grandparent caregivers commonly perceive themselves as "invisible," wherein they belong with neither their same-age friends nor the younger parents of their grandchildren's friends (Erhle, 2001). While their friends may be retired and enjoying hobbies and travel, custodial grandparents often find their time occupied with the grandchild's leisure activities (Robinson and Wilks, 2006). Consequently, it is not uncommon for custodial grandparents to report losing friends when they take on a caregiving role, increasing their risk for social isolation (Cox, 2000). The added financial obligation of raising a grandchild and the unexpected nature of this role change can also create strain in the grandparents' marital relationship (Robinson and Wilks, 2006). In addition, grandparent caregivers commonly report feeling alienated from social networks such as churches and other prior sources of support (Fuller-Thomson and Minkler, 2000). Consequently, it is possible that the disruption of their social networks accompanied by such feelings (Emick and Hayslip, 1999; Fuller-Thomson and Minkler, 2000) may undermine their physical and mental health, as well as their ability to parent.

From an interpersonal perspective, just as traditional grandparent peers may be a source of shame or guilt about custodial grandparents' failures as a parent, they may also be an important source of social support and serve as an implicit benchmark for grandparent caregivers' evaluations of changes in their lifestyle, mental and physical health, and interpersonal relationships as a function of becoming full-time caregivers to their grandchildren (Dolbin-MacNab, Roberto, and Finney, 2013; Hayslip, Herrington, Glover, and Pollard, 2013). Indeed, their own perceptions about their current roles as noncaregiving grandparents impact their perceptions of grandparents who raise a grandchild (Hayslip et al., 2013). As social support has been shown to affect one's physical (Krause, 2001) and emotional health (Antonucci, 2001), it may also be an important factor affecting the successes or difficulties of grandparent-headed household (see Dolbin-MacNab et al., 2013). The aforementioned perspectives also reinforce the mutually interactive nature of the connection between traditional and custodial grandparents and underscore the importance of viewing custodial grandparenting within the larger framework of relationships with others, which impact and are impacted by how such persons define such relationships (Hayslip and Patrick, 2003).

Rationale for the Present Study

Traditional grandparents thus may compose the reference group against which custodial grandparents define themselves in terms of personal adjustment, grandchild outcomes, and parental success (Hayslip et al., 2013). Indeed, as most custodial grandparents were traditional grandparents prior to becoming caregivers of their grandchildren, such expectations and self-appraisals regarding one's parenting skills are likely. Smith and Dolbin-MacNab (2013) found that the extent to which grandparent caregivers' self appraisals were either negative or not influenced their well-being as well as their parenting practices. In contrast, taking an authoritative parenting style and engaging in benefit finding were found to positively influence grandparent caregiver well-being and lessen parental stress (Castillo, Henderson, and North, 2013). At the same time, the redefined social-interpersonal context and associated stigma with having failed as a parent (see above) may contribute to more negative perceptions held by age peers and subsequently internalized by some custodial grandparents (Hayslip et al., 2013). From a social support perspective, however more traditional grandparent peers who were once friends, coworkers, or neighbors may also constitute an important dimension of the custodial grandparent's convoy of support (Antonucci, 2001) and, therefore, directly or indirectly influence (a) the grandparents' access to social or educational services, (b) the availability of instrumental or emotional support to them, and/or (c) the affirmation of a caregiver grandparent's values as a competent parent in the face of chronic health difficulties, social isolation, lessened income, depression, or the stigma associated with raising a grandchild (Dolbin-MacNab et al., 2013; Fruhauf and Bundy-Fazioli, 2013).

Gettinger and Guetschow (1998) argue that the involvement of any parent in a child's life requires a clear "understanding of role expectations" by both society and the parent. However, in many custodial grandparent homes, the clarity with which they define their parental role may be marginal in light of a comparative lack of recent childrearing experience and the fact that many grandparents indeed suffer from role confusion (Hayslip et al., 1998), that is, "How am I supposed to behave now that I am no longer a traditional grandparent; am I my child's parent or grandparent?" As the feelings and attitudes of grandparent caregivers have been well documented (see above), which in part may reflect how others might feel toward them, that is, feelings of isolation, shame, depression, it becomes important to explore the bases for views others might hold about custodial grandparents and their grandchildren. Indeed, we can learn a great deal about custodial grandparenting by viewing it from "the outside," in that others' perceptions, biases, and attitudes can have a powerful influence on the well-being of custodial grandparents themselves. Further, such feelings held by others may be related to the perceived stigma attached to the reasons for the assumption of the grandparent caregiving role.

As the majority of custodial grandparents are women (Hayslip and Kaminiski, 2005; Park and Greenberg, 2007), the present study focused on factors influencing perceptions held by traditional noncaregiving grandparents of custodial grandmothers utilizing multiple measures of such views. Over and above their value in understanding the interpersonal context defining custodial grandparenting, these data might also provide a baseline against which caregiving grandparents' views about what others think of them as parents can be compared. An understanding of the basis for the perceptions of custodial grandparents by others, that is, traditional grandparents, might assist in understanding influences on parental efficacy among custodial grandparents and, thus, may benefit both these grandparents and their grandchildren.

The parameters chosen here to operationalize traditional grandparents' perceptions of custodial grandparents reflect several important themes that have defined the literature regarding concerns custodial grandparents have of their adjustment to their newly acquired parental roles as well as concerns they perceive others to have about them, that is, personal adjustment and/or parental efficacy, the impact of custodial grandparenting on one's physical and psychological well-being, the importance of social support, and needs for a variety of social services (see Hayslip et al., 2008, 2013; Hayslip and Kaminiski, 2005; Hayslip and Page, 2012; Hayslip and Patrick, 2003; Park and Greenberg, 2007).

The current experimental study approached this question in using random assignment of traditional noncaregiving grandparents (traditional grandparents) to levels of independent variables. These independent variables were manipulated aspects of a hypothetical scenario, that is, grandchild sex, grandchild problems, reasons for assuming the caregiver role, to assess the impact of these factors on traditional grandparents' perceptions of grandparent caregivers. This allowed for all extraneous variables, for example, other characteristics of either the custodial grandparent in the scenario or noncaregiving grandparent demographics, to be evenly distributed among the manipulated conditions described in a scenario describing a caregiving grandmother and her grandchild. Thus, such factors could conceivably influence perceptions of caregiving grandparents; their systematic evaluation via their manipulation was not the focus of the present experimental study. Indeed, their effects, if they exist, are randomly distributed and/or constant across conditions in the present design. Thus, their systematic impact, if any, remains a topic for future research.

Method

Participants

Participants in this study were 610 traditional grandparents recruited via newspapers and public announcements at schools, churches, and other community groups and agencies in northern Texas. The only exclusion criterion was that none of the participants could coreside with or have custodial responsibility for any of their grandchildren, all of whom were reportedly being raised by their parent(s) on a full-time basis. Participants ranged in age from 40 to 94 years (M age = 63). Less than 2% of the participants reported ever having had full-time responsibility for their grandchildren in the past, and among those who reported having had some responsibility, it had been at least a year since such responsibilities had ended. Table 1 presents the demographic characteristics of the grandparent sample here.

Table 1. Percentage of Sample in Each Demographic Category

	Percentage		Percentage
Race		Gender	
Caucasian	82	Male	23.4
African American	10	Female	71.6
Hispanic	4	Missing	4.8
Asian American	1		
Other/not specified	3	Education	
		< 12	10.4
Marital status		12 years or greater	89.6
Married	71		
Single	9.8	Self-rated health	
Widowed	1.5	Very poor	0.7
Divorced	16.4	Poor	3.2
Missing	1.7	Fair	21.4
		Good	40.4
Annual income		Very good	30.9
(in thousands of dollars)		Missing	3.5
< 10	5.3		
10–20	7.0	Self-rated health relative	
20–30	12.3	to age peers	
30–40	12.8	Very poor	2.2
40–50	11.8	Poor	15.8
50–60	6.3	Fair	38.5
60+	37.7	Good	26.9
Missing	6.8	Very good	10.1
		Missing	6.5

Procedure

This study was approved by the University of North Texas Institutional Review Board. Participants completed a paper-pencil survey containing demographic questions as well as those relating to their relationship to their own grandchildren, contact with and personal knowledge of grandparents raising their grandchildren, and the extent of their own experiences in caring for their own grandchildren. Each grandparent participant was randomly assigned to one of two orders of administration to control for order effects. Half of the sample first completed the demographic survey before reading a randomly assigned scenario depicting a relationship between a custodial grandmother and her grandchild (see Appendix). Such participants then responded to a series of questions as they applied to the scenario. The remaining half of the sample first read the scenario to which they had been randomly assigned and responded to the questions pertaining to it, and then answered the demographic questions.

Elements of the scenario provided to each participant varied systematically so that the custodial grandmother depicted in the story (a) was raising either a male or female grandchild; (b) was responsible for a child who was or was not experiencing emotional, behavioral, peer-related, or school problems; and (c) had assumed parental responsibility for a grandchild resulting from either parental death, divorce, incarceration, abandonment, drug abuse, job loss, or child abuse. Each scenario, therefore, reflected a unique combination of the above three factors. Manipulation of these factors via the presentation of a given scenario permitted an independent estimate of each factor's effect on attitudes toward grandparent caregivers held by traditional grandparent-age peers. Via the separation of factors influencing traditional grandparent's views about those who are raising their grandchildren that are in everyday life inseparable, the experimental manipulation of grandchild gender, grandchild problem presence or absence, or reason for role assumption constitutes the use of an analogue research approach to understanding the nature of a problem that is not amenable to other means of gathering data about behavior (see Borkovec and Rachman, 1979; Kasdin and Rogers, 1978).

Grandparent Perceptions Measures

After reading each scenario, traditional grandparent participants rated the scenario using the following scales developed for the present study, wherein responses varied between 1 to 5: (a) *Life Disruption* - alpha = .77: Participants responded to 10 items measuring the extent to which the life of the custodial grandmother depicted in the scenario had been disrupted by assuming caregiving responsibilities of the grandchild; higher scores indicated more disruption. Sample items included "The life of this grandparent is disrupted by caring for her grandchild," "Caring for this grandchild will put a strain on this grandparent's marriage," "This grandparent needs time away from parenting," "Raising this grandchild will speed up the aging process for this grandparent," and "This grandparent does not have time for herself." (b) *Need for Social/Mental Health Services* - alpha = .73, developed for the current project, included 12 items providing a measure of the traditional grandparent's perception of the custodial grandparent's need for services to assist her in raising the grandchild; higher scores indicated greater need. Sample items included "Being able to parent again makes this parent feel young," "This grandparent is fearful about what will happen to her in the future," "The grandparent is feeling frustrated," "This grandparent is in need of help from a mental health professional," and "This grandparent is personally well adjusted." (c) *Need for Social Support* - alpha = .72. After reading the scenario, participants also responded to 9 items developed for the present study to measure the extent to which the custodial grandmother was perceived as being in need of social support from friends, family, and such; higher scores indicated greater need. Sample items included "This grandparent is being taken advantage of," "This grandparent is feeling ignored by her friends," "This grandparent is feeling ignored by her family," "This grandparent helped create the situation she is in," "It is the grandparent's fault that she must care for her grandchild."

Independent Variables

The independent variables were defined with regard to those that were manipulated via the construction of the scenario: sex of the grandchild, the presence/absence of grandchild problems, that is, behavioral/learning problems, and reason for role assumption, for example, abandonment, child abuse, death of a parent, a parent's drug abuse, imprisonment of a parent, loss of employment, divorce. As noted above, as individuals were randomly assigned to read a given scenario, it follows that other characteristics of the hypothetical grandmother not explicitly mentioned in the scenario (e.g., variations in her age, marital status, or socioeconomic status) were also randomly distributed and consequently not manipulated here, and that grandparent respondent demographic characteristics that might also influence responses to the scenarios were also randomly distributed/held constant and thus, not manipulated here.

Results

Data were analyzed via a $2 \times 2 \times 7$ MANOVA manipulating Grandchild Gender-2 levels, Grandchild Problem-2 levels, and Reason for Role Assumption-7 levels, followed by univariate tests and post hoc comparisons as appropriate. The above perceptual dimensions, that is, needs for social support, needs for social and mental health services, and life disruption, served as dependent variables. As no main effects for ethnicity had been found in a separate prior study with young adults (Hayslip et al., 2009) and due to difficulty recruiting an ethnically heterogeneous sample (requiring at least 1,300 traditional grandparents), the impact of ethnicity was not explored here. The above-described MANOVA yielded multivariate main effects for Grandchild Sex, Grandchild Problem, and for Reason for Role Assumption. There were no multivariate interaction effects.

As seen in Table 2, univariate analyses related to the main effect for Grandchild Sex indicated custodial grandmothers raising female grandchildren to be perceived by traditional grandparents as experiencing significantly greater life disruption, greater need for social and mental health services, and greater need for social support than custodial grandmothers raising male grandchildren. As seen in Table 3, univariate analyses related to Grandchild Problem indicated that grandmothers raising grandchildren who had emotional/behavioral problems or problems with peers or at school were also perceived to be experiencing significantly greater life disruption, to be in greater need of social and mental

Table 2. Main Effects for Grandchild Gender

	Male		Female		
Variable	Mean	SD	Mean	SD	F
Life disruption	21.53	6.50	22.46	6.09	5.54[a]
Need for services	31.37	7.69	33.50	7.26	18.36[a]
Need for support	19.52	6.48	20.55	6.16	3.91[a]

[a]$p < .05$; Cell sizes (complete data) ranged from 14 to 25, with the average cell size being 15. Multivariate $F_{3,512} = 6.53$, $p < .001$, $eta^2 = .037$.

Table 3. Main Effects for Grandchild Problem

	Male		Female		
Variable	Mean	SD	Mean	SD	F
Life disruption	23.69	5.76	20.11	6.37	45.92[a]
Need for services	36.13	6.06	28.31	6.89	200.21[a]
Need for support	21.62	5.72	18.49	6.57	36.60[a]

[a]$p < .01$; Cell sizes (complete data) ranged from 14 to 25, with the average cell size being 15. Multivariate $F_{3,521} = 74.15$, $p < .001$, $eta^2 = .303$.

health services, and to be in greater need of social support than grandmothers raising grandchildren without similar problems.

As seen in Table 4, univariate analyses regarding the impact of Reason for Role Assumption indicated custodial grandmothers to be perceived as having experienced greater life disruption, as per inspection of 95% confidence intervals, when the reason for role assumption was the result of parental drug abuse, abandonment of the grandchild, and parental incarceration. Intermediate in this respect were parental job loss and parental divorce. Custodial grandmothers were perceived as having experienced the least life disruption when the reason for role assumption was related to child abuse and parental death. Custodial grandmothers were perceived as needing more social support when the reason for role assumption was the result of parental divorce, parental drug abuse, parental incarceration, abandonment of the grandchild, and parental job loss. Custodial grandmothers were perceived as needing the least social support when the reason for role assumption was the result of either child abuse or parental death. As presented in Table 3, univariate analyses yielded no main effect for Reason for Role Assumption for needs for social/mental health services.

Table 4. Main Effects for Reason for Role Assumption

	Parent death		Divorce		Imprisonment		Job loss		Child abuse		Abandonment		Drug abuse		F
	Mean	SD	Mean	SD	Mean	SD	Mean	SD	Mean	SD	Mean	SD	Mean	SD	
Disruption[1]	20.27	6.25	21.62	6.18	22.57	7.18	21.91	5.71	20.74	6.52	22.83	5.92	23.25	6.11	2.41[a]
Services[2]	31.45	7.38	31.45	8.76	32.90	8.24	32.67	6.43	31.57	8.23	32.48	6.51	33.36	7.30	1.07
Support[3]	18.04	6.00	20.91	6.42	20.79	6.79	20.21	5.77	18.65	6.90	20.49	5.52	21.21	6.43	2.83[a]

Notes: [1]Life disruption; [2]Need for services; [3]Need for Support.

[a]$p < .05$; Cell sizes (complete data) ranged from 14 to 25, with the average cell size being 15. Multivariate $F_{18,1542} = 1.68$, $p < .05$, $eta^2 = .019$.

Discussion

In general, findings of this study indicate that perceptions of custodial grandparents held by traditional grandparents are in some cases consistent with data reported by custodial grandparents themselves, but in other cases indicate that traditional/noncaregiving grandparents misunderstand or underestimate the challenges custodial grandparents face. Findings regarding the main effect for grandchild sex indicated that traditional grandparents perceived raising a granddaughter to create greater life disruption and greater need for both social services and social support relative to raising a grandson. This finding is in contrast to reports from custodial grandparents themselves and research examining the impact of raising grandsons (Baird, 2003; Hayslip, 2010; Hayslip et al., 1998; King et al., 2006; Wohl et al., 2003) as well as separate data finding no main effect of grandchild sex on young adults' perceptions of custodial grandparents (Hayslip et al., 2009). Differences in such perceptions between traditional grandparents and either custodial grandparents or young adults could indicate that traditional grandparents in this study may underestimate the demands of raising grandsons. These findings might also reflect the gendered attitude of older adults who are now traditional grandparents, having completed child rearing in past decades when boys might have been perceived as being easier to raise than girls or whose disruptive or aggressive behavior was tolerated to a greater extent relative to that of girls, based upon gender stereotypes (see Bee and Boyd, 2010).

The results regarding effect of grandchild problem are more consistent with findings from the above-cited self-report data from custodial grandparents (Baird, 2003; Wohl et al., 2003) as well as findings published elsewhere pertaining to young adults' perceptions of grandparent caregivers (Hayslip et al., 2009). They indicated that children with emotional, behavioral, social, or academic problems are perceived as eliciting more life disruption as well as greater need for both social services and social support, for either the grandchild or the grandparent. While this may be an accurate perception, it may also suggest that traditional grandparents and young adults (see Hayslip et al., 2009) *underestimate* both the role demands and personal adjustment difficulties faced by custodial grandparents raising grandchildren who are *not* experiencing adjustment problems (see Hayslip et al., 1998).

Findings here regarding reason for role assumption are unique. Keeping in mind that the absolute differences between means across reasons for role assumption were small, we target here only those that are most different from one another. Consistent with perceptions held by young adults (Hayslip et al., 2009), traditional grandparents in this study perceived the least life disruption for grandmothers raising grandchildren as a result of parental death, as well as child abuse, which was not the case in the Hayslip et al. (2009) study, relative to other reasons for role assumption. This may be a manifestation of the disenfranchised nature of grief over the loss of a child for grandparent caregivers (Miltenberger et al., 2003–2004) as seen by traditional grandparents, or it may reflect either a lack of experience with the death of a child or a lack of awareness of the potential impact of a child's death, which may be emotionally isolating (Reed, 2000). Similarly, the very nature of child abuse and a relative lack of experience with it may explain traditional grandparents' perceptions of its likely impact on caregiving grandparents. Parental death is certainly the most unambiguous of reasons to assume this role and may be thought to predict less life disruption because it presents both the grandparent and grandchild with more clearly defined expectations of each's role and perhaps more finality about the grandchild's placement in the grandparent's care. It is worth noting, however, that even grandparents whose reason for assuming the parenting of a grandchild is less ambiguous and possibly less stigmatizing nevertheless need social support and services (Dolbin-MacNab et al., 2013; Hayslip et al., 1998; Smith, 2003).

In contrast, traditional grandparents in this study perceived the most life disruption to be related to parental incarceration, drug abuse, or abandonment, perhaps because these factors lend themselves more easily to stigmatization or blame of the grandparent. The perceived impact of these additional reasons for role assumption may also reflect older adults' attitudes that incarceration, drug use, or parental abandonment reflect negatively on the parenting skills of both generations, resulting in greater stigmatization and perhaps greater perceived life disruption. Unfortunately, such perceptions indeed parallel those held by traditional grandparents that a grandchild's difficulties are caused by the poor parenting skills of the caregiving grandparent (Hayslip and Glover, 2008; Smith and Dolbin-MacNab, 2013). They are also consistent with the found relationship between grandparent caregiver well-being and grandchild strengths (Goodman and Hayslip, 2008).

Previous research has found that young adults perceived custodial grandparents as needing less social support when the reason for role assumption resulted from parental death relative to other reasons for raising grandchildren (Hayslip et al., 2009). Here, traditional grandparents also cited child abuse, in addition to parental death, as eliciting less need for social support relative to other reasons, which parallel the above findings for life disruption, and may be explained similarly, that is, the underestimation of and disenfranchisement of grief over a child, a lack of direct experience with or the stigma surrounding child abuse. Likewise, perceived stigma, presumed parental incompetence, or perhaps the ambiguity of the placement's finality may explain the greater perceived need for social support in cases of parental divorce, drug abuse, incarceration, child abandonment, or job loss, which may be viewed as involving more choice on the part of the parent.

In contrast to findings with young adults wherein parental death, incarceration, job loss and divorce were seen as eliciting less need for social services among custodial grandparents (Hayslip et al., 2009), the present data gathered from traditional grandparents yielded no significant main effects for reason for role assumption on need for social or mental health services. This lack of difference suggests that, in contrast to young adults, traditional grandparents perceive all custodial grandparents as being in equal need of mental health or social services regardless of the reason for role assumption. This in itself is an overgeneralization and ignores the fact that many grandparents grow and prosper emotionally and are resilient in taking on the responsibility of raising a grandchild (Hayslip and Smith, 2013).

We acknowledge the speculative nature of our interpretation of those factors explaining traditional grandparents' perceptions of custodial grandparents and the fact that such attitudes may or may not translate into behaviors during interactions with custodial grandparents or via the use of provided services. Nevertheless, these findings contribute to an interpersonal/contractual understanding of the perceptions of traditional grandparents regarding what gives rise to the needs of custodial grandparents as they deal with life changes and challenges. Based upon the present findings, it may be that the nature of traditional grandparents' perceptions contribute to situations where those in positions to be helpful and supportive are, to varying degrees, more or less sensitive to (a) the circumstances bringing about the necessity for custodial grandparenting, (b) to the effects of the potential stigma attached to raising a grandchild (Hayslip, 2010), and (c) to the unique challenges in raising granddaughters versus grandsons, or to those associated with raising a grandchild experiencing emotional, behavioral, or (d) school-related difficulties. Collectively, these difficulties may contribute to social isolation and poor health (see Hughes, Waite, LaPierre, and Luo, 2007) or depression, born of the perception that one's age peers cannot understand or empathize with the experience of raising a grandchild (Erhle, 2001; Kelley, Whitley, Sipe, and Croft, 2000; Wohl et al., 2003), leading to an even greater chance that grandparent caregivers will not seek formal or informal social support and/or will not access social, medical, or mental health services (Baker and Silverstein, 2008; Dolbin-MacNab et al., 2013; Hayslip and Shore, 2000). Additional observational and/or experimental research could help clarify how such attitudes translate into traditional grandparents' behaviors and perhaps those of others, such as service providers, toward custodial grandparents and into how those interactions affect grandparent and grandchild functioning.

Limitations of the Present Study

It should be noted that the applicability of these findings to other subgroups of traditional grandparents, for example, grandfathers, those from other ethnic backgrounds and geographic locations, to custodial grandparents themselves, and/or to those who provide services and support are largely unknown. Indeed, the present study is one of the first to attempt to understand views held toward grandparent caregivers by others. While some evidence suggests that grandparent caregivers are stereotyped by service providers (Janicki, McCallion, Grant-Griffin, and Kolomer, 2000), public assistance employees perceive them more positively than some other types of caregivers, older adults in general, and social service clients in general (Waldrop and Gress, 2002). We speculate that increased experience with grandparent caregivers could improve employees' perceptions of them, given public assistance workers' more extensive contact with custodial grandparents. This is in contrast to the 40% of the current sample who did not know anyone who was raising a grandchild; this topic requires future study. Likewise, other variables particular to noncaregiving grandparents potentially impacting their perceptions of custodial grandparents that were not examined here (e.g., ethnicity, marital status of the grandparent, grandparent gender, grandparent age) are worthy of future research attention.

We acknowledge that the absolute differences between means found here regarding the impact of grandchild sex and reason for role assumption were not as great as those associated with grandchild problems. Yet, as seen in Tables 2 and 3, such effects were statistically reliable, and especially with regard to reason for role assumption, consistent across measures of perceived life disruption and needs for social support. Future research directions include exploring the effects of traditional grandparents' attitudes on their behaviors toward custodial grandparents and their grandchildren, as well as the effects of these behaviors on custodial grandparents' and grandchildren's well-being in the context of everyday interactions or their receipt of services.

Conclusions and Implications

By interpersonalizing the experience of custodial grandparenting, these data help us to understand grandparents who are raising their grandchildren from the "outside," that is, in the context of others' attitudes toward them. Consequently, they provide valuable information that could be a key to changing older adults' and indeed societal attitudes toward custodial grandparents. Negative attitudes and underestimation of custodial grandparents' needs could result in such grandparents not receiving needed help and support from others in their convoy, resulting in the grandchild receiving less than adequate parenting from someone who feels overwhelmed and who is receiving little formal or informal assistance. Such attitudinal influences may contribute to social isolation, feelings of both invisibility and rejection by one's age peers, and underutilization of available services (Hayslip, 2010; Wohl et al., 2003).

In addition, findings here underscore the need for interventions at multiple levels to impact not only the attitudes of others, but also the interpersonal and emotional functioning of custodial grandparents themselves. It will be important that programs that can help custodial grandparents be accessible and made known to them. One example of interventions that may help could be support groups for grandparent caregivers (Smith, 2003) in which meeting others in a similar situation may reduce feelings of being stigmatized, blamed, and isolated. Clinicians working with custodial grandparents may wish to consider how others' attitudes may affect social support in conceptualizing the social stressors and resources of their clients. Others' expectations of them may further impair grandparent caregivers' own efforts to redefine their roles or simultaneously maintain their relationship with their other children and grandchildren while caring for a grandchild, which may include custody disputes or disagreements about the level of the biological parent's involvement in the grandchild's life. In this respect, empowering grandparents to confront and overcome such attitudinal barriers and express their feelings and needs clearly becomes an increasingly important issue for service providers, educators, and therapists who work with custodial grandparents (Cox, 2000).

Appendix

Mrs. Smith is a married grandparent and has several adult children. She has recently become a full-time grandparent caregiver to one of her grandchildren. Mrs. Smith has been caring for her elementary school–age granddaughter for one year, and her good health has allowed her to provide for the grandchild. Her granddaughter has exhibited some behavior and learning problems in school and has been involved in fights with friends. Also her grandchild has begun to experience some symptoms of depression such as not eating and trouble sleeping at night. Mrs. Smith became the primary caregiver of her granddaughter when the child's parents abandoned the child. Due to these circumstances, Mrs. Smith will remain the primary caregiver of her grandchild for an indefinite period of time.

REFERENCES

Antonucci, T. C. 2001. Social relations: An examination of social networks, social support, and sense of control. In J. Birren and K. W. Schaie (Eds.), *Handbook of the psychology of aging* (5th ed., pp. 427-453). San Diego, CA: Academic Press.

Baird, A. 2003. Through my eyes: Service needs of grandparents who raise their grandchildren, from the perspective of a custodial grandmother. In B. Hayslip and J. Patrick (Eds.), *Working with custodial grandparents* (pp. 59-68). New York, NY: Springer.

Baker, L. A. and Silverstein, M. 2008. Preventative health behaviors among grandmothers raising grandchildren. *Journals of Gerontology: Social Sciences,* 63: S304-S311.

Bee, H., and Boyd, D. 2010. *The developing child* (12th ed.). Boston, MA: Allyn & Bacon.

Borkovec, T. and Rachman, S. 1979. The utility of analogue research. *Behaviour Research and Therapy,* 17: 253-261.

Castillo, K., Henderson, C., and North, L. 2013. The relation between caregiving style, coping, benefit finding, grandchild symptoms, and caregiver adjustment among custodial grandparents. In B. Hayslip and G. Smith (Eds.), *Resilient grandparent caregivers: A strengths-based perspective* (pp. 25-37). New York, NY: Routledge.

Cox, C. 2000. Empowering grandparents raising grandchildren. In C. Cox (Ed.), *To grandmother's house we go and stay: Perspectives on custodial grandparents* (pp. 253-267). New York, NY: Springer.

Dolbin-MacNab, M., Roberto, K., and Finney, J. 2013. Formal social support: Promoting resilience in grandparents raising grandchildren. In B. Hayslip and G. Smith (Eds.), *Resilient grandparent caregivers: A strengths-based perspective* (pp. 134-151). New York, NY: Routledge.

Emick, M. and Hayslip, B. 1999. Custodial grandparenting: Stresses, coping skills, and relationships with grandchildren. *International Journal of Aging and Human Development,* 1: 35-61.

Erhle, G. 2001. Grandchildren as moderator variables in the family: Social, physiological, and intellectual development of grandparents who are raising them. *Family Development and Intellectual Functions,* 12: 223-241.

Erhle, G. and Day, H. D. 1994. Adjustment and family functioning of grandmothers raising their grandchildren. *Contemporary Family Therapy,* 16: 67-82.

Fruhauf, C. and Bundy-Fazioli, K. 2013. Grandparent caregivers' self-care practices: Moving toward a strength-based approach. In B. Hayslip and G. Smith (Eds.), *Resilient grandparent caregivers: A strengths-based perspective* (pp. 88-102). New York: Routledge.

Fuller-Thomson, E. and Minkler, M. 2000. America's grandparent caregivers: Who are they? In B. Hayslip and R. Goldberg-Glen (Eds.), *Grandparents raising grandchildren* (pp. 3-31). New York, NY: Springer.

Gettinger, M. and Guetschow, K. 1998. Parental involvement in schools: Parent and teacher perceptions of roles, efficacy, and opportunities. *Journal of Research and Development in Education,* 32: 38-52.

Goodman, C. C. and Bert Hayslip. 2008. Mentally healthy grandparents' impact on their grandchildren's behavior. In B. Hayslip and P. Kaminski (Eds.), *Parenting the custodial grandchild: Implications for clinical practice* (pp. 41-52). New York, NY: Springer.

Hayslip, B. 2010. *Final report to the North Central Texas Area Agency on Aging: Conducting focus groups for grandparents raising grandchildren in the North Texas area: May-July, 2010.* Denton, TX: University of North Texas.

Hayslip, B. and Glover, R. 2008. Traditional grandparents' views of their caregiving peers' parenting skills: Complimentary or critical? In B. Hayslip and P. Kaminski (Eds.), *Parenting the custodial grandchild: Implications for clinical practice* (pp. 149-164). New York, NY: Springer.

Hayslip, B., Glover, R. J., Harris, B., Miltenberger, P. B., Baird, A., and Kaminski, P. L. 2009. Perceptions of custodial grandparents among young adults. *Journal of Intergenerational Relationships,* 7: 209-224.

Hayslip, B., Herrington, R., Glover, R., and S. Pollard. 2013. Assessing attitudes toward grandparents raising their grandchildren. *Journal of Intergenerational Relationships,* 11: 1-24.

Hayslip, B. and Kaminski, P. 2005. Grandparents raising their grandchildren: A review of literature and suggestions for practice. *Gerontologist,* 45: 262-269.

Hayslip, B., and Page, K. S. 2012. Grandparent-grandchild/great-grandchild relationships. In R. Blieszner and V. Bedford (Eds.), *Handbook of families and aging* (2nd ed., pp. 183-212). Westport, CT: Praeger.

Hayslip, B., King, J., and Jooste, J. 2008. The adjustment of children and grandparent caregivers in grandparent-headed families. In B. Hayslip and P. Kaminski (Eds.),

Parenting the custodial grandchild: Implications for clinical practice (pp. 17-40). New York, NY: Springer.

Hayslip, B. and Patrick, J. 2003. Custodial grandparenting viewed from a life span perspective. In B. Hayslip and J. Patrick (Eds.), *Working with custodial grandparents* (pp. 3-12). New York, NY: Springer.

Hayslip, B. and Shore, R. J. 2000. Custodial grandparenting and mental health services. *Journal of Mental Health and Aging,* 6: 367-384.

Hayslip, B. and Smith, G. 2013. *Resilient grandparent caregivers: A strengths-based perspective.* New York, NY: Routledge.

Hayslip, B., Shore, R. J., Henderson, C. E., and Lambert, P. 1998. Custodial grandparenting and the impact of grandchildren with problems on role satisfaction and role meaning. *Journal of Gerontology: Social Sciences* 3: S164-S173.

Hughes, M., Waite, L., LaPierre, T., and Luo, Y. 2007. All in the family: The impact of caring for grandchildren on grandparents' health. *Journals of Gerontology: Social Sciences,* 62: S108-S119.

Janicki, M., McCallion, P., Grant-Griffin, L., and Kolomer, S. 2000. Grandparent caregiver: Characteristics of the grandparents and the children with disabilities for whom they care. *Journal of Gerontological Social Work,* 33: 35-55.

Jendrek, M. 1993. Grandparents who parent their grandchildren: Effects on lifestyle. *Journal of Marriage and the Family,* 55: 609-621.

Joslin, D. 2000. Grandparents raising grandchildren orphaned and affected by HIV/AIDS. In C. Cox (Ed.), *To grandmother's house we go and stay: Perspectives on custodial grandparents* (pp. 167-183). New York, NY: Springer.

Kasdin, A. E. and Rogers, T. 1978. On paradigms and recycled ideologies: Analogue research revisited. *Cognitive Therapy and Research,* 2: 105-117.

Kelley, S. J., Whitley, D., Sipe, T., and Croft, B. 2000. Psychological distress in grandmother kinship care providers: The role of resources, social support and physical health. *Child Abuse & Neglect,* 24: 311-321.

King, J., Hayslip, B., and Kaminski, P. 2006. Variability in the need for formal and informal social support among grandparent caregivers: A pilot study. In B. Hayslip and J. Patrick (Eds.), *Custodial grandparenting: Individual, cultural, and ethnic diversity* (pp. 55-74). New York, NY: Springer.

Kolomer, S., McCallion, P., and Overynder, J. 2003. Why support groups help: Successful interventions for grandparent caregivers of children with developmental disabilities. In B. Hayslip and J. Patrick (Eds.), *Working with custodial grandparents* (pp. 111-116). New York, NY: Springer.

Krause, N. 2001. Social support. In R. H. Binstock and L. K. George (Eds.), *Handbook of aging and the social sciences* (5th ed., pp. 273-294). San Diego, CA: Academic Press.

Miltenberger, P., Hayslip, B., Harris, B., and Kaminski, P. 2003–2004. Perceptions of the losses experienced by custodial grandmothers. *Omega: Journal of Death and Dying,* 48: 245-262.

Park, H.-H. and Greenberg, J. 2007. Parenting grandchildren. In J. Blackburn and C. Dulmus (Eds.), *Handbook of gerontology: Evidence-based approaches to theory, practice, and policy* (pp. 397-425). New York, NY: John Wiley.

Reed, M. 2000. *Grandparents cry twice: Help for bereaved parents.* Amityville, NY: Baywood.

Robinson, M. and Wilks, S. 2006. "Older but not wiser": What custodial grandparents want to tell social workers about raising grandchildren. *Social Work and Christianity,* 33: 164-177.

Smith, G. 2003. How caregiving grandparents view support groups: An exploratory study. In B. Hayslip and J. Patrick (Eds.), *Working with custodial grandparents* (pp. 69-92). New York, NY: Springer.

Smith, G. and Dolbin-MacNab, M. 2013. The role of negative and positive caregiving appraisals in key outcomes for custodial grandmothers and grandchildren. In B. Hayslip and G. Smith (Eds.), *Resilient grandparent caregivers: A strengths-based perspective* (pp. 3-24). New York, NY: Routledge.

Waldrop, D. and Gress, C. 2002. Public assistance employees' perceptions of older adults and caregivers who apply for benefits. *Gerontology and Geriatrics Education,* 23: 73-91.

Wohl, E., Lahner, J., and Jooste, J. 2003. Group processes among grandparents raising grandchildren. In B. Hayslip and J. Patrick (Eds.), *Working with custodial grandparents* (pp. 195-212). New York, NY: Springer.

About the Authors

Ynesse Abdul-Malak is a doctoral candidate in sociology at Syracuse University. Her work focuses on understanding how social structures impact the aging processes of individuals over the life course with a special emphasis on U.S. Caribbean immigrants. She is currently co-authoring a book manuscript, *Grandparenting Children with Disabilities*.

Peter D. Brandon is a social demographer in the Department of Sociology, at the University at Albany. His research includes exploring extended family networks, investigating formal and informal child care settings, and monitoring the social and economic well-being of grandparents. His other research on childhood disabilities has shown the value of using time use data for understanding the burdens and barriers that parents confront when raising children with disabilities. Currently, he serves on a Committee on National Statistics panel that is reviewing and evaluating the content and design of the 2014 Survey of Income and Program Participation.

Lynne M. Casper is professor of sociology and director of graduate studies at the University of Southern California. She is co-editor of the books *Work, Family, Health, and Well-being* (2005, Erlbaum) and *The Handbook of Measurement Issues in Family Research* (2006, Erlbaum). Casper is recipient of the American Sociological Association's 2002 Otis Dudley Duncan Award for outstanding scholarship in social demography for her book *Continuity and Change in the American Family*. She currently serves as vice president of the Population Association of America. She has published extensively in the areas of families and households, work, family and health, cohabitation, fatherhood, child care, voting and demographic methods.

P. Lindsay Chase-Lansdale is the Frances Willard Professor of Human Development and Social Policy at the School of Education and Social Policy, a faculty fellow in the Institute for Policy Research (IPR), and Associate Provost for Faculty, Northwestern University. She is an expert on the interface between research and social policy for children and families.

Megan L. Dolbin-MacNab is associate professor of human development, associate professor of health sciences, and a faculty affiliate of the Center for Gerontology at Virginia Tech. She is also a licensed marriage and family therapist. Her research on grandfamilies has explored grandchild experiences and well-being, parenting and family dynamics, and best practices for community- based interventions. She is the author of numerous journal articles and book chapters about grandfamilies, as well as resources for practitioners working with custodial grandparents and their grandchildren. Dolbin-MacNab also consults with local and state support programs on delivering effective services to grandparents raising grandchildren.

Rachel Dunifon is professor in the Department of Policy Analysis and Management at Cornell University, where she is also associate director for the Bronfenbrenner Center for Translational Research. Her research focuses on child and family policy, with a focus on factors influencing the development of less-advantaged children.

Sandra M. Florian is a Ph.D. candidate in sociology at the University of Southern California. Broadly, Sandra's research interests are in the sociology of the family, inequality and social mobility, and variations by race, class, and gender. Her research has focused on identifying socioeconomic and demographic factors associated with family structure and fertility trajectories, and the different ways in which family forms shape broader patterns of social stratification, and individuals' opportunities for social mobility. Her research has also explored the different types of family structure, living arrangements, and patterns of multigenerational support in coresident grandparent families in the USA.

Rebecca J. Glover is professor of human development in the Department of Educational Psychology at the University of North Texas. Her scholarship has focused on examinations of interpersonal interactions and comprehension of others based on differing developmental contexts and experiences. With specific regard to adult development and aging, collaborative efforts with Dr. Hayslip have resulted in findings which personalize the unique experience of custodial grandparents, clarify attitudes of others (e.g., service providers), and demonstrate how these interactions affect grandparent/grandchild functioning.

Madonna Harrington Meyer, is Laura J. and L. Douglas Meredith professor and chair of sociology, and faculty associate of the Aging Studies Institute, at Syracuse University. She is co-editor, with Elizabeth Daniele, of the forthcoming *Gerontology: Changes, Challenges, and Solutions*. She is author of *Grandmothers at Work: Juggling Families and Jobs*, winner of the 2014 GSA Kalish Book Award. She is co-author with Pamela Herd of *Market Friendly or Family Friendly? The State and Gender Inequality in Old Age*, winner of the 2008 GSA Kalish Book Award. She is also editor of *Care Work: Gender, Labor, and the Welfare State*.

Bert Hayslip Jr. is Regents Professor Emeritus at the University of North Texas. He is a fellow of the American Psychological Association, the Gerontological

Society of America, and The Association for Gerontology in Higher Education. An Associate Editor of *Experimental Aging Research* and of *Developmental Psychology*, his coauthored books include *Emerging Perspectives on Resilience in Adulthood and Later Life* (Springer, 2012), *Resilient grandparent caregivers: A strengths-based perspective* (Routledge, 2012), *Adult Development and Aging* (Krieger, 2011), and *Parenting the Custodial Grandchild* (Springer, 2008). He is Co-PI on a NINR funded project exploring interventions to improve the functioning of grandparent caregivers.

Micah Ioffe is a doctoral student in clinical psychology at Northern Illinois University. Her research interests focus on the influence of family dynamics and relationships on children's and adolescents' psychological functioning.

Christine R. Keeports is a doctoral student in clinical psychology at Northern Illinois University. Her research interests include the impact of interparental conflict on young adults and on the parent-child relationship.

Kimberly Kopko is a Senior Extension Associate in the Department of Policy Analysis and Management at Cornell University, and an affiliate of the Bronfenbrenner Center for Translational Research. Her research focuses on family processes during adolescence.

Yooumi Lee is pursuing a PhD in social science at Syracuse University. Her work focuses on aging families and their living arrangements, intergenerational relationships and social support systems (parental care and grandchild care), and in the health and well-being of older people with a special emphasis on East Asian families.

Laura Pittman is associate professor of clinical psychology and director of clinical training at Northern Illinois University. She takes a risk and resilience approach to understand how family processes and broader contextual factors influence children's and adolescents' socioemotional and cognitive functioning. Much of her research has considered the role grandparents play in the lives of children at risk due to family stress or poverty.

Sarah Pollard earned her undergraduate degree in 2004 with a major in psychology and French from Austin College in Texas, and received her doctorate in counseling psychology from the University of North Texas in 2013. She was a post doctoral fellow at the Emory School of Medicine and Children's Healthcare of Atlanta, where conducted family therapy, diagnostic evaluations and referrals for children who had experienced trauma. Since August, 2014, she is on the staff as a licensed psychologist and certified trauma-focused cognitive behavioral therapist with the Children's Medical Center in Dallas, Texas.

C. Brady Potts is visiting assistant professor of sociology at Occidental College and co-editor of *The Civic Life of American Religion*. His research focuses on the politics of risk, civic engagement in disaster response, and public responses to catastrophe. His current research focuses on the changing role of experts and the politics of expertise in civil engineering in California state government in the 1920s and 1930s.

Merril Silverstein is inaugural holder of the Marjorie Cantor Chair in Aging Studies at Syracuse University in the Maxwell School, Department of Sociology and School of Social Work. He received his doctorate in sociology from Columbia University. In over 150 publications, his research focuses on aging in the context of family life, with an emphasis on life course and international perspectives. He serves as principal investigator of the Longitudinal Study of Generations and has projects in China, Sweden, the Netherlands, and Israel. He was a Brookdale and Fulbright Scholar and recently served as editor-in-chief of *Journal of Gerontology: Social Sciences*.

Lauren Wakschlag is a developmental/clinical psychologist. She is currently professor & vice chair for scientific & faculty development in the Department of Medical Social Sciences, Northwestern University Feinberg School of Medicine. Dr. Wakschlag's research is focused on developmentally-sensitive characterization of disruptive behavior, its prenatal origins and its underlying mechanisms, including the protective role of family processes.

Index